Acclaim for Michael Bérubé's

Life As We Know It

"One cannot escape the chilling conclusion that thousands of people have been grossly misunderstood, neglected and brutalized, not because of their mental limitations but because of ours. . . . Bérubé's arguments are brilliantly persuasive." —*Washington Post Book World*

"Moving and engrossing . . . Bérubé writes with care and feeling." —*Commonweal*

"Bérubé is a wonderful writer . . . one cannot read this book without coming to care for this lovely child." —*Boston Sunday Globe*

"An engaging personal account of raising a son with Down syndrome, by a loving father for whom the experience raises serious question about the nature of social justice, natural rights, and our obligations to one another." —*Kirkus*

"[Bérubé's] passion [is] channeled but not muted by his elegant prose."
—*Los Angeles Times Book Review*

"This is a book that needed to be written, asking hard questions that must be asked, and Michael Bérubé has had the courage and insight to write it. Buy a copy for yourself. Buy another for a friend. Send one to your favorite legislator. It's enough—and more than enough—to redeem 'family values' from the mouths of demagogues and place them right where they belong: in your soul."   —Nancy Mairs, *The Nation*

"With skillful prose, always tempered with laugh-out-loud humor, Bérubé not only argues compellingly for Jamie's place at 'our' table, but also demands that we look long and hard at our definition of table and at our definition of us. . . . A beautifully written book."
   —*American Journal of Human Genetics*

Michael Bérubé

Life As We Know It

Michael Bérubé is director of the program for research in the humanities at the University of Illinois at Urbana-Champaign. He is the author of five books, including *Public Access: Literary Theory and American Cultural Politics*, and has written for *The New Yorker, The Village Voice,* and many academic journals. He lives in Champaign, Illinois, with his wife, Janet Lyon, and their two sons, Nick and James.

Life As We Know It

A Father, a Family,

and an

Exceptional Child

Michael Bérubé

Vintage Books
A Division of Random House, Inc.
New York

FIRST VINTAGE BOOKS EDITION, APRIL 1998

Grateful acknowledgment is made to the *Children's Television Workshop*
for permission to reprint an excerpt from the song "Heavy and Light,"
from the television show *Sesame Street*. Copyright © 1990 by Sesame
Street, Inc./Splotched Animal. Reprinted by permission of the
Children's Television Workshop.

The Library of Congress has cataloged the
Pantheon Books edition as follows:

Bérubé, Michael, 1961–
Life as we know it : a father, a family, and an exceptional child
/ Michael Bérubé
p. cm.
Includes bibliographical references and index.
ISBN 0-679-44223-5
1. Bérubé, Michael, 1961-   2. Parents of handicapped children—
United States—Biography.
3. Mentally handicapped children—United States—Biography.
4. Down's syndrome—United States—Case studies.
5. Parent and child—United States—Case studies. I. Title.
HQ759.913.B47 1996
649'.1528'092—dc20 96-12805
CIP

Vintage ISBN: 0-679-75866-6

Author photograph © Corley Photography

Random House Web address: http://www.randomhouse.com/

Printed in the United States of America
10 9 8 7 6 5

For Jamie

with love and admiration

Contents

▲

INTRODUCTION   ix

CHAPTER ONE
Genetic Destiny   3

CHAPTER TWO
Humans Under Construction   40

CHAPTER THREE
Sapping the Strength of the State   95

CHAPTER FOUR
Walking the Talk   134

CHAPTER FIVE
Bragging and Rights   179

EPILOGUE   250
ACKNOWLEDGMENTS   265
SOURCES   268
INDEX   275

Introduction

▲

My little Jamie loves lists: foods, colors, animals, numbers, letters, states, classmates, parts of the body, days of the week, modes of transportation, characters who live on Sesame Street, and the names of the people who love him. Early last summer, I hoped his love of lists—and his ability to catalogue things *into* lists—would stand him in good stead during what would undoubtedly be a difficult "vacation" for anyone, let alone a three-year-old child with Down syndrome: a three-hour drive to Chicago, a rush-hour flight to LaGuardia, a cab to Grand Central, a train to Connecticut—and *then* smaller trips to New York, Boston, and Old Orchard Beach, Maine. Even accomplishing the first of these mission objectives—arriving safely at O'Hare—required a precision and teamwork I do not always associate with my family. I dropped off Janet and nine-year-old Nick at the terminal with the baggage, then took Jamie to long-term parking with me while they checked in, and then entertained Jamie all the way back to the terminal, via bus and shuttle train. We sang about the driver on the bus, and we counted all the escalator steps and train stops, and when we finally got to our plane, I told Jamie, *Look, there's Mommy and Nick at the gate! They're yelling that we're going to lose our seats! They want to know why it took us forty-five minutes to park the car!*

All went well from that point on, though, and in the end, I suppose you could say Jamie got as much out of his vacation as might any toddler being whisked up and down New England. He's a seasoned traveler, and he thrives on shorelines, family gatherings, and New Haven pizza. And he's good with faces and names.

Then again, as we learned toward the end of our brief stay in Maine, he doesn't care much for amusement parks. Not that Nick did either, at three. But apparently one of the attractions of Old Orchard Beach, for my wife and her siblings, was the small beachfront arcade and amusement park in town, which they associated with their own childhoods. It was an endearing strip, with a roller coaster just the right size for Nick—exciting, mildly scary, but with no loop-the-loops, rings of fire, or oppressive G forces. We strolled among bumper cars, cotton candy, games of chance and skill, and a striking number of French-Canadian tourists: perhaps the first time our two little boys had ever seen more than one Bérubé family in one place. James, however, wanted nothing to do with any of the rides, and though he loves to pretend-drive and has been on bumper cars before, he squalled so industriously before the ride began as to induce the bumper cars operator to let him out of the car and refund his two tickets.

Jamie finally settled in next to a train ride designed for children five and under or thereabouts, which, for two tickets, took its passengers around an oval layout and over a bridge four times. I found out quickly enough that Jamie didn't want to *ride* the ride; he merely wanted to stand at its perimeter, grasping the partition with both hands and counting the cars—one, two, three, four, five, six—as they went by. Sometimes, when the train traversed the bridge, James would punctuate it with tiny jumps, saying, "Up! up! up!" But for the most part, he was content to hang onto the metal bars of the partition, grinning and counting—and, when the train came to a stop, pulling my sleeve and saying, "More, again."

This went on for about half an hour, well past the point at which I could convincingly share Jamie's enthusiasm for tracking the train's progress. As it went on my spirits began to sink in a way I do not recall having felt before. Occasionally it will occur to Janet or to me that Jamie will always be "disabled," that his adult and adolescent years will undoubtedly be more difficult emotionally—for him and for us—than his early childhood, that we will never *not* worry about his future, his quality of life, whether we're doing enough for him. But usually these moments occur in the relative comfort of abstraction, when Janet and I are lying in bed at night and wondering what will become of us all. When I'm *with* Jamie, by contrast, I'm almost always fully occupied by taking care of his present needs rather than by worrying about his future. When he asks to hear the Beatles because he loves their cover of Little Richard's "Long Tall Sally," I just play the song, sing along, and watch him dance with delight; I do not concern myself with extraneous questions such as whether he'll ever distinguish early Beatles from late Beatles, Paul's songs from John's, originals from covers. These questions are now central to Nick's enjoyment of the Beatles, but that's Nick for you. Jamie is entirely sui generis, and as long as I'm with him I can't think of him as anything but Jamie.

I have tried. Almost as a form of emotional exercise, I have tried, on occasion, to step back and see him as others might see him, as an instance of a category, one item on the long list of human subgroups. *This is a child with Down syndrome*, I say to myself. *This is a child with a developmental disability*. It never works: Jamie remains Jamie to me. I have even tried to imagine him as he would have been seen in other eras, other places: *This is a retarded child*. And even: *This is a Mongoloid child*. This makes for unbearable cognitive dissonance. I can imagine that people might think such things, but I cannot imagine how they might think them in a way that prevents them from seeing Jamie *as* Jamie. I try to recall how I saw such children when I was a child, but here I guiltily draw a blank: I don't remember seeing them at all, which very likely means that I never quite saw them *as* children. Instead I remember a famous passage from Ludwig Wittgenstein's *Philosophical Investigations*: " 'Seeing-as' is not part of perception. And for this reason it is *like* seeing, and then again *not* like." Reading Wittgenstein, I often think, is something like listening to a brilliant and cantankerous uncle with an annoying fondness for koans. But on this one, I know exactly what he means.

As Jamie counted the train cars and urged them up, up, up for maybe the sixteenth time, I actually began to see him differently—and then to catch myself doing it. Seeing, then seeing-as, then seeing. He was not like the other children his size, who were riding the train with the usual varieties of distress and delight, and he was *noticeably* different. I began to see other parents looking at him with solicitude, curiosity, pity . . . and I thought, well, it's better than fear or disgust, but I still don't like it. Once last year, on our way back from visiting a local apple orchard, Janet told me that she'd seen other parents looking at James with an expression she read as *So that's what they're like when they're little*, and she said she'd sent those parents telepathic messages saying, *Don't be looking at my child, who's perfectly well behaved; keep an eye on your own child, the one who's pushing everybody else out of the wagon*. But this was different. Here, at a ride for small children, Jamie seemed clearly . . . limited. Not just unwilling, but somehow *unable* to enjoy the ride as "normal" children were supposed to enjoy it.

Finally, one mother approached us and asked Jamie (I was glad she asked us by asking Jamie directly, instead of asking me) if he would like to ride the train with her daughter. "Would you like to go on the train with this little girl?" I said, hoisting him up. "Noooooooo," said James, arching his back and repelling as best he could. "Down, down," he added, pointing to the ground. "Thanks very much," I said to the girl's mother. "He just loves watching the train, but he really doesn't want to go on. It was very nice of you to ask." She stayed by us for the duration of her daughter's ride, during which I engaged Jamie in a discussion of whether his classmates might ride the train:

"Does Madison ride a train?"

Jamie nodded "hm" (a shorthand "yes" he learned from his mother), then cocked his head and went into his "list" mode: "How 'bout . . . um . . . Keegan." Sometimes when Jamie gets pensive and says, "How 'bout, um," he's really thinking hard; sometimes, I think, he's just going through a routine he's learned from watching what pensive people do.

"Oh yes, Keegan rides a train," I assured him.

"How 'bout . . . um . . . Thaniel."

"Yes, Nathaniel also rides a train." (Good *th*, I thought.)

"How 'bout . . . um . . . Timmy."

"Timmy can ride a train."

"Are those his friends?" the girl's mother asked me.

"Yeah," I replied. "I'm hoping he'll get the idea that he can go on the train, too. Failing that, I'll settle for reminding him that he goes back to day care next week." But by this time I couldn't care less whether he went on the damn train; I just wanted him to vary his routine, to stop clutching the bars and saying "up, up, up." Not only for his benefit, or for the benefit of anyone who might be looking at him, but for my benefit: I was getting thoroughly bored with Jamie's take on the amusement park.

Suddenly I realized why Jamie's demeanor had been bothering me, why he had begun to seem like a "limited" child, a mere member of a *genus*: He was reminding me of a passage in William Faulkner's *The Sound and the Fury*, an image of Benjy Compson clutching the front gate and watching the "normal" children fearfully pass him by:

> *Aint nothing going to quiet him, T.P. said. He think if he down to the gate, Miss Caddy come back.*
> *Nonsense, Mother said.*
> I could hear them talking. I went out the door and I couldn't hear them, and I went down to the gate, where the girls passed with their booksatchels. They looked at me, walking fast, with their heads turned. I tried to say, but they went on, and I went along the fence, trying to say, and they went faster. Then they were running and I came to the corner of the fence and I couldn't go any further, and I held to the fence, looking after them and trying to say.

And then I remembered the very young Benjy, held tenderly by his sister Caddy after their mother has called him a "poor baby":

> we stopped in the hall and Caddy knelt and put her arms around me and her cold bright face against mine. She smelled like trees.
> "You're not a poor baby. Are you. Are you. You've got your Caddy. Haven't you got your Caddy."

It's one of the novel's earliest portraits of Caddy Compson: unlike her obsessively self-dramatizing mother, she loves Benjy too much to allow herself the distance of pity. The scene could not be more important to the emotional drama of Faulkner's novel. Caddy is so compelling and sympathetic a character precisely because she alone, of all the Compsons, consistently treats Benjy with a tenderness and compassion that never descends to condescension. Benjy is in this sense the key to the novel's moral index: *Whatsoever you do to the least of my brothers* . . . and when Caddy is banished from the household Benjy loses the only blood relative who has empathy enough to understand his desires. Not for nothing are Caddy and Benjy among the most unforgettable characters in the literature of our century. For all its famous narrative pyrotechnics, *The Sound and the Fury* is at bottom a novel of characters: doomed Caddy, brooding Quentin, demonic Jason, stoic Dilsey, and retarded Benjy, whose primary senses and emotions are painfully acute but who has no sense of the passage of time, no sense of good or evil. Most of Faulkner's readers know that the title of the novel alludes to the final soliloquy of Shakespeare's *Macbeth*:

> *Life's but a walking shadow, a poor player*
> *That struts and frets his hour upon the stage,*
> *And then is heard no more. It is a tale*
> *Told by an idiot, full of sound and fury,*
> *Signifying nothing.*

And, I suppose plenty of people (though all too few of my students) know that Benjy is part of a noble lineage in Western Lit, from *King Lear* to Dostoyevsky to *Forrest Gump*. But not too many readers know that Faulkner based his portrait of Benjy Compson on a local Mississippi man with Down syndrome.

▲

Later that night we went out for—what else?—seafood. Jamie loves fish, particularly salmon, and he is both entertained and perplexed by picture-book portraits of grizzly bears plucking and devouring live salmon from the river. "Are you like a hungry bear?" I ask James. "Do you gobble the salmon all up?" "Hm," Jamie nods, and he's not kidding: we've seen him pack away half a pound of salmon at a sitting, all the while putting one index finger to pursed lips and saying, "More."

So James had a great time at dinner, as we expected. Then, after dinner, he felt like tooling around the restaurant a little. It was a large place and touted itself as a "family" restaurant, which meant it allowed for a lot of high chairs, booster seats, small portions, spills, dropped utensils, and noise. I figured a wandering toddler, supervised by Dad, wouldn't constitute a breach of decorum. Luckily, a whole section of the restaurant lay empty—about ten tables against the wall, on a platform raised two steps above the rest of the floor, punctuated by a bar and a TV. For now, the area was serving as a station for waitresses on break and hockey fans watching game four of the Stanley Cup finals between Detroit and New Jersey. "Well, I know you want to see the game," Janet said to me. "Why don't you just shepherd him over there?"

So I kept one eye on the Stanley Cup finals and one eye on Jamie, as he methodically walked to each table, babbled spiritedly to himself, and shuttled back and forth to a small slate fireplace—dormant, of course, in late June. But it wasn't until he got to a table near me that I overheard some of his babbling: "Taco," he was saying. "Hm. Chicken. Okay." He nodded, and then off he went to the fireplace.

I frowned. *No, it can't be.* But then, he *is* awfully mimetic, isn't he? Doesn't he pretend to make coffee in the morning? Doesn't he try to toss the salad, set the table, and sweep up all the debris under his chair after dinner? *But he wouldn't come up with something so elaborate. Not at three years of age.* Well, wait. Here he comes. He stops at one table, then proceeds to another where he seems, by his account, to be depositing pizza and burgers. I know the menu: all of these are items from his list of favorite foods. I abandon the hockey game, take a seat at a nearby table, and call him over. "Jamie?" He walks over. "Are you the waiter?"

"Hm," he hms brightly, eyes wide, clearly delighted that I've picked up on this.

"Can you get me . . . let's see . . . a tuna sandwich?"

"Tuna!" he half-shouts in a hoarse little voice, and heads back to the fireplace. Did I imagine him pretending to write that down? I must have imagined it. He's extraordinarily mimetic, all right, as so many children are, but he doesn't usually get the tiny details; he's more comfortable with the general idea. I mean, he moves the dustbuster around, but he doesn't get *all* the rice, not by a long shot. He knows the route Janet traverses to make coffee, but he doesn't understand that the water has to go *into* the coffee pot. He's three years old, and like the Cat in the Hat, he makes a mess. But I know I *wanted* to think he wrote down my order.

He eventually got back to my table, but I don't remember whether he remembered that I'd asked for a tuna sandwich. By this point I was lost in the same kind of reverie that had possessed me at the amusement park, only this time I knew Jamie had no literary antecedents. He had decided that this wing of the restaurant was his, that these tables were peopled by customers wanting tacos, chicken, pizza, burgers, fries, and tuna (no green beans, no peach melba, no broccoli, no strawberries), that the fireplace was the kitchen, and that he was the waiter. This was the child who'd seemed so "limited" at the amusement park? The adults who'd seen him that afternoon may have seen him as a retarded child, as a disabled child, as a child to be pitied; and the children, if they were children like the child I was, may not have "seen" him at all. They certainly wouldn't have seen the distinct little person with whom I went to the restaurant that evening—a three year old whose ability to imitate is intimately tied to his remarkable ability to imagine, and whose ability to imagine, in turn, rests almost entirely on his capacity to imagine *other people*. Sure, his imagination has its limits; they're evident in the menu. He imagines people who order *his* list of foods, and yes, that list is (by any nutritionist's standards) limited. But the ability to imagine what other people might like, what other people might need—that seems to me a more crucial, more *essential* ability for human beings to cultivate than the ability to ride trains round and round. After we got back to our motel, after New Jersey had won the Cup, after the kids were finally asleep, I looked out over the beach and wondered whether Janet and I would always be able to understand what Jamie wants and needs, and whether our ability to imagine his desires will be commensurate with his ability to imagine ours.

Meanwhile, as Jamie was fussing about bumper cars, serving entrees to imaginary diners, and splashing in the waves, the 104th U.S. Congress was debating how to balance the federal budget by slashing programs for the disabled and the mentally handicapped; electricians and construction workers in New Haven were putting the final touches on preparations for the 1995 Special Olympics World Games; researchers with the Human Genome Project were trying to locate the biochemical basis for all our variances; and millions of ordinary human beings, all of them women, were undergoing prenatal testing for "severe" genetic defects like Down syndrome.

Jamie has no idea what a busy intersection he's landed in: statutes, allocations, genetics, reproduction, representation—all meeting at the crossroads of individual idiosyncrasy and sociopolitical construction. "Value" may be something that can only be determined socially, by collective and chaotic human deliberation; but individual humans like James are compelling us daily to determine what *kind* of "individuality" we will value, on what terms, and why. Perhaps those of us who can understand this intersection have an obligation to "represent" the children who can't; perhaps we have an obligation to inform our children about the traffic, and to inform the traffic about our children. As those children grow, perhaps we need to foster their abilities to represent themselves—and to listen to them as they do. I strongly suspect that we do have those obligations. I am not entirely sure what they might entail. But it is part of my purpose, in writing this book, to represent Jamie as best I can—just as it is part of my purpose, in representing Jamie, to ask about our obligations to each other, individually and socially, and about our capacity to imagine other people. I cannot say why it is that we possess the capacity to imagine others, let alone the capacity to imagine that we might have *obligations* to others; nor do I know why, if we possess such things, we so habitually act as if we do not. But I do know that Jamie has compelled me to ask these questions anew, just as I know how crucial it is that we collectively cultivate our capacities to imagine our obligations to each other.

■

CHAPTER ONE

Genetic Destiny

▲

In my line of work I don't think very often about carbon or
potassium, much less about polypeptide chains or transfer-
RNA. I teach American and African-American literature; Janet
Lyon, my wife and general partner, teaches modern British literature and women's studies. Nothing about our jobs requires us to
be conscious of the biochemical processes that made us—and,
more recently, our children—into conscious beings. But in 1986,
when Janet was pregnant with our first child, Nicholas, I would
lie awake for hours, wondering how the baseball-size clump of
cells in her uterus was really going to form something living, let
alone something capable of thought. I knew that the physical
processes that form dogs and drosophila are more or less as intricate, on the molecular level, as those that form humans; but pup-
pies and fruit flies don't go around asking how they got here. And
though humans have been amazed and puzzled by human gestation for quite a while now, it wasn't until a few nanoseconds ago
(in geological time) that their wonder began to focus on the
chemical minutiae that somehow differentiate living matter from
"mere" matter. The fact that self-replicating molecules had eventually come up with a life form that could actually pick apart the

workings of self-replicating molecules . . . well, let's just say I found this line of thought something of a distraction. So much so that finally a friend of ours decided that what I needed was a good dose of demystification. "Michael," he said, stopping me in the middle of one of my frantic father frenzies, "I know this is all new to you, but look at it this way—it's just DNA making a home for itself."

I recall replying that the spectacle of DNA making its home was plenty worthy of our attention, but I also thought, at the time, that I would never again devote so much attention to it. Not in my line of work—and probably not even with a second or third child, either. I figured the miracle of human birth, like the miracle of humans landing on the moon, just wouldn't have the same emotional impact the second time around.

Five years later, in September 1991, Janet was pregnant again, another fall semester was beginning, and I was up late writing. At 2 A.M., Janet asked when I was coming to bed. At 4 A.M. she asked again. "Soon," I said. "Well, you should probably stop working now," she replied, "because I think I'm going into labor." At which point she presented me with an early birthday present, a watch with a second hand. "You'll find it easier to time contractions with one of these."

That was the first unexpected thing: James wasn't due for another two weeks. Then came more unexpected things, in rapid succession.

Eight hours later, in the middle of labor, Janet spotted a dangerous arrhythmia on her heart monitor. The only person in the room was an obstetrics staff nurse; Janet turned to her and barked, "That's V-tach. We need a cardiologist in here. Get a bolus of lidocaine ready, and get the crash cart." Being an ex-cardiac-intensive-care nurse comes in handy sometimes—but as for me, I hadn't the faintest idea what Janet's orders meant. I only knew they were urgent, and "crash cart" certainly sounded ominous. Pounding on her chest and forcing herself to cough, Janet broke out of what was possibly a lethal heart rhythm. Labor stalled; up to this point everything had gone perfectly according to plan, and we'd been diligently doing our breathing exercises and timing those contractions. Now we found ourselves staring at each other for an hour in a standard-issue, pastel-blue hospital "birthing room," too apprehensive even to say a word about what we were apprehending, afraid that if we talked about what might happen, it just might. Suddenly, at a strange moment when Janet and I were the only people in the room, James's head presented. A few minutes earlier it had looked as if the "pushing" phase of labor was still hours away; now the delivery itself was upon us. I hollered down the hall for help. James appeared within minutes, an unmoving baby of a deep, rich, purple hue, his neck wreathed in his umbilical cord. "He looks downsy around the eyes," I heard. Downsy? He looks stillborn, I thought. They unwrapped the cord, cut it, gave him oxygen. Quickly, incredibly, he revived. No cry, but who cared? They gave him an Apgar score of 7, on a scale from 1 to 10. I remember feeling an immense relief. My wife was alive, my second child was alive. At the end of a teeth-grating hour during which I'd wondered if either of them would see the end of the day, Down syndrome seemed like a reprieve.

Over the next half hour, as the nurses worked on James, and Janet and I tried to collect our thoughts, I realized I didn't know very much about Down's, other than that it meant James had an extra chromosome and would be mentally retarded. I must have looked as if I were horribly lost, because through her tears Janet

was actually trying to comfort me: "We can handle this," I remember her saying. "We can handle this together. This is not a
stopper. We can handle this." I knew even then, somehow, that
Janet was neither predicting nor describing but *decreeing* it so.
From here on, we *could* handle this, because my soulmate and
partner said we could. She was telling me, and telling herself as
well, that we could bear anything this child might bear with
him.

But could we believe our own hope? Could we meet even the
simplest of challenges this child might pose? Would we ever have
normal lives again? We'd struggled for eight years on salaries that
left us able to peer at the poverty line only if one of us stood on
the other's shoulders. A mere three weeks earlier, the university
had hired Janet, thus making us one of the extremely rare dual-
career academic couples working in the same department; we
knew how lucky we were, and we thought we were finally going
to be "comfortable." But now were we going to spend the rest of
our days caring for a severely disabled child? Would we have even
an hour to ourselves? Christ, we'd only just finished paying off
the bills for *Nick's* birth two months earlier, and now were we
going to plunge into the kind of catastrophic medical debt that
only American health care can make possible? These were selfish
thoughts, and the understanding that selfish thoughts might be
"natural" at such a time didn't make them any less bitter or insis-
tent.

We went over the past few months. The pregnancy had been
occasionally odd but not exactly scary. We'd decided against getting an amniocentesis at twelve weeks, on the grounds that a
sonogram would pick up nearly any serious problems with the
fetus *except* Down syndrome, and the chances of having a child
with Down syndrome at Janet's age, thirty-six, were roughly

equal to the chances of an amniocentesis-induced miscarriage (1 in 225 and 1 in 200, respectively). Later in the pregnancy there were some hitches: reduced fetal movements, disproportionate fetal measurements on sonograms, low weight gain, and so on. Our worries were persistent but vague.

Back in the present, over on his table in the birthing room, James wasn't doing very well. He still wasn't moving, he had no sucking reflex, and he was getting bluer. How could his Apgar have been 7? We'd been told everything was all right for a newborn with Down's, but it wasn't, as we found a bit later when James was transferred from the nursery to the intensive care unit and put on 100 percent oxygen. It turned out that a fetal opening in his heart hadn't closed fully. You and I had a similar arrangement until just before we were born, when our heart's ventricles sealed themselves off in order to get us ready to start conducting oxygen from our lungs into our bloodstream; in Jamie's case, there was an opening between his pulmonary artery and the descending aorta. He had a hole where no hole should be and wasn't oxygenating properly.

There was more. Along with his patent ductus arteriosus and his trisomy 21, there was laryngomalacia (floppy larynx), jaundice, polycythemia (an excess of red blood cells), torticollis, vertebral anomaly, scoliosis (curvature of the spine), hypotonia (low muscle tone), and (not least of these) feeding problems. That's a lot of text to wade through to get to your kid.

Basically, James was in danger. If he made it through the night, he would still be a candidate, in the morning, for open heart surgery *and* a tracheostomy. Because of the laryngomalacia, which isn't closely related to Down's, he couldn't coordinate sucking, swallowing, and breathing, and his air supply would close off if he slept on the wrong side. Surgery (the tracheostomy) was therefore a very real option. The vertebral problems, we learned, occur in roughly one of six kids with Down's; his first three vertebrae were malformed, his spinal cord vulnerable. And his neck muscles were abnormally tight (that's the torticollis), leaving him with a 20-degree head tilt to the left. He was being fed intravenously and had tubes not only in his arm but in his stomach as well, run neatly through one of his umbilical arteries. Before this I had not known that there *was* such a thing as an umbilical artery. Our first Polaroid of him shows a little fleshy thing under a clear plastic basin, lost in machinery and wires. I remember thinking, it's all right that they do all this to him now because he'll never remember it. But it can't be a pleasant introduction to the world.

By the time Jamie was settled in the ICU and Janet was sleeping in her recovery room, it was late afternoon. Early that morning, we had dropped Nick at a friend's house for the day, along with instructions about how to get him to and from school; now mother and infant had been assigned their relevant medical staff, and I could briefly turn my attention elsewhere. But somehow I would have to break the news to Nick.

Nick had followed the past eight months' events with great enthusiasm. He had skimmed fetal development books, noting how the fertilized egg would progress from "yucky" to "weird" to "okay-looking," and he had even learned that a baby starts growing when the daddy adds something to the egg. We decided the rest of the details of human fertilization could wait until the day of Nick's wedding. When, in April, the first sonogram revealed that the baby would be a boy, we told Nick that afternoon, upon getting him from school, that he would soon have a baby brother. Nick sat up in the back seat of the car, jaw agape, then clenched his fists and rolled himself into fetal position, saying, "Yes! yes!"

That summer, on July 4, the baby suddenly stopped moving—in retrospect, our first sign that something might be wrong. Janet checked into the hospital, and while she underwent various tests, Nick and I visited the maternity waiting room, where we found pamphlets on how to prepare for the arrival of siblings. Nick started reading through these and quickly turned to me in puzzlement, unable to understand the part about how some big sisters and brothers don't want the new baby to come home from the hospital. Sibling rivalry? Nick had to read about it to discover that it was an emotional option. He was merely hoping the little baby was all right. Now, two and a half months later, I would have to tell him that the baby brother he wanted so badly might not be the kind of baby he had in mind. I would not only be asking my precocious five year old to understand something as unfathomable as Down syndrome; I would also be asking him to amplify his imagination, extend his soul. I didn't know myself whether it was safe to love Jamie yet, whether it was appropriate to think of him and talk about him as my son, Nick's brother.

So Nick learned that the baby was born alive and whole but was very sick; some things, we hoped, would get better, but at least one thing would be with him all his life. Down syndrome was kind of complicated that way. Nick wanted to know what it was; in return, I asked him how much he wanted to know about it. Did he want the long explanation or the short one? Characteristically, Nick chose the long one, and I was thankful that ever since he'd been hospitalized for severe asthma at the age of two, we'd given him pretty comprehensive explanations of medical emergencies. He wouldn't understand everything about a genetic disorder, since he didn't yet know that cells carried chromosomes and genes, but at least he'd have someplace to put the information until he *could* understand it all. At three, he had been very young to understand what bronchioles and oxygenation were, and now he'd be very young to understand what nondisjunction and DNA were as well. We ordered a pizza, talked about amoebas and eye color, and stayed up well past his normal bedtime.

The next morning I drove Nick to school, canceled my classes for the day, and checked into the NICU. I still didn't know how to greet James, or how to conduct myself around this bruised baby wrapped in wires and leads: I couldn't pick him up and hold him, and I couldn't even make eye contact because he still hadn't opened his eyes. I remember staring at him through his basin, mumbling, "Hey, little man," but even that lame hello came out sounding forced, insincere. Janet and I tried to read Jamie's prospects from machines and from the faces of his doctors and nurses, and for most of that first day the outlook was so cloudy that we spent our time distracting ourselves from thinking about the various kinds of surgery Jamie might have to undergo. Fortunately, our car was stalling out, frequently, for no discernable reason, so we deflected some of our anxiety onto the more quotidian question of how to go about getting a new car; we had arranged for Janet's classes to be taught for the next few weeks by a friend and graduate student, and we kicked ourselves for not having made any similar arrangements for *my* classes. Like many universities, Illinois doesn't have any policy on maternity leave; Janet would have to rely on her "sick leave" instead. *Paternity* leave hadn't even occurred to us, probably because we'd both grown up in the United States. Sometimes I think it would be a good idea to bring Western civilization to the United States after all.

But even as we groused about American business as usual, American medicine was keeping our little boy afloat. We were afraid that Jamie might require extraordinary measures to stay alive, and we were afraid that we would have to decide what we thought about such measures—that is, if the hospital staff should happen to honor our sense of when "life" is meaningful and when it's just a legal fiction. Would Jamie's doctors perform miraculous technological feats ostensibly on his behalf, and would we be granted the right to refuse such treatment if we considered it excessive? We didn't want to think about the conditions under which we would actually have to answer such a question. In the meantime, all Jamie needed was IV feedings, supplemental oxygen, and a blood gas machine: marvels in almost any other century, but routine in 1991. Some months later, the writer Kirkpatrick Sale, a renowned environmentalist and technophobe, came to speak at Illinois, and when he was through with his excoriation of Western science, pollution, waste, and rapacity, I asked him whether blood gas machines might not have been, on balance, a good thing to have introduced into the world. Not that I don't agree that our corporations have poisoned much of the planet and that advanced medicine raises as many questions as it answers; it's just that I don't have the option of feeling nostalgia for a cleaner, less spoiled past in which both of my children would have died in infancy, one at two years and the other at two days.

Gradually Jamie's prospects improved, and one anxiety after another peeled away: Jamie's duct closed, and as I entered the intensive-care unit one morning I found that the staff had erased from his chart the phone number of the emergency helicopter service that would have flown him to Peoria for heart surgery. His blood oxygen levels got up to the high 90s and stayed there, even as he was weaned from 100 percent oxygen to a level just above the atmospheric norm. A tracheoscopy (that is, a viewing of his throat with an eyepiece at the end of a tube) determined that he didn't need a tracheostomy. He still wasn't feeding, but he was opening an eye now and then and looking out at his brother and his parents.

We established a routine of visits, morning and evening. In the morning, we would arrive after we'd dropped Nick at school, and in the evening we'd arrive with Nick in tow. We were told that children weren't allowed in the ICU, but we assured everyone that Nick would scrub in like everyone else and wouldn't go near any of the equipment. We just couldn't leave him standing at the window for an hour, cordoned off from saying hello and bringing presents to his baby brother. Nick's presence was important to us, we said, but for all we knew it was vastly more important to Nick and to Jamie, too.

One of the benefits of having your child stationed in a small-town ICU, we found, was that your ICU nurses weren't so numbed by trauma and overwork that they couldn't accommodate a big brother like Nick. So in the evenings, while Janet and I talked to the nurses and watched Jamie's gauges, Nick deflected his own anxieties by filling pages upon pages of scrap paper with drawings of new cars and taping them to the sides of Jamie's ICU bed for his entertainment. Misspelled Festivas, Lamborghinis, and Corollas soon formed a frieze around Jamie's clear plastic bassinet, and although Nick had thoughtfully taped his pictures facing inward so that Jamie could see them, I finally had to say to Nick, "it's very sweet that you're drawing so many cars for your brother, but maybe it would be a good idea to draw him something else, like a face." Nick immediately saw the wisdom in this and began peppering his cars with faces.

One evening, as I looked up from a long, bleary stare at Jamie and his apparatus, I was startled to see what looked like large, ungainly praying mantises moving slowly about the room: spindly and fragile, they seemed to be gliding erratically through a thin, clear fluid, stopping, starting, and making random bursts of noise to each other. In the next instant I knew that these creatures were *humans*, nurses and parents, and with an odd regret I knew I would never again be so estranged from everything as to see my own species from such a distance. "Dad?" Nick asked a moment later, bringing me firmly back to myself, or at least to my identity as understood by someone else. He looked up at me somberly from his makeshift drawing-table. "I think I'm like those bad children."

This did not help to reorient me. "What bad children, hon?"

Nick looked away. "The ones who don't want their baby brothers to come home."

I had no idea that this would come next on the agenda. I inhaled sharply and took Nick in my arms. "Oh, sweetie. Those weren't *bad* children, Nicholas. It's completely normal to feel funny about having a baby brother. *That's* what that little book was about. When a baby arrives, they need so much attention, and the bigger kid sometimes feels left out. Especially when the baby is like Jamie."

"A silly Mister Down Syndrome Baby," Nick half-smiled, not yet sure whether this was something to make light of.

"Yes, indeed. A silly Mister Down Syndrome Baby." Later that night, though I forget exactly how, it became clear that while Nick was festooning Jamie's corner of the ICU with Corvettes and Cavaliers and Tracers and Tercels, he was also thinking that his own ambivalence about these boring visits to the ICU was one reason his baby brother was so sick—as if he were somehow prolonging Jamie's hospitalization by being like those bad children who didn't want their baby siblings to come home.

Outside the ICU, the social apparatus of "disability" was

forming around us with remarkable speed. Within days we were known to, and put in touch with, a bewildering number of social agencies responsible for different aspects of James' care. We tried to sort out the DSC (Developmental Services Center), DSCC (Department of Specialized Care for Children), and the DSACC (Down Syndrome Association of Champaign County). There were visits from Diversified Healthcare, speech pathologists, physical therapists, social workers. One overly helpful person started giving us the statistics on the incidence of leukemia in people with Down's and warned us that James might display "inappropriate affection," a phrase I've been tumbling around in my head ever since. One staffer told us Jamie's vertebrae might require corrective surgery, if not now then in early adolescence; another staffer said Jamie's neck was nothing to worry about, nothing that would prevent him from playing football in high school.

I got hold of everything within reach on genetics, reproduction, and "abnormal" human development, dusting off college textbooks I hadn't touched since before Nick was born. At one point a staff nurse was sent in to check on *our* mental health, and she found us babbling about meiosis and monoploids, wondering anew that Jamie had "gotten" Down syndrome the second he became a zygote. When the nurse inadvertently left behind her notes, Janet sneaked a peek. "Parents seem to be intellectualizing," we read. "Well," Janet shrugged, "that seems accurate enough."

Looking over the fossil record, I really don't see any compelling logic behind our existence on the planet. I'm told that intelligence has obvious survival value, since organisms with a talent for information processing "naturally" beat out their competitors for food, water, and condos, but human history doesn't convince me that *our* brand of intelligence is just what the world was waiting for. Thus I've never believed we were supposed to survive the Ice Age, or that some cosmic design mandated the cataclysmic collision in the late Cretaceous period that gave us an iridium layer deep in our soil and may have ended the dinosaurs' 200 million-year reign. Bacteria and horseshoe crabs unmodified for eons are still with us; but what has become of Eusthenopteron, introduced to me by then five-year-old Nicholas as the fish that could walk on land? If you were fighting for survival 350 million years ago, you'd think you'd have had a leg up on the competition if you developed small bones in your fins, enabling you to shimmy up onto shore. But you'd be wrong. These days, Eusthenopteron is nothing more than a card in Nick's "prehistoric animals" collection, alongside the ankylosaur, the mastodon, and the lounge lizard. I figured we were here thanks to dumb luck and blame cussedness, and though we have managed to understand our own biochemical origins and take neat closeup pictures of a crescent Saturn (quite a feat, if you think about it, since you have to position a camera *behind* Saturn to see the planet as a crescent), we also spend much of our time exterminating ourselves and most other species we meet. And nothing in Nick's cards says we too won't wind up as a card in nature's deck of "prehistoric" animals.

A lot of the problem with human neonates is the dang head. It's too big. As the neck is to the giraffe and the tail is to the peacock, so is the cerebral cortex to the human. Our brains are so outsized and unwieldy that in order to get out of the mother's body, our young have to slide one half of their skulls over the other half, and they come out all distended and asymmetrical (which is one reason why our film renditions of alien intelligent species fixate so obsessively on elongated skulls). Even after we're born, we can't hold our heads up, for though we've got the ecosystem's most elaborate neural net in our trust, its control center is perched atop a weak, skinny, and extremely vulnerable tube called the neck, through which all our food, air, and water have to pass in order to do us any good. As Arthur C. Clarke once pointed out, it's not a very well-designed system, especially for one's first few months on the planet. What's even stranger about those first few months is that human babies' big, impressive brains are actually the *least* developed at birth of all the primates. Every other primate baby arrives armed with "bonding" skills humans don't develop for four months or so. Yet, for some reason, human parents put up with 2 A.M. feedings, postpartum depressions, and random neonatal excretions all in the hope that their offspring will eventually distinguish them from all the other noisy, nattering bipeds galumphing about. I don't know why we're designed this way, but it seems as if natural selection has somehow made us a species whose reproduction depends inordinately on parental faith.

Still, it wasn't until I got to college and started thinking about sex and drugs in rather immediate ways that I began to realize that the workings of chance on the molecular level are even more terrifying than on the evolutionary plane. Of course, the molecular and the evolutionary have everything to do with each other; it's just that the minutiae of mitosis are more awe-inspiring to me, *because* more quotidian, than the thought of random rocks slamming into my home planet every couple hundred million years. For those who don't feel like cracking open old textbooks, Richard Powers's novel *The Gold Bug Variations* offers some idea of what happens when your DNA gets involved in cell division: "seven feet of aperiodic crystal unzips, finds complements of each of its billion constituents, integrates them perfectly without tearing or entangling, then winds up again into a fraction of a millimeter, all in two minutes." And this is just the ordinary stuff your cells are doing every moment. Sex, as always, is a little more complicated.

So let's talk about sex. But let's leave aside the difficult, political stuff like infant mortality rates and the quality of prenatal and postnatal care for just a second—although I tend to believe there's not much that's more indicative of a society's values than these. (Imagine a country in which deeply religious people blockaded streets, harassed pedestrians, screamed at the top of their lungs, and terrorized their ideological adversaries *all in order to insure adequate prenatal care for impoverished mothers*. Then remember that the United States has the industrialized world's only *rising* infant mortality rate.) Anywhere from fifteen to twenty of every hundred pregnancies end in miscarriage; if you count miscarriages that occur within hours of fertilization, that number may begin to look more like *fifty* of every hundred. Chromosomal abnormalities account for over half of all miscarriages, and trisomies—three chromosomes where there should be a pair—account for half of those. Frightening as these statistics may be, I prefer to see the glass half full: it's a wonder that so many fertilizations actually *work*.

Mitosis, that bewildering unzipping of a seven-foot chain of chemicals, is actually just ordinary cell division; meiosis is another process altogether. After mitosis, a cell whose nucleus contains forty-six chromosomes becomes two identical cells whose nuclei each contain the same forty-six chromosomes. After meiosis, a cell with forty-six chromosomes has divided into two new cells genetically *different* from the parent cell and often different from each other: each new cell now contains twenty-three chromosomes, one from each "chromosome pair" possessed by the parent cell. Then there's a second meiotic division of each new cell, so that meiosis winds up producing *four* new "daughter nuclei" from one original cell whereas mitosis produces two. Meiosis is the first step in human sexual reproduction, occurring well before anyone's asked anyone out on a date. It's the reason you inherited half your genes from your mother and half from your father, each of whom gave you half of theirs. One of the advantages of meiosis, in the long run, is that it produces a great deal of genetic variety in a species: if you shuffle two half-sets of human chromosomes you can get something like 64 trillion possible outcomes. When the outcome is Down syndrome, it's almost always because somebody's twenty-first chromosome failed to divide during the "anaphase" stage of meiosis—and then when the resulting twenty-four-chromosomed nucleus eventually hooked up with a properly divided nucleus (this would occur at fertilization, at some point during or after the first date), the resulting zygote got three sets of twenty-first chromosomes. Trisomy 21.

Normally, each of us has twenty-two pairs of autosomes, and then two sex chromosomes—XX or XY. Abnormalities of the sex chromosomes, like Klinefelter's syndrome (47 chromosomes, XXY), Turner's syndrome (45, XO), and other unnamed possibilities (XXX, XYY, and so on) can turn out to be unnoticeable in childhood. Because the Y chromosome contains so few genes and extra X chromosomes are deactivated in multiple configurations (like XXY), people with sex chromosome abnormalities are sometimes not diagnosed until puberty or adulthood, when their genetic makeup manifests itself in "observable" phenomena such as infertility. Trisomies can apparently happen anywhere; there's nothing special about the twenty-first chromosome that makes it uniquely susceptible to faulty self-replication. Of the myriad possible genetic mistransmissions in the autosomes, it appears that only three kinds of trisomies have made it to term often enough to acquire the name of their discoverers: trisomy 13 (Patau's syndrome), trisomy 18 (Edwards' syndrome), and trisomy 21 (Down's syndrome, now more often referred to as Down syndrome). Trisomy 21 is far and away the most common of these; trisomy 16 is more common still, but is universally lethal. Trisomies 9 and 10 are next in frequency, and there are records of all kinds of partial trisomies as well—first chromosome, fifth, fourteenth. "Partial" trisomies are a slight misnomer, since they don't really involve three chromosomes where there should be a pair. They occur when a chromosome *has* managed to divide during meiosis but has done so inaccurately, leading to a fertilized egg that has excessive genetic material on (for example) the first chromosome pair, but not three first chromosomes. Partial trisomies are often referred to by the chromosome *arm*: thus, if the *p* arm of chromosome 1 failed to divide correctly during meiosis, then the child will have a 1 pair with an extra *p* arm, and that's called "trisomy 1p syndrome."

Just about anything can go wrong between meiosis and fertilization, in other words, and it often does. Down syndrome alone accounts for one of every 600 to 800 live births; it's one of the most common birth "defects" on the planet. But from another angle, Down syndrome is actually far more common than that, because roughly 80 percent of fetuses with Down's are eventually miscarried. It's hard to say for certain, since miscarriage can have so many causes (not all of them genetic in origin), but it's possible that trisomy 21 happens quite frequently, perhaps once in every 100 to 200 fertilizations. It turns out, actually, that Down's results from an undivided *twenty-second* chromosome rather than an undivided twenty-first, as had been thought for as long as chromosomes and Down's were known things; but to keep the literature on Down's unconfused, geneticists have renumbered chromosomes 22 and 21, even though the rest of our numbers correspond to the length of the chromosome (starting with 1). Trisomy 21 is not only the most frequent but also, so far as we know, the least dangerous of the trisomies. Edwards' and Patau's syndromes were both named in 1960, the year before I was born. Kids with Edwards' or Patau's syndrome are born with serious skeletal deformations, multiple systems failures (digestive, circulatory, nervous), and profound levels of mental retardation; they normally don't live more than a few months. When I first studied genetics, those were the kind of effects I expected of genetic anomalies, regardless of the size of the chromosome. Although the twenty-first chromosome is the smallest we have, little James still has extra genetic material in every single cell. Trisomy 21 isn't one of the lethal trisomies, but it's still a major genetic error, and most major genetic errors are catastrophic biochemical events. You'd think the effects of such a basic transcription error would make themselves felt pretty clearly.

By contrast, what's odd about Down's is how extraordinarily subtle it can be. Mental retardation is one well-known effect, and it can sometimes be severe, but anyone who's watched Chris Burke in *Life Goes On* or the 1995 Special Olympics World Games knows that the extent of such retardation can be next to negligible. The *real* story of Down's lies not in intelligence tests but in developmental delays across the board, and for the first two years of James' life the most important of these were physical more than mental (although thanks to James I've come to see how interdependent the mental and physical really are). His muscles are weaker than those of most children his age, his nasal passages imperceptibly narrower. His tongue is slightly thicker; one ear is crinkly. His fingers would be shorter and stubbier but for the fact that his mother's are long, thin, and elegant. His face is a few degrees flatter through the middle, his nose delicate.

Down's doesn't cut all children to one mold; the relations between James' genotype and phenotype are lacy and intricate. It's sort of like what happens in Ray Bradbury's short story "A Sound of Thunder," in which a time traveler accidentally steps on a butterfly while hunting T. Rex 65 million years ago and returns home to find that he's changed the conventions of English spelling and the outcome of the previous day's election. As he hit the age of two, James was very pleased to find himself capable of walking; by three, he had learned to say the names of colors, to count to ten, and to claim that he would *really* be turning four. Of all our autosomal nondisjunctions, only Down syndrome produces so nuanced, so finely articulated a variation on human reproduction. James is less mobile and more susceptible to colds than his peers, but as his grandparents have often attested, you could play with him for hours and never see anything "wrong" with him.

Then there's a variant form of Down's, called mosaicism, which results from the failure of the chromosome to divide not *before* fertilization but immediately *after*, during the early stages of cell division in embryogeny. Only one in a hundred people with Down's are mosaics, but it's possible for such folks to have some normal cells and some with trisomy 21; there's something about our chromosomes, then, that can produce anomalies during either meiosis *or* mitosis. There's also *translocation*, in which the twenty-first chromosome splits off and joins the fourteenth or fifteenth, producing people who can be called "carriers"; they can give birth to more translocation carriers, normal children, or translocation kids with Down's. At this point we get into an area of genetic complexity that's beyond my ability to synopsize, but it's possible for "carriers" to have the right number of chromosomes even though one of their twenty-firsts is attached to one of the fourteenths. So they don't have Down's, but they do have some complicated meioses.

Although everyone knows that incidence of Down's increases

with maternal age, almost no one knows that three quarters of all such children are born to mothers under thirty-five, or that fathers are genetically "responsible" for about one-fifth of them. Nor did I know, until James was born, that there are now two competing theories for why older women are more likely to have children with Down's. The older theory is the "sticky chromosomes" theory, which holds that nondisjunctions happen during meiosis because the eggs have been lying around longer (or, as one textbook eloquently puts it, "nondisjunction during oogenesis is thus a function of senescence of the oocytes"). But the newer theory, a "with age comes wisdom" theory, suggests that what happens as women get older isn't that their chromosomes get stickier but that their uteruses get more tolerant of fetal abnormality. The body starts taking a more liberal attitude toward difference, perhaps.

So, then, how shall we craft a theory of "difference" sufficient unto humans such as James? Most contemporary analyses of difference focus on relatively visible (and politically charged) variables like race and gender, and for over a hundred years the West has been plagued by biologists and social scientists obsessed with the project of ascribing human differences to genetics and assigning traits by race (intelligence, criminality, musical talent, and so on). But "race" accounts for only a minuscule proportion of human differences, whereas the vast majority of our genetic differences are to be found *among local populations*. From the geneticists' perspective, in other words, we've been led astray by our focus on visible markers like skin color and facial features. Or as one textbook has it, the question has to do with which genes you're looking for (or at):

In humans, some gene frequencies (for example, those for skin color or hair form) obviously are well differentiated among populations and major geographical groups (so-called geographical "races"). If one looks at identifiable structural genes, however, rather than these outward phenotypic characters, the situation is rather different. . . . The study of polymorphic blood groups and enzyme loci in a variety of human populations has shown that about 85% of total human genetic diversity is found within local populations, about 8% between local populations within major geographical "races," and the remaining 7% between the major "races."

That analysis dates from 1981; a more recent textbook, reporting genetic variances among 11,900 individuals from 59 different populations around the world, reports even more dramatic findings: "98.5% of the observed variation lies between individuals within populations, about 0.8% of the observed variation is between racial groups, and about 0.6% of the variation is between populations in the same racial group." As Richard Powers writes, "The growth of genetics has been the growth of realizing how huge the gap between individuals is." By themselves, the percentages alone may be astonishing, but they're even more astonishing when you contemplate the sheer numbers involved. Let's say the human genome consists of around 100,000 genes. About 80 percent—80,000—of these are identical in all humans. That leaves 20,000 genes to shuffle, and $2^{20,000}$ possible variations you and your mate can pass on to your children ($2^{20,000}$ is one of those numbers that run from one side of Kansas to the other). Well over a hundred times as many of those variations will be attributable to your "local population" inheritances as will be attributable to your racial status. In a genetic sense, then, "race" and gender matter hardly at all (indeed, most feminists would argue that gender, unlike sex, is not genetic); by far the most dynamic sites of human variation are to be found in different local populations.

Yet, whatever else they might be, forms of human social organization are largely a matter of determining *which* differences make a difference: skin color remains a more significant mark of human differentiation than eye color. Since any two people of the same group (with the exception of identical twins) will always differ in many millions of biological details, it's always possible to divide humans into many billion categories consisting of one person each. Human "difference," then, is always a matter of negotiating the competing claims of difference *within* and difference *between*, such that perceived differences within European peoples (say, English and French, German and Polish, Norwegian and Swede), however crucial they may be to the bloody history of Europe, may pale by comparison to perceived differences between Europeans and Africans. By the same token, the recognition of likeness may itself be the source of mortal conflict, as in the so-called "narcissism of minor differences," where English and Irish, Arabic and Turkish, Chinese and Japanese peoples frantically find rationales for conceiving each other as radically Other. Depending on how you cut your "we," we're more like apes than like our fellow Americans. Either we humans are hopelessly atomized, each sealed within the biochemical prison of the self, or we're more closely related to each other than we can bear to think.

Parents seem to be intellectualizing. And why not?

There has never been a better time to be born with Down syndrome—and that's really saying something, since Down syndrome appears to have been with us for ten million years or more. How do we know? Because in the 1970s, Down syndrome was reported in gorillas and chimpanzees. Since there's no chance that we humans "gave" Down syndrome to other primate species, it would seem that trisomy 21 has been an integral part of being "human" ever since our evolutionary tree split off from that of apes. Cro-Magnons and Neandertals had babies with Down syndrome; *Australopithecus* had children with Down syndrome; *ramapithecus*, the chattering, quadruped ancestor of *Australopithecus*, had children with Down syndrome; even those ape-men and ape-women in the opening scene of Stanley Kubrick's *2001: A Space Odyssey*—they had kids with Down syndrome, too. For whatever reason, we've produced offspring with Down syndrome with remarkable regularity at every point in our history as hominids—even though it's a genetic anomaly that's not transmitted hereditarily (except in extremely rare instances) and has no obvious survival value. The statistical incidence of Down's in the current human population is no less staggering: there may be almost half a million people with Down's in the United States alone, or just about one on every other street corner.

But although *Homo sapiens* and all our hominid forebears have always experienced some difficulty dividing our chromosomes properly, Down syndrome was not identified and named until 1866, when British physician J. Langdon Down diagnosed it as "mongolism" (because it produced children with almond-shaped eyes reminiscent, to at least one nineteenth-century British mind, of Central Asian faces). At the time, the average life expectancy of children with Down's was under ten. And for a hundred years thereafter—during which the discovery of antibiotics lengthened the lifespan of Down's kids to around twenty—Down syndrome was known as "mongoloid idiocy."

The 1980 edition of my college genetics textbook, *The Science of Genetics: An Introduction to Heredity*, opens its segment on Down's with the words, "An important and tragic instance of trisomy in humans involves Down's Syndrome, or mongoloid idiocy." It includes a picture of a toddler-age mongoloid idiot along with a cellular photograph of his chromosomes (called a "kary-otype") and the completely erroneous information that most people with Down's have IQs in the low 40s. The presentation is objective, dispassionate, and strictly "factual," as it should be in a college textbook. But reading it again in 1991, I began to wonder: Is there a connection between the official textual representation of Down syndrome in medical discourses (including college textbooks) and the social policies by which people with Down syndrome are understood and misunderstood?

You bet your life there is. Now, anyone who's paid attention to the "political correctness" wars on American campuses knows how stupid the academic left can be. We're always talking about language instead of reality, whining about "lookism" and "differently abled persons" instead of changing the world the way the real he-man left *used* to do. But you know, there really is a difference between calling someone a "mongoloid idiot" and calling him or her "a person with Down syndrome." There's even a difference between calling people "retarded" and calling them "delayed." These words may appear to mean the same damn thing when you look them up in Webster's, but I remember full well from my days as an American male adolescent that I never taunted my peers by calling them "delayed." Even for those of us who were shocked at the frequency with which "homo" and "nigger" were thrown around in our fancy Catholic high school, "retard" aroused no comment, no protest. In other words, a retarded person is just a retard. But *delayed* persons will get where they're going eventually, if you'll only have some patience with them.

One night I said something like this to one of the leaders of what I usually think of as the other side in the academic culture wars, just to make the point that our terminology *can* matter to our social lives in a nontrivial way. Being a humane fellow, he replied that although epithets like "mongoloid idiot" were undoubtedly used in a more benighted time, there have always been persons of good will who have resisted such phraseology. It's a nice thought, the kind you usually hear from traditionalists when you point out the barbarism and brutality of our human past. But it just ain't so. Right through the 1970s, "mongoloid idiot" wasn't an epithet; it was a *diagnosis*. It wasn't uttered by callow, ignorant persons fearful of "difference" and Central Asian eyes; it was pronounced by the best-trained medical practitioners in the world, who told families of kids with Down's that their children would never be able to walk, talk, dress themselves, or recognize their parents. Best to have the child institutionalized and tell one's friends that the baby died at birth. Only the most stubborn, intransigent, or inspired parents resisted such advice from their trusted experts. Who could reasonably expect otherwise?

It's impossible to say how deeply we're indebted to those parents, children, teachers, and medical personnel who insisted on treating people with Down's as if they *could* learn, as if they *could* lead "meaningful" lives. In bygone eras, the parents who didn't keep their children home didn't really have the "option" of doing so; you can't talk about "options" (in any substantial sense of the word) in an ideological current so strong. But in the early 1970s, some parents did swim upstream against all they were told and brought their children home, worked with them, held them, provided them physical therapy and "special learning" environments. These parents are saints and sages. They have, in the broadest sense of the phrase, uplifted the race. In the 10 million–year history of Down syndrome, they've allowed us to believe that we're finally getting somewhere.

Sometimes these parents acted out of religious conviction, believing they should play the hand God dealt them, whatever His plan might be. Sometimes they acted pragmatically: one family decided not to institutionalize their baby when one doctor informed them that, at a state hospital, "perhaps the care would be so minimal that he would not survive past the first year of life." That one piece of advice wound up offsetting the counsel of every other physician they heard from. Another family drove across two Midwestern states, on the advice of doctors, to speak to the headmaster of the nearest institution. The father told me the story some thirty years after it happened. After hours on the road, they met the headmaster, who appeared to have stepped out of a famous Grant Wood painting. But despite his dour appearance, he wound up being the first person who'd given them any hope for their child, advising them to keep the baby home at first and see whether they'd be interested in bringing him in anytime in the first year—but there was no rush. The parents thanked the headmaster, left the institution, and never made the return trip. As the father put it, they had finally been given permission to try to love and care for their child themselves, and that turned out to be all they needed.

What's interesting about stories like this is that they were common even in the 1940s and 1950s. After the war, there were various news items about the unsatisfactory and even scandalous conditions of mental hospitals, but there was also a very strong social consensus that the "retarded" would do best among "their own kind"—regardless of the specifics of their disability. The textual record of those decades reveals a kind of national schizophrenia about institutionalization. For every complaint about the sorry state of the state's hospitals, there are a handful of moving testimonials by parents who'd institutionalized their child in the sincere belief that it was the best thing for all concerned. One such parental testimonial, *Barbara: A Prologue*, published in 1958, was actually written by a professor of what would now be called "special education." Barbara was placed in an institution soon after birth but died there after only four months, having suffered both pneumonia and a heart attack. Her father, Willard Abraham, addressed his narrative to her posthumously, in apology and explanation. Of the decision to release Barbara to Arizona's Valley of the Sun School, Abraham writes,

> We felt we had all the facts that were available. They included these: Your condition was unquestioned by the medical men on whom we depended most; the intelligence range of the tremendous majority of mongoloid children is limited; institutionalization is apparently almost inevitable after a few or more years. . . .
>
> We are convinced, Barbara, that for you at that time our decision was right, but now, months later, we wonder whether it would have been right if you had been with us longer. We'll always wonder about that.

The Abrahams' decision was not an ignorant one. On the contrary, it was all the more agonizing *because* the father was himself an expert in the field and knew intimately the details of the relevant research on "mongolism." He was told to expect an IQ of 20 to 60, and he was told that although the home environment might boost that number, it probably wouldn't boost it more than ten points. He was thus put in the position of asking whether "those few IQ points were worth it" to Barbara or to the rest of the family. If, indeed, institutionalization was inevitable after a few years, and the social stigma of retardation so severe as to scar the parents and their two-year-old nondisabled son, might not it be better for such children to be raised elsewhere, in an environment more suited to their needs and abilities?

So ran the logic of institutionalization. Sometimes parents were encouraged to keep their "mongoloid" babies at home briefly, say, for a few months. Although this might make parting more difficult for the parents later on, the conventional wisdom was that the babies themselves wouldn't mind at all, since, as Willard Abraham was told, mongoloids are "the most adjustable" of all mentally retarded children and "don't have any difficulty" leaving the home. Most parents apparently discovered, during that few months' trial period, that their infant with Down syndrome wasn't very responsive and concluded that the experts were probably right after all: the baby would be better off elsewhere. Often, parents looked for signs of the inevitable, interpreting every "delay" as further proof of the diagnosis. But what's odd about this is that the vast majority of *all* human infants aren't very responsive in their first four months, and many, though not most, "fail" to learn to grasp toys, roll over, or babble baby talk in that time.

So how did those first "early intervention" parents manage to buck the current? Frankly, we're not sure how they did it, and often, neither are they. In 1974, when Emily Perl Kingsley was told by her obstetrician to institutionalize her baby Jason and tell her family and friends the child was stillborn, she refused to listen—but, she says, she does not know where her resolve came from: "I am not exactly sure what it took to disregard the advice of this man, but whatever it was, we summoned it up and decided to bring Jason home." Jason turned out not to be a very responsive child—until, that is, he reached the age of four months. But if Emily and Charles Kingsley had listened to their doctor, they wouldn't have given Jason even that four-month window. As Emily writes,

Our obstetrician took my husband aside and told him that this was a child who was never going to accomplish anything. This was a child who, he said, would probably never sit up, stand, walk, talk, or have any meaningful thoughts whatsoever. He would never recognize us as his parents. He would never be able to distinguish us from any other adults who were halfway nice to him. . . .

This is about as rock-bottom as you can get. The expectations he gave us were nil. After the obstetrician gave Charles this terribly gloomy advice, Charles said one of his most brilliant lines ever. He said to the obstetrician, "Okay, maybe my son will never grow up to be a brain surgeon. Maybe all he'll ever be is an obstetrician!"

You would like to think the bond between mother and child is "natural," infinitely resistant to cultural and ideological solvents. It's a reasonable thought. But it's only cultural. If, like the Kingsleys, you were told by an expert in special education that "in my twenty three years of experience I've never yet seen a mongoloid who could read," it is extremely unlikely that you would expect your disabled little boy to grow up and write his own response to the obstetrician who delivered him. But that's exactly what Jason did at the age of seventeen, as part of a class assignment in high school: "I have a disability called Down syndrome. My bad obstetrician said that I would never learn and send me into a institution and never see me again. No way Jose! Mom and Dad brought me home and taught me things." A year later, Jason was working with his friend Mitchell Levitz, born with Down syndrome in 1971, on a book called *Count Us In: Growing Up with Down Syndrome*. Writing the book with Mitchell gave Jason a few more thoughts about the circumstances of his birth, and about how best to reply to his bad obstetrician:

He never imagined how I could write a book. I will send him a copy of this book so he'll know.

I will tell him that I play the violin, that I make relationships with other people. I make oil paintings, I play the piano. I can sing. I am competing in sports, in the drama group, that I have many friends and I have a full life.

So I want the obstetrician will never say that to any parent to have a baby with a disability any more. If you send a baby with a disability to an institution, the baby will miss all the opportunities to grow and to learn in a full life, and also to receive a diploma. The baby will miss relationships and love and independent living skills.

I am glad that we didn't listen to the obstetrician. If we tell the obstetrician about this, he will responded differently to all other families with a baby with a disability. . . .

And then he will be a better doctor.

So we beat on, boats against the ideological current.

In retrospect, it's beginning to look as if many of the developmental deficits attributed to Down syndrome could instead be attributed to institutionalization. Of course, the phrase "mongoloid idiocy," and its attendant policies, did not cause Down syndrome. But words and phrases are the devices by which we beings signify what homosexuality, or Down syndrome, or anything else, will mean. There surely were, and are, the most intimate possible relations between the language in which we spoke of Down's and the social practices by which we understood it—and refused to understand it. You don't have to be a poststructuralist or a postmodernist or a post-*anything* to get this; all you have to do is meet a parent of a child with Down syndrome. Not long ago, we lived next door to people whose youngest child had Down's. After

James was born, they told us of going to the library to find out more about their baby's prospects and wading through page after page of outdated information, ignorant generalizations, and pictures of people with Down's in mental institutions, face down in their feeding trays. These parents demanded the library get some better material on Down syndrome and throw out the garbage they had on their shelves. Was this a "politically correct" thing for them to do? Damn straight it was. That garbage has had its effects *for generations*. It may look to you like it's only words, but perhaps the fragile neonates whose lives were impeded by the policies—and conditions—of institutionalization can testify in some celestial court to the power of mere language, to the intimate links between words and social policies.

Some of my friends tell me this sounds too much like "strict social constructionism"—that is, too much like the proposition that culture is everything and biology is only what we decide to make (of) it. But although James is pretty solid proof that human biology exists independent of our understanding of it, every morning when he gets up, smiling and babbling to his family, I can see for myself how much of his life depends on our social practices. On one of those mornings I turned to my mother-in-law and said, "He's always so full of mischief, he's always so glad to see us—the only thought I can't face is the idea of this little guy waking up each day in a state mental hospital." To which my mother-in-law replied, "Well, Michael, if he were waking up every day in a state mental hospital, he wouldn't *be* this little guy."

As it happens, my mother-in-law doesn't subscribe to any strict social constructionist newsletters; she was just passing along what she took to be good common sense. But every so often I wonder how common that sense really is. Every ten minutes we hear that the genetic basis of something has been "discovered," and we rush madly to the newsweeklies: Disease is genetic! Homosexuality is genetic! Infidelity, addiction, adventurousness, obsession with mystery novels—all genetic! The discourses of genetics and inheritance, it would seem, bring out the hidden determinist in more of us than will admit it. Sure, there's a baseline sense in which our genes "determine" who we are. We can't play the tune unless the score is written down somewhere in the genome. But one does not need or require a biochemical explanation for literary taste, or voguing, or faithless lovers. In these as in all things human, including Down's, the genome is but a template for a vaster and more significant range of social and historical variation. That's true even for human attributes that are clearly more "biological" than voguing and reading. Figuring out even the most rudimentary of relations between the genome and the immune system (something of great relevance to us wheezing asthmatics) involves so many trillions of variables that a decent answer will win you an all-expense-paid trip to Stockholm. Nor can you predict allergic reactions from the genes alone: because the body's immune system takes a few years to go on-line, your environmental variables (from dioxin to cat dander) are very likely going to be more important to you than most hereditary "constants" you care to name.

Yet even if you don't think that biology is destiny, and even if you don't believe evolution follows any plan, there's still something very seductive about the thought that Down syndrome wouldn't have been so prevalent in humans for so long without good reason. Indeed, there are days when, despite everything I know and profess, I catch myself believing that people with Down syndrome are here for a specific purpose—perhaps to teach us patience, or humility, or compassion, or mere joy. A great deal can go wrong with us *in utero*, but under the heading of what goes wrong, Down syndrome is among the most basic, the most fundamental, the most common, *and* the most innocuous, leavening the species with children who are somewhat slower, and usually somewhat gentler, than the rest of the human brood. It speaks to us strongly of design—if design govern in a thing so small.

After seventeen days in the ICU, James was scheduled for release. We would be equipped with the materials necessary for his care, including oxygen tanks and an apnea monitor that would beep if his heart slowed, became extremely irregular, or stopped. To compensate for his inability to take food orally, James would have a gastrostomy tube surgically introduced through his abdominal wall into his stomach.

Janet and I balked. If James was going to be sent home into conditions identical to those of the ICU, why wasn't he staying in the ICU? There was no shortage of beds; the only other occupants of the ICU were a few preemies, some born as early as 24 weeks. James had recently made progress in his bottle feeding; why do pre-emptive surgery? He had a wonderful, aggressive, and imaginative nurse named Kay, who'd just thought of feeding him with special new bottles angled to accommodate his need to eat on his side, and she'd boosted Jamie's daily oral intake from 7 cc to 30 cc in the past two days. We got suspicious. Was the HMO sending James home just to cut costs? Were they recommending a gastrostomy because they considered surgery to be a quick fix? We recalled one doctor's proposed solution to Jamie's tight neck muscles: cut the muscles and resew them. You don't have to be a consulter of crystals and channelers to think that stretching and massage might be better first options.

In fact, James was born just as hospitals started introducing their "up and out" policies for neonates and their moms. A few weeks before Janet went into labor, our HMO had sent us hundred-dollar coupons redeemable if mother and child were discharged from the hospital within forty-eight hours. These days, by contrast, that kind of offer almost looks like the stuff of nostalgia: at least they gave us forty-eight hours; at least they offered us cash back on our new family acquisition. I think of the recent cartoon in which parents of a newborn drive up to the express maternity center and are told by a nurse with a headset, "Congratulations! Do you want fries with that?" But of course we didn't take advantage of the once-in-a-lifetime opportunity to cash in our rebates on Jamie. Instead, here we were in an office just off to the side of the NICU, insisting to the NICU's head physician that we didn't want our child to come home yet.

I was rather uneasy about this. The last thing I wanted was to appear as if we weren't eager to clutch our child to the very bosom of our household—such as it was. I literally wanted to know if you could hug and hold a child with a gastrostomy tube. But Janet, as usual, had a much more complicated relationship to medical professionals than I. On the one hand, she's more knowledgeable, more authoritative in dealing with hospital staff. Inevitably, sooner or later, I mispronounce an important procedure or forget that Orthoxin is simply the brand name for euleithromyasone, a cognate of phryxolaticin (also known as whattheglutamate), and the doctors exchange significant glances with each other, thinking, *We don't have to listen to this guy, he can't tell his duodenum from his jejunum.* But by the same token, although Janet's medical expertise gives her a credibility I envy, it's sometimes perceived as threatening: *This one knows too much. Let's take her to the river.* Most doctors are vastly relieved that they can talk details with Janet, but a few can get weird. This isn't terribly surprising: the severe and longstanding power imbalance between nurses and doctors can make some doctors arrogant or sheepish in dealing with a former nurse with a Ph.D. and a large vocabulary. Since Janet was, to her credit, much more adamant than I about keeping Jamie in the ICU and avoiding surgery, our conferences with the NICU medical staff involved a good deal of verbal maneuvering and feeling-out.

We nixed the gastrostomy tube, saying we'd prefer to augment his bottle feedings with a nasal tube and we'd do it ourselves. But this time, when I say "we," I'm eliding a great deal of discussion and debate. One reason the NICU physician proposed surgery for James, no doubt, was that he did not want to give parents the burden of doing nasal feedings on their own child: I remember thinking that however suspicious we might be of the decision to send Jamie home, we certainly couldn't expect the NICU staff to start with the assumption that Jamie's parents would rather run small tubes through their infant's nose than have practiced surgeons insert a larger tube *for* them. When Jamie's doctors agreed to forgo the surgery, we knew not only that we were being listened to after all, but also that they'd been using their best medical judgment from the start—and their best medical judgment told them to trust Janet on this one. For it was Janet, needless to say, who knew more about nasal feedings than I did, Janet who convinced me that I could learn to do them nearly as competently as she—though we had nothing to practice on.

A year or two later, a friend of ours asked Janet to conduct a seminar for medical students at Illinois, recounting her experiences and offering advice on how to deal with parents after difficult or traumatic childbirth. Only then, as Janet prepared her remarks for the seminar, did I realize that our obstetrician had disappeared almost immediately after delivering James. We had no complaints whatsoever about Jamie's care: most of the story Janet told was a lesson in how to do things right. But, Janet added, if you're the ob-gyn and you deliver a child like James, *do not disappear*. Do not leave the room. Make eye contact. Look me in the eye and ask me what you can do to help me deal with this. We don't know why Janet's obstetrician left and never contacted us again. Perhaps she herself was surprised and overcome. Perhaps she feared that we would associate her with a "tragic" event. Perhaps she thought that we would *blame* her for the delivery, as if we would consider suing an obstetrician for a chromosomal nondisjunction that had occurred sometime around New Year's Day eight and a half months earlier. But then again, our obstetrician simply needed a little advice, maybe a little more courage. We've since heard of a doctor who broke the news to parents by explaining that human children had forty-six chromosomes, whereas their child would have forty-seven.

So it was decided. Jamie would stay another weekend in the ICU, during which we would train ourselves in how to care for him when he came home on Monday, October 7. For Sunday night, we arranged to stay in a room in the maternity wing, with James in a basinette between our beds. This would give us practice in listening for the apnea monitor and in watching his oxygen overnight. On Saturday night, we went out to Urbana-Champaign's fanciest restaurant: surprisingly good French cuisine marooned in east central Illinois, where the French had once blown through, named the place "flat land," and then hightailed it to the bayou, where the nightlife was better. We thought it would be our last night out for some time—and besides, we had a few things to celebrate. September 21 had marked our sixth wedding anniversary; five days later I turned thirty.

The restaurant has long since closed, but all Janet has to do is mention it to me to bring back everything about that night. We exchanged vows more solemn than those with which we had plighted our troth six years earlier: that we would not merely get through the next year but get through it with grace and great emotional agility; that we would always stay passionately in love; and that we would take both our children to Maine or Virginia every summer, that they might learn to travel, bodysurf, and knit their lives ever more closely to those of their aunts, uncles, grandparents, and honorary relatives. After finishing a dinner we couldn't afford, we went home and made plans to rent a house in York, Maine, which we couldn't afford either.

Then we prepared Jamie's nursery, with its bright colors, mobiles, stuffed animals, and oxygen tanks.

■

CHAPTER TWO

Humans Under Construction

▲

After Jamie had been in the ICU for two weeks or so, he started becoming a narrative. We didn't feel like we were his parents yet, since we weren't taking care of him daily. Instead, because we had to report on him to myriad friends, colleagues, and relatives, we found ourselves engaged in an odd process of manufacturing updates, progress reports, and brief explanations of things like tracheoscopy and congenital heart defects. Soon we had concocted an entire discourse *about* James, well before we were able to feed him or hold him. I remember remarking, at the time, that Jamie was beginning to seem less like a baby to me than like a policy: every day the public briefings, the updates, the attempts to keep our friends and family reassured or just well informed. *His 0-sats have stabilized, but we're going to watch him overnight and hold a consult in the morning. The X-rays didn't reveal any bowel obstruction, but we continue to be concerned about his bilirubin numbers and we're not ruling out the option of sending in troops.* Anyone who's served as a patient's official LDH (liaison during hospitalization) knows what the procedure is like. Did the chemo work? Do they have to do exploratory surgery? What exactly does an MRI *do*, anyway?

When Jamie finally came home, then, he came home as a thoroughly medicalized child. Not merely "medicated," but medicalized: to talk about him was also to talk about his procedures and prospects in medical terms, and he already had a hefty medical chart to prove it.

Where there's a hefty medical chart, there's bound to be a hefty medical bill. To all who asked, we spoke about Jamie in medical terms, cautiously optimistic; to our immediate families, we also spoke about him, once or twice, in financial terms. Our parents and our siblings possessed that unique form of intimacy with us that allowed them to say, "The two of you must be going through a very difficult time," and then to say, half an hour later under the same heading, "And what are your bills like?" To our infinite relief, Janet and I happened to be among that dwindling number of Americans who can say, *We're fully insured, thank goodness. Now, as for those X-rays.* . . . Even still, when we did receive the thick, heavy envelope containing a list of Jamie's procedures, their costs, and the related doctor's charges and fees for hospital beds, we pored over the details in shock, stunned by the weight of a medical bill we weren't even paying.

Jamie came home without the gastrostomy tube, so he didn't require any surgery. I recall his pediatrician, Donald Davison, telling us, "He's just scooting by," meaning that he'd barely avoided heart surgery, barely avoided throat surgery, and was now barely avoiding stomach surgery. It's probably indicative of our psyches at the time that we found this news encouraging rather than terrifying. But even without undergoing a single surgical procedure, Jamie had managed to consume thirty thousand dollars' worth of medical treatment during his three-week stay in the ICU. When we gasped at the thought of a child costing ten thousand dollars a week, however, we actually thought not of ourselves (since we weren't footing that ten thousand) but of the other parents we'd met in the ICU. If we compared our position with theirs, we knew at once that we were getting off light. Jamie was hospitalized for less time than any of his mates in the ICU, some of whom were in the unit for months. In fact, we developed a curious relation to some of the other ICU parents. Jamie was the biggest—and, by some measures, the healthiest—little guy in the unit, but ten years from now, chances were that any one of these premature infants would be doing much better than he. Then again, some of our fellow ICU parents would conceivably be paying hospital bills for those ten years and more, having racked up over half a million dollars in health care costs. One couple, who took their baby home just before Jamie was released, looked as if they had just attended their high school prom that spring. We hoped their baby's birth wouldn't drive them into bankruptcy before they turned twenty.

The reason Jamie's hospitalization was fully covered was that we had chosen "high option" insurance as University of Illinois employees. Five and a half years earlier, when we were graduate students at Virginia, we'd been the proud owner of a health insurance policy that covered Janet's hospitalization but not Nick's. Our intrepid insurers billed the room and the doctor's fees to Nick, leaving us to conclude that if only we'd given birth to a nonbillable entity such as a cat, we'd have been all right financially. When we took Jamie home from the ICU, I don't believe a day went by when we didn't shake our heads and wonder what would have happened if Jamie had been born when we were graduate students. Yet fortunate as we were, we weren't entirely in the clear, either. Jamie was sent home with an apnea monitor and supplemental oxygen. We found that O_2 cannisters aren't as free as the wind blows, but the oxygen wasn't too expensive—$20 or

$30 a month. The apnea monitor, however, rented for $800 a month, $200 of which we were responsible for. The purpose of the monitor was simple. If anything happened to Jamie's heart, the monitor would let off a piercing electronic scream no human could sleep through. Since sleep apnea is quite a common problem among children with Down syndrome, the monitor was unquestionably a necessity. But the monitor also went off whenever its batteries ran low, or whenever Jamie moved enough in his sleep to jostle the leads and wires that were attached to a foam strap around his chest. The monitor had three different beeping patterns for three different kinds of apnea, and although Jamie's breathing was never in great danger that winter, we did hear the machine's range of shrieks and beeps quite often enough to satisfy our curiosity. And it scared the bejeezus out of us every single time.

We have no idea whether the cost of the monitor bears any relationship to what it costs an HMO to provide us with one. We do know that when an orthopedic surgeon advised us to get a neck collar for James, we took him in to be "fitted," only to find that a tiny, two-inch-thick piece of foam, cut by hand to the shape of his neck, would run us $100. Perhaps the foam itself costs a quarter and the knifework costs $99.75 per collar, but we tend to doubt this. We could not, in any case, have put a price on an object whose purpose it was to keep our baby's neck straight when he was sleeping, nor could we have dreamed of trying to get through those early nights without a monitor or without supplemental oxygen. In fact, I was initially afraid that our home ICU for James wouldn't have *enough* machines. After our long vigils in the hospital, I had gotten to the point where I did not trust myself to gauge Jamie's condition without looking at a blood gas machine for a readout of his O-sats. Now we began to get the idea that we inhabited a medical system wherein providers bilk insurers and vice versa. Whatever it was, it was a system too opaque for human comprehension.

A few weeks after Jamie came home, I stopped into a convenience store where two men were arguing about health care. "But who's going to pay for it?," shouted one man in a frantic tone one does not often hear in convenience stores. "You can put everybody on national health, but who's going to pay for it"? For a moment I felt like intervening: *You're already paying for it*, I wanted to say. *My family pays $175 a month for coverage, and the University of Illinois kicks in another $250. That's more than $5,000 a year in premiums, which is pretty considerable, but we've just run up a bill of $30,000. One way or another, as taxpayer or as policyholder, you're paying the difference.* But I kept my mouth shut, not only because it would have been rude, even according to the etiquette of Kwik-Marts, to jump into the discussion, but also because I knew there was no way I could pull off the kind of omniscient narration that would show plainly and convincingly that we're all in this one together.

One of the barriers to national health care in the United States is that Americans usually don't think of themselves as "all in this together" unless they're at war. Thus, for instance, the paradox that one cultural commentator after another can speak of the "disuniting" or the "fraying" of America without being able to propose a moment in the past when our unity as a people was something other than wishful thinking. (The 1960s? The era of segregation? The Great Depression? Prohibition? The Progressive Era, when unionizers were beaten and women didn't have the vote? The Gilded Age, with all its lynchings? The Civil War? The period of slavery? Even during World War II our troops were segregated by race. . . .) Only at odd, singular historical moments do we Americans have fits of wondering about whether we should join the rest of the industrialized world in offering our citizens universal health care. But what I find truly disturbing about those fits is that for many Americans, the prospect of being all in this together becomes an occasion for imagining new forms of personal policing. *Why should I subsidize the health care of my neighbors who smoke a pack a day? Why should I cover the binges of alcoholics? Why should I foot the bill for all those fat, lazy people who consume bacon cheeseburgers, large fries, and a side portion of my taxes?*

I imagine a Kwik-Mart scenario of the future in which I choose to violate the decorum of the store and argue with one of my fellow customers about health care and fiscal policy, but when my interlocutor learns that I have a "disabled" child, he turns on me furiously, demanding to know why I would expect any of my fellow Americans to help me pick up the tab for my family's decision to bear a child who eats more than his proper share of the national health budget.

No one has ever said such a thing to me. No one has asked us to account for the decisions that brought James to us; no one, not even those family members who were solicitous enough to ask about James's medical bills, has asked us why we decided to forgo amniocentesis, or whether *that* decision entailed a host of corollary decisions about abortion and fetal disabilities. There are only a few people who know us well enough to ask about such things, and those people also know how to extend to us, without saying so explicitly, an agreement of mutual circumspection under which we will only discuss matters so private if we feel the desire or the necessity to do so. Every so often, someone asks us whether we knew Jamie would have Down syndrome or whether it was a surprise. When we reply that it was a surprise, we imagine to ourselves the follow-up question we've never gotten:

Would we have chosen to have the child if we had known?

▲

Our decision to forgo amniocentesis was deliberate; we debated it for some time, knowing full well that for us, this constituted a "passive" decision to carry the pregnancy to term if the child did in fact have something like Down syndrome, something that a mere sonogram wouldn't detect. I honestly do not recall the conversation Janet has often related to me, in which she said, "You realize that we're taking the chance that the baby will be born with Down syndrome," and I apparently replied, "Well, we'll just love him all the more, then." This seems to me a nice—if somewhat blithe and uninformed—thing to have said, but I cannot actually vouch for having said it. I remember very clearly arguing against amniocentesis, figuring that it was an invasive procedure that would only "catch" things we didn't think we wanted caught, and that might induce a miscarriage to boot. Under those circumstances, it seemed unquestionably better to take the chance that our child would have Down's than to take the chance that he would not be born at all. But although Janet will tell you that she and I certainly did discuss the subject explicitly at least once before Jamie's birth, I have managed to repress any such memory.

So I suppose that if we had found out that James had Down syndrome when he was still in the third or fourth month of fetal development, we would have started learning about Down's earlier than we did, and we'd have done what we could to prepare for a potentially difficult birth. We are as strongly pro-choice today as we were before James was born, and our personal decisions regarding Janet's pregnancy with James were consequences of, not exceptions to, our deeply held convictions about abortion and reproductive rights. But what if we had been told, upon receiving the results of an amniocentesis, that our baby would never be able to live a "normal" life? What if we had been told that he would never become a conscious being, never learn to talk, read, or recognize his parents? What, in other words, if we had been as seriously misinformed about Jamie's prospects in the spring of 1991 as were most previous generations of parents and providers? In that case, I have to admit, we would have been faced with an extremely difficult decision, and if we were persuaded that our child's life would be nothing but suffering and misery for all concerned, James included, then it's quite possible that we would have chosen to have an abortion instead. Perhaps we would have sought a string of second opinions; perhaps we would have clung to the hope that our child would be an exception. But so much depends on what kind of information is available to whom. If we had no way of knowing how loving, clever, and "normal" a child like Jamie can be, we would simply have to rely on the advice of "experts." And if those experts told us there was no way to raise such a child, we would probably believe them. I can't say that with certainty; after all, we're very much in the realm of the hypothetical here, with two sets of "what if"s—what if we had gotten a prenatal diagnosis, and what if we had been grievously misadvised about our child's prospects. But I can say that I have some general idea of how agonizing such a decision can be.

The questions themselves are as complex as any moral dilemmas we humans have yet devised. Who has a right to know about possible fetal abnormalities, and what should be done (and by whom?) when abnormalities are detected? What about "quality of life" considerations for the parents and child? At what point, if any, do the unborn accrete to themselves a "right" to life? Should parents' decisions to bear children rest on financial concerns, on the state of their medical care and health insurance? Should some forms of prenatal testing be mandatory—or prohibited?

I'm not sure my words can convey an accurate sense of how extremely difficult it is to discuss James in this sense. It was hard to talk about him as a medicalized being back when he was in the ICU; it's harder still to talk about him in terms of our philosophical beliefs about abortion and prenatal testing. That's partly because these issues are so famously divisive and emotionally charged, but it's also because we can no longer frame any such questions about our child now that he's here. And abortion is, as everyone knows, one of those issues on which the framing of the questions is practically dispositive. If you ask people whether the state should have the right to override an individual woman's jurisdiction over what happens in her body, you'll probably get a rather different set of answers than you would if you asked whether a woman should have the right to kill an innocent unborn child. Personally, I find the second version of this question infinitely more toxic and coercive than the first, but I can't deny that both versions are circulating in my culture and helping to determine policy initiatives and political mobilizations on a daily basis.

Indeed, you could write the history of the abortion debate since the 1960s by charting how the issue has been framed. During the early years of the women's movement, reproductive rights were one of the foundations of women's political autonomy. Why, indeed, should legislative bodies of wealthy white men dictate what can and can't happen in the flesh-and-blood bodies of women? How can women assume the status of fully independent moral and political agents if they don't even have the right to decide for themselves whether or not to terminate unwanted pregnancies? It is rare that I see abortion publicly discussed in this way today. I'm not talking about the extent to which anti-abortion conservatives have set the terms for debate; I'm talking about the way moderates and liberals, both men and women, have defended women's reproductive rights. For some time now, the abortion debate has been presented as a clash between the state's right to establish moral guidelines, on the one side, and the individual's right to be free from state intervention, on the other. This is only a tiny slippage from the way abortion was discussed in the 1970s, but its consequences are significant. For many liberals, the question has now become one of defending the individual's right to do a bad thing. The pro-life forces have taken the broadly moral position that it is wrong to take a potential human life; more extreme activists have equated abortion with murder. Liberals, in response, have adopted a more or less libertarian position that says *Keep your laws off our reproductive systems.* Principled as this response may be, it leaves the door open for a "moderate" middle term: *All right, go ahead and have an abortion; the state will not interfere. But remember that you're doing a bad, selfish thing, and should feel very guilty about it.*

This, in a nutshell, was Naomi Wolf's argument in an October 1995 issue of the *New Republic*. Starting from the entirely plausible premise that feminism "has ceded the language of right and wrong to abortion's foes," she proceeds to cede the language of right and wrong to abortion's foes, insisting that "the pro-choice movement is not listening" to the voices of women who feel guilt and grief at having an abortion. Abortion, in these terms, can be understood as a political "right"—but only if women first admit that it is wrong.

So if some impossibly rude hypothetical person were to ask us, *Would you have chosen to abort your child?,* we might say (assuming we gave such a person the courtesy of a reply at all) that we've already made that decision in different terms, thank you. Jamie the four-year-old child is not the same creature he was when he was a fetus in the third or fourth month of prenatal development, and we do not project onto the fetus our feelings for the child. As far as we're concerned, the question is moot. The important thing for us now is picking Jamie up from school on time and getting him over to speech therapy—or perhaps the important thing is discovering a way to get him to eat vegetables or to tell us when he needs to use the bathroom. The Down syndrome discussion groups I've taken part in to date, both on the Internet and in the tangible world, have been loath to discuss abortion precisely because it involves a host of issues so important and so emotionally compelling that they will only divide us and distract us from the task at hand, namely, caring for our children now that they're here. Every time someone brings up the question on the listserv, he or she is met with dozens of e-mail responses reading, "NO! NO! NOT ON THIS LIST! PLEASE don't have this discussion here! There are plenty of other newsgroups for this debate. This is about children with disabilities." But then again, the world into which Jamie was born is riven by questions about rights to life and to reproductive freedom, and the prospects of people with disabilities—and fetuses with disabilities—depend urgently on how we come to terms with them.

It wasn't long after Jamie was born that we began to realize the peculiar plight of children with disabilities in the United States. Jamie, like so many other children, is caught between politicians and pragmatists—between people who craft party platforms on protecting the unborn and people who are trying to get our society to care for the children who've already been born. For Jamie is exactly the kind of child who gets overlooked by your average pro-life politician who extends "rights" to fetuses, embryos, and even zygotes (since life, so they claim, begins at conception), while denying those rights to living persons. What in the world can we make of legislators who oppose abortion rights but also oppose social programs for the care of infants and small children? The logical consequences of this political position are simply staggering. Humans, it would appear, have an innate "right to life"—but only until they're born. After that, it's their job to become self-sufficient. No one owes anyone a living, as the saying goes, not even if the "anyone" in question is physically or mentally disabled. Certainly, when we take up the moral claims of abortion opponents who also oppose Head Start, parental leave laws, the Women, Infants, and Children food program, and school lunch programs, we can say that among those who argue that the state has a compelling interest in a fetus's right to life, there are very few indeed who would also burden the state with the imperative not to let living children starve.

It is a strange land, no doubt, adequate only to the imagination of Dickensian satire, where leading politicians and self-appointed moralists talk endlessly about "family values" while kicking the crutches out from under Tiny Tim. Of course, no one, not even the most ardent free-market ideologue, conceives of himself as a crutch kicker. But that was Dickens's point in *A Christmas Carol*: unless Scrooges are miraculously vouchsafed some reasonably comprehensive vision of the social fabric, either by supernatural forces or by an omniscient Victorian novelist, they will not see that their fiscal policies and political beliefs have anything to do with the fate of Bob Cratchit's children.

But the world is not run by Dickens's most sympathetic readers, nor is it run by those who score the most debating points. And what if it were? Regardless of the outcomes of political elections and the passage of public laws, we will never have a society in which each citizen gets every kind of nutritional, physical, financial, and psychological support he or she needs. We can argue on pragmatic grounds that we should be more immediately concerned with the born than with the unborn, but even this argument does nothing to address the dilemma with which children like James present us. That dilemma can best be framed, I think, by three related questions: What does it mean to have the technological capacity to care for the "disabled" without the political will to do so? What does it mean that we have developed a society in which people with Down syndrome can flourish as never before (thanks to antibiotics, modern surgery, and/or early intervention programs), but in which they are too often denied the chance to flourish? And finally, how should we understand the politics of contemporary medical practice, in which the technological advances that make it possible for disabled persons to lead "normal" lives are inextricable from the advances that make it possible to screen for fetal "defects"?

The danger for children like Jamie does not lie in women's freedom to choose abortion; nor does it lie in prenatal testing. The danger lies in the creation of a society that combines eugenics with enforced fiscal austerity. In such a society, it is quite conceivable that parents who "choose" to bear disabled children will be seen as selfish or deluded. Among the many things I fear coming to pass in my children's lifetime, I fear this above all: that children like James will eventually be seen as "luxuries" employers and insurance companies cannot afford, or as "luxuries" the nation or the planet cannot afford. I do not want to see a world in which human life is judged by the kind of cost-benefit analysis that weeds out those least likely to attain self-sufficiency and to provide adequate "returns" on social investments. It is not a comforting thought that the disabled and the "retarded" were among the *first* groups to be pathologized in 1930s Germany, on the grounds that they were insupportable burdens on the hardworking, able-bodied citizens of the nation. Why, indeed, should our taxes go to support the infirm, the unable, the defective? Are there no private charities, no chain gangs, no poorhouses? The distinction beloved of our contemporary free-market conservatives—between "productive" and "unproductive" citizens—should send a chill down any spine, even the picture-perfect spines of all us supremely able-bodied persons.

In the final days of 1994, Janet's brother, Bud, and his wife, Sarah, suddenly found themselves the parents of twins. They had done an amniocentesis, and later confessed to feeling guilty about this, as if Janet and I, having made a different decision, would disapprove of their desire for a definitive cytogenic diagnosis. Thus it was that they knew they would have twin boys, each of whose karyotypes looked just fine. What they didn't know was that Sarah would deliver those twins after only twenty-four weeks of gestation. Trevor spent four months in the ICU; his brother Dashiell, nine. Trevor is now doing very well, and Dash, though slowed down somewhat by a colostomy, is a feisty, alert little boy with a mischievous smile. Trevor and Dash will likely require the same kind of social support system on which Jamie relies; in the fall of 1995, Bud and Sarah even wrote to President and Mrs. Clinton to tell them so and to urge the president not to approve Congress's proposal to turn Medicaid over to the states, on the grounds that Dash's life was literally hanging in the balance.

If anyone thinks that amniocentesis can screen out the vicissitudes of chance, they'd do well to think again. No amount of fetal testing can guarantee parents the birth of perfect children. All the amniocenteses we can muster will not bequeath us a brave new world without such children as Jamie, Trevor, or Dash in it. I must admit that for some months after Jamie was born, I had my doubts about the politics of amniocentesis. I had my moments of imperiousness: why should anyone want to know more about their pregnancy than we knew about ours? Then I read about a couple who, upon getting an amniocentesis and learning that their child would be born with Down syndrome, decided not to have a natural birth at home but to deliver the baby in a large city hospital where there would be ample facilities to handle a complicated birth—and perhaps save the infant's life, if need be. What would be gained by dissuading parents such as these from undergoing prenatal tests? Conversely, what would be gained by dismantling—or at least retooling—the enormous sociomedical apparatus of prenatal testing?

It's true that many parents who test the fetus for Down syndrome will abort if the test is positive. Most of them are looking for genetic defects for a reason, regardless of whether I or anyone else might regard that reason as sufficient. But there's no reason to conclude that testing *in itself* constitutes a threat to the existence of people with Down syndrome.

It's alarming to me how often this point gets lost in the debates over prenatal testing. Not long ago, an old high school friend got in touch with me, sending me a copy of the summer 1989 issue of the *Human Life Review*. The journal is published by the Human Life Foundation and describes itself as being devoted to the overturning of *Roe* v. *Wade*; it shares some of its editorial board with the better-known *National Review*. The reason I was sent this particular issue is that it contained an essay by a woman named Christine Allison, who offered a moving and forceful account of her daughter Chrissie, born with Down syndrome, along with the dire warning that Chrissie and Jamie are members of a "dying species." As far as Allison is concerned, prenatal testing is but a prelude to abortion:

The world of prenatal testing is without doubt the most perilous of all: a place where a child may find an adversary even in his own mother.

It is a terrible irony that the world which has given Chrissie . . . a chance to lead a normal life is the same world that may well extinguish the last person of her kind. But these are the terms of the new medicine. Over the past two decades, while one branch of the medical sciences has sought with extraordinary success to eradicate the worst effects of retardation in Down Syndrome people, another branch has sought simply to eradicate people with Down Syndrome.

Allison was primarily concerned with what was a new test in 1989, the so-called triple screen, that can spot unusually high levels of human chorionic gonadotropin and correspondingly low levels of estriol and alphafetoprotein in the maternal bloodstream, all of which suggest a good possibility that the fetus has Down syndrome. "By measuring the protein levels in all pregnant women in the 16th week," Allison writes, "doctors can determine whether the more conclusive amniocentesis test should be recommended." The result, for Allison, can only be that potential children with Down syndrome will be "silently and methodically targeted for extinction," adding yet more thousands of fetal bodies to what she calls "the quiet genocide that is now taking place."

Allison's essay is, among other things, a good reminder of why most parents of disabled children don't want to talk about abortion. Though I cannot do otherwise than to advocate for the services and policies her Chrissie needs to live a "normal" life, I also cannot read an essay like hers without feeling a disabling anger and pain that prevent me from resting on the common ground we're supposed to share. At the kernel of Allison's argument is the idea that parents should be kept ignorant of their children's health lest they make the wrong decision about whether to bear the child. What basis is there, I wonder, for substantive exchange with someone who presumes a priori that other people are not fit to be considered moral agents? Where do you begin to discuss ethics and public policy with someone who insists that "there is no such thing as not being able to 'afford' a Down Syndrome child" because "every bit of therapy and special education is paid for by the state"—as if there were no such thing as a family unable to afford another *non*disabled child?

The reason prenatal testing is so controversial to pro-life advocates, I think, is that it introduces a new level of moral complexity into a debate many pro-lifers regard as settled. I don't mean to suggest that the pro-life argument isn't morally complex; at its best, it certainly is. Even though it's based on the premise that life begins at conception, it formulates this position with a good deal more logical rigor than most of the activists who are currently lobbying state legislatures to enact statutes based on that premise. Let me explain. When the pro-life movement advocates the legal standard that life begins at conception, its opponents usually rely on two counterarguments: one, the libertarian argument, which holds that the state should not have the power to decide such a question; two, the scientific argument, which holds that definitions of "life" are too slippery to be settled by legislative fiat. As long as the pro-life position insists that life *objectively begins* at conception, these counterarguments are, I believe, more than sufficient rebuttals, appealing to political and scientific prudence. But when the pro-life position is stated not as "objective fact" but as a matter of *probabilities*, then we're on different philosophical ground altogether.

The "probabilities" argument is the basis of the anti-abortion position in John T. Noonan's classic *The Morality of Abortion*, published in 1970, three years before the Supreme Court decided *Roe* v. *Wade*. Noonan's book is a painstaking explanation and defense of the history and philosophy of the Catholic Church on the subject of abortion, so it's all the more interesting that Noonan bases his argument not on "objective fact" but on "objective *discontinuities*." The argument, in a nutshell, runs like this: There are roughly two hundred million spermatozoa in the typical ejaculation, therefore each spermatozoon has around a one-in-two-hundred-million chance of developing into a human being. Once an ovum is fertilized by that spermatozoon, however, the resulting being has something like a four-in-five chance of becoming a human being. Noonan's conclusion is twofold: first, that such "an immense jump in potentialities" provides a good basis for making a moral distinction at the point of the jump; and second, that abortion is therefore wrong even if we do not define the fertilized egg as a "person."

The first of these conclusions is extremely problematic, and deserves close examination. But it's worth noting, as a matter of logic (and morality, and public policy), that the second conclusion is much more complicated—and plausible—than pro-choice advocates usually assume it is. In her 1971 defense of abortion rights, for instance, Judith Jarvis Thomson concedes the possibility that the fetus may be a person, but goes on to argue, with considerable wit and intelligence, that there is no reason to grant the proposition that every "person" has a right to life. Her example is intriguing: "You wake up," she writes,

> and find yourself back to back in bed with an unconscious violinist. A famous unconscious violinist. He has been found to have a fatal kidney ailment, and the Society of Music Lovers

has canvassed all the available medical records and found that you alone have the right blood type to help. They have therefore kidnapped you, and last night the violinist's circulatory system was plugged into yours, so that your kidneys can be used to extract poisons from his blood as well as your own. The director of the hospital now tells you, "Look, we're sorry the Society of Music Lovers did this to you—we would never have permitted it if we had known. But still, they did it, and the violinist is now plugged into you. To unplug you would be to kill him. But never mind, it's only for nine months. By then he will have recovered from his ailment, and can safely be unplugged from you."

Thomson goes on from here to discuss the vastly different circumstances by which eggs are fertilized and violinists are plugged into other people's bloodstreams, but the general point remains the same: Does the violinist, as a "person," have an absolute right to life?

Most people would say no, Thomson suggests. But Noonan's thesis, unlike most pro-life arguments, does not require that we understand the fetus as a rights-bearing person; his thesis is based on probable outcomes. "If the chance is 200,000,000 to 1 that the movement in the bushes into which you shoot is a man's," Noonan writes, "I doubt if many persons would hold you careless in shooting; but if the chances are 4 in 5 that the movement is a human being's few would acquit you of blame." What Noonan misses here is the fact that if you're a pregnant woman, the fetus is not a movement in the bushes; it's attached to you, like the violinist. But the larger principle at stake goes to the heart of our controversies over the ethics of prenatal testing: Is conception the only place where we can draw a definitive line beyond which a mother has no right to seek abortion? According to Noonan, the argument from probabilities is grounded both in nature and in "common sense." As he frames it, his "probabilities" standard "seems in accord with the structure of reality and the nature of moral thought" and is "the most commonsensical of arguments" because it "is not aimed at establishing humanity but at establishing an objective discontinuity which may be taken into account in moral discourse." In other words, we're not drawing the line, we're merely acknowledging the line that's already there in reality:

> The probabilities as they do exist do not show the humanity of the embryo in the sense of a demonstration in logic any more than the probabilities of the movement in the bush being a man demonstrate beyond all doubt that the being is a man. The appeal is a "buttressing" consideration, showing the plausibility of the standard adopted. The argument focuses on the decisional factor in any moral judgment and assumes that part of the business of a moralist is drawing lines. One evidence of the non-arbitrary character of the line drawn is the difference of probabilities on either side of it.

At first blush, this may indeed sound like the soul of (common) sense; no doubt our feelings about probable outcomes have something to do with the fact that many of us feel differently about fetuses than about hypothetical violinists. Nevertheless, the "probabilities" standard raises a host of insuperable difficulties. First, it is not clear how big a "difference of probabilities" you need to claim an "objective discontinuity." It is entirely possible that when prospective parents learn—say, in the seventeenth week of a pregnancy—that their child will be born with Down syndrome, they will interpret this as an objective discontinuity. If they are told by their physician that their child will never learn and never have a meaningful thought, then they are all the more likely to make a decision based on "probabilities": *Yesterday we thought we were having a "normal" child; today we learn she will be a vegetable*. Second, as Lewis Schwarz points out in his discussion of Noonan, it is not clear whether every "objective discontinuity" is a sound basis for moral reasoning. "Consider the situation," Schwarz writes, "when someone's brain is severely injured and there is a large shift in the probability that the person will ever have another thought, let alone possess human wisdom. Can we draw a morally well-founded line here and maintain that he or she may be killed?" And third, there is no reason, other than intuition, for us to associate objective discontinuities with clean moral lines. It might *feel* right to draw a line between clearly different probabilities, but it may often be more necessary—and even more justifiable—to draw a line between *small* differences in probability.

This last objection may sound like a logical quibble, but in fact, for my purposes, it's the most important of the three. Pro-choice advocates, including myself, are often stymied by what seem to be unanswerable questions. Why is it all right to abort a pregnancy in the seventh week, or even with a "morning-after" pill, but not at thirty weeks' gestation? At what point between week seven and week fifteen, say, or week twelve and week twenty-four, does abortion become wrong? If you rely on Noonan's theory of conception as an objective discontinuity, you can't possibly answer. But if you propose instead that a pregnancy may contain numerous "objective discontinuities," or that moral decisions can be as legitimately made in "gray areas" as in "immense jumps in potentialities," then you're on different terrain. When does a fetus become sufficiently babylike as to make abortion wrong? We don't know. When does a person definitively acquire the moral reasoning and moral status of an adult? Where can you draw the line between movement and nonmovement? What precisely is the difference between the novel and other literary genres? We don't know, we don't know. Very likely the edges are blurry, or our vision is. But let's talk about it and see whether we can't come to some sort of provisional agreement about where we need to draw lines and where we can get by instead with loosely demarcated gray zones.

For a time, I used to believe that birth itself afforded us the best line we could draw, thinking that although Noonan is right about the odds of human life pre- and postconception, still, the fetus is only a *potential* human. But this left me unable to account for my opposition to third-trimester abortions. Then I thought I must have been relying instead on the criterion of viability: any fetus that can survive independently outside the womb has a right to life equal to that of a living human being. But medical technology has made it unclear what it means to "survive independently," and what's more, beings with equal rights often come into conflict anyway. Then I read a short essay in the British journal *The Spectator*, in which Peter Singer, author of *Rethinking Life and Death* and of the entry on "ethics" in the *Encyclopedia Britannica*, complicates matters still further by arguing that neither viability *nor* birth should be considered "objective":

> Why, for example, should the life of a premature baby born at 23 weeks' gestation be more worthy of protection than the life of a foetus at 24 weeks? One possible answer is that in the absence of any sudden change in the foetus or newborn infant itself birth is as good a place as any to draw a line that the law can uphold. But it would also be possible, if less neat, to ac-

cept that just as the human being develops gradually in a
physical sense, so too does its moral significance gradually increase. We do not, as our treatment of disabled newborn infants shows, consider the newborn as full members of the
community immediately on birth.

Singer here overlooks the possibility that some hospitals *do* treat
disabled newborns as "full members of the human community,"
sometimes even to the point of insisting on heroic "lifesaving"
measures that the parents themselves do not want for their child.
This objection, however, is beside the point, because Singer's argument is itself strongly opposed to those "lifesaving" measures.
For Singer, there is no compelling case that neonatal care should
be extended to every "live" birth. Yet, under current British law,
Singer argues, anencephalic infants and "cortically dead" babies,
because they are not legally brain-dead, must be kept alive even if
their vital organs could save the lives of babies down the hall who
need only a working pair of kidneys to survive. Few people, I
think, would insist on the justice of maintaining the lives of babies who will literally never become conscious of their own existence if this means that other infants with easily correctable birth
defects must die instead.

So what, then, is to be our guide as we draw our moral lines?
Where other commentators have proposed conception, viability,
or birth, Singer proposes the capacity for self-consciousness—
and, leading his argument out to its conclusion, endorses what
many people would call infanticide:

Perhaps, like the ancient Greeks, we should have a cere-
mony a month after birth, at which the infant is admitted to
the community. Before that time, infants would not be recog-

nized as having the same right to life as older people. Such a date would still be early enough to ensure that the rights of all those who are self-aware would be fully protected, but it would be late enough to detect most cases of severe and irreparable disability.

I trust that none of my readers will be surprised to learn that I find this solution as questionable as any other. Singer may be right to juxtapose the interests of a premature baby born at twenty-three weeks, a fetus at twenty-four, and living babies who need transplants or transfusions; but his one-month waiting period solves nothing for babies, like Bud and Sarah's, whose first four weeks outside the womb leave them nearly as fragile and as indeterminate as they were at birth.

My point is that "reality" does not make itself apparent to us in the way Noonan suggests: *Here are my objective discontinuities— you may cut me at the joints.* If we are to draw lines between acceptable and unacceptable treatment of humans and human fetuses, then those lines will depend on our collective deliberations as we try to sort out the competing claims of religious beliefs, medical practices, human rights, and legal interpretations. There are doubtless infinite gradations, infinite possibilities for splitting hairs and sketching moral lines, between conception and birth. The reason prenatal testing is so unsettling, for some people, is that even if it does nothing else, it makes us all the more aware of how bewildering it can be to live in a world in which every point is potentially part of a line.

Noonan himself admits as much in a curious passage of his book. Because he means to base his argument on "objective" realities and moral values, he needs to argue against the idea that morals are simply matters of human deliberation. Specifically, he

wants to maintain the position that each human being has a "natural" right to being recognized as human by his or her fellow humans, and that this "natural" right supersedes any social
determination of what "human" means. Unfortunately, as he begins to acknowledge that entire groups of people can be and have
been "dehumanized," he comes close to making the point he's arguing against:

> If humanity depends on social recognition, individuals or
> whole groups may be dehumanized by being denied any status
> in their society. Such a fate is fictionally portrayed in *1984* and
> has actually been the lot of many men in many societies. In the
> Roman Empire, for example, condemnation to slavery meant
> the practical denial of most human rights; in the Chinese
> Communist world, landlords have been classified as enemies of
> the people and so treated as non-persons by the state. Human-
> ity does not depend on social recognition, though often the
> failure of society to recognize the prisoner, the alien, the het-
> erodox as human has led to the destruction of human beings.

This is eloquent enough, but it's also deeply self-contradictory. If
humanity depends on social recognition, writes Noonan, why,
then, we would have a world that is . . . very much like the one
we actually live in. Because the fact is that very few societies have
ever taken seriously the proposition that every human has an
equal moral claim on his or her existence in the world. Noonan's
formulation here leaves him in the uncomfortable position of arguing that human rights are natural and universal even though
humans have acted otherwise throughout their history. *These
things are universally acknowledged*, one concludes, *except when they're
not acknowledged at all.*

Noonan would reply, no doubt, that we humans have dehumanized each other because we failed to acknowledge the universal law governing our common humanity; but this answer is much more troubling than it appears, because it repeats the signal error committed by the world's previous universalists when they've proposed "natural" laws that most people aren't observing. Take, for instance, the European and American intellectuals of the Enlightenment, who bequeathed us the proposition that all men are created equal. At the same time that they were devising such an egalitarian moral standard, they were also claiming that Africans were not "men" in this sense because they lacked the capacity for reason. That is, all humanity is governed by universal law, *except for you people over there, who therefore cannot be human.* Is there something wrong with the logic of universalism when it can't account for variances and exceptions, or were Immanuel Kant, David Hume, and Thomas Jefferson simply not smart enough to see the contradictions between their theory and their practice? Whether there's a small or a large difference between these probabilities, I'm inclined to lean toward the first of them.

If every point in our world is potentially part of a line, does this mean that all moral lines are therefore equally valid or defensible? No: some lines have tremendous consequences, and some have none, regardless of whether they were drawn over "objective discontinuities" or not. For an example we need look no further than the daily news. In recent years, the logic of the anti-abortion movement has begun to have literally murderous consequences. The movement's staggering refusal to distinguish between the living and the unborn has become the basis for the killing of abortion providers, and even though those killings (and their supporters) have been officially denounced by mainstream pro-life organizations, there isn't one pro-life organization that disputes the killers' premise—that life begins at conception. Absent that premise, there is no justification for likening family planning workers to the perpetrators of the Holocaust, or for claiming that 30 million American "babies" have been "killed" since *Roe* v. *Wade*. On the American right, of course, these kinds of claims are as common as rain. Yet it follows clearly from this line of argument that the killing and terrorizing of family planning workers is justified on the grounds that murdering one doctor or closing one clinic by force will "save" innumerable lives of the unborn. If zygotes and embryos, as well as fetuses not yet capable of surviving outside the womb, are to be understood as having the same rights to "life and liberty" as every living human, then there is no way to combat the pro-life/pro-murder position except by appealing to its internal inconsistency: you can't be pro-life and take life. However, if embryos have the same moral status as abortion providers, then this charge of internal inconsistency is not terribly important, and anti-abortion terrorists can very well reply that it is right to take one life in order to save many more, just as it would have been right, if one had the opportunity, to stop the Holocaust by any means necessary, including the murder of SS officers and German high officials.

It is possible, I know, to hold the belief that life begins at conception and yet to support abortion rights. You can grant that the fetus is a potential person from the moment of fertilization and yet believe, as Peter Singer wrote in his *Spectator* essay, that "the argument that we should bring all potential people into existence is not persuasive." It's rare, however, to hear this argument advanced, especially by religious leaders who *are* concerned as much about the fate of the living as the fate of the unborn. The contemporary Catholic Church, in fact, not only espouses the belief that all potential people should be brought into existence once a spermatozoon fertilizes an ovum; it also holds that the category of "potential people" *exceeds* the category of fertilized ova, and therefore deems all forms of contraception sinful, including unauthorized celibacy (since this too prevents the creation of life). Again, this is not to say that I find Singer's solution attractive; believing that life begins at one month after birth merely substitutes one fuzzy line for another while absolving us of the obligation to try to keep people here once they've arrived. And even John Paul II himself, when he came face to face with some of the thousands of street children of São Paulo, had to admit that we're not doing a very good job of caring for postnatal humans as matters now stand. Rumor has it that in São Paulo the Pontiff even began to rethink the Holy See's medieval position on contraception. Perhaps he thought about whether the ethical imperative to be fruitful and multiply might be a historically bounded law: *Be fruitful and multiply until you overrun the globe. Then start thinking about collective self-destruction.* Perhaps he wondered what God could have in mind to order the production of another few thousand street children every year. Perhaps he wondered whether he really could be God's representative on earth, or whether he could fulfill the task of bringing the Word to Nineveh now that the city's population exceeded twenty million. What instruments we have agree that if John Paul II did ponder these things, he did not end his ruminations by changing his mind.

In a fascinating essay, "Accounting for Amniocentesis," anthropologist Rayna Rapp explores the social settings in which prenatal testing takes place. One case study involves a little Haitian boy named Étienne St.-Croix, born with additional chromosomal material on the number 9 chromosomes; his mother, Veronique, 37, told Ms. Rapp that she would have considered abortion if the fetus had Down's, but not for something as indeterminate as a partial trisomy 9:

> If it had been Down's, maybe, just maybe I would have had an abortion. Once I had an abortion, but now I am a Seventh Day Adventist, and I don't believe in abortion anymore. Maybe for Down's, just maybe. But when they told me this, who knows? I was so scared, but the more they talked, the less they said. They do not know what this is. And I do not know, either. So now, it's my baby. We'll just have to wait and see what happens. And so will they.

Another mother tells Rapp that when her amniocentesis revealed a fetus with Down syndrome, her obstetrician immediately recommended abortion, but she hesitated; she was also thirty-seven, single, a Mormon, and the mother of an eighteen-year-old by a previous marriage when she accidentally became pregnant. She bore the child. When Rapp meets her, the child, Stevie, is six, and the mother says, "I should warn you first, I'm against this amniocentesis business and abortion of these kids." Her explanation for her decision is dotted with the same crucial "maybes" as is Veronique's:

> I did some research, I visited this group home for adult retardeds in my neighborhood. You know, it was kind of nice. They looked pretty happy, they had jobs, they went bowling. I thought about it. Maybe if I was married, maybe if I had another shot at it. But this was it: take it or leave it. So I took it. . . . Stevie's doing really well, he'll learn to read this year, I know he will. And if he doesn't, that's okay, too. This kid has been a blessing, he makes me ask myself, "why are we put

here on this earth?" There must be a reason, and Stevie's reason was to teach love, to stop haters dead in their tracks. Everyone who meets him loves him. . . . So when I see a girl who's pregnant, I always tell her about Stevie, I always say, "don't have that test, you don't need that test to love your baby the way it is." Oh, for some of them, maybe abortion is a good thing, I don't know. But for me, Stevie was just what I needed.

How different is different? One mother says "maybe if it had been Down's"; another says, "maybe if I were married." Both mothers argue against aborting disabled fetuses—maybe. Maybe because we were put here for a reason; maybe because the doctors themselves don't know what to expect. Maybe, these women think, just maybe I can deal with this; maybe if things were different . . . but we don't know. Sometimes the most liberal attitudes toward abortion and human life inhabit the same woman who opposes amniocentesis; sometimes social organizations one might consider deeply conservative turn out to promote positively aggressive policies in favor of prenatal testing. In heavily Hasidic Crown Heights, writes Rapp, "the *Chevras Dor Yershurim* (Organization for the Generations) recruits more participants for Tay-Sachs screening than any medical institution. Here, reinforcement of patriarchal authority to arrange marriages goes hand in hand with state-of-the-art prenatal screening."

I find it impossible to say what a "conservative" or a "progressive" position might be with regard to these moirés of patriarchy, single motherhood, fetal disability, and religious conviction. Accordingly, I find it impossible to imagine that we mere humans can compose a uniform moral calculus that will operate with perfect justice in circumstances so various and overdetermined.

Perhaps I am utterly wrong about this, and we mere humans are in fact on the verge of devising a uniform moral calculus. What, in such a calculus, would be gained by compelling prospective parents to remain in the dark about the health of their baby? Women with complicated medical histories, women with abnormally high blood pressure in their eighth week, women who've had miscarriages in the past, or just women who worry a lot—why should these women be denied the chance to assess, as fully as possible, what their babies might mean to them psychologically, physically, financially, whether they choose to abort or choose to book a bigger hospital? Certainly if we had known that James would turn out to be the complicated little guy he is, there would have been no time during the labor when Janet and I were left alone, no time when Janet had to issue emergency orders because the obstetrics staff nurse couldn't spot a V-tach quickly enough. We should not assume, therefore, that the technology of prenatal testing itself will impel specific human responses, as if there will be a mass extinction of fetuses with Down's should we develop the capacity to detect trisomy 21 in the eighth gestational week. However, it *is* possible—and increasingly necessary—to ask about how the sociomedical apparatus works, and whether our ability to spot fetal abnormalities might not eventually become more coercive than descriptive.

For instance, it's still relatively uncontroversial to request a prenatal test for Huntington's disease. The test is complicated—it involves gathering a genetic family history—but not prima facie outrageous. What would be outrageous, I suggest, is a social dispensation under which doctors and parents understand that it is *always* their duty to spot Huntington's in utero and stamp it out. If I am told that my child stands a good chance of developing a disease at age fifty-five, this does not prevent me from worrying that she may be hit by a train at age six or hoping that she will invent a car that runs on water at age thirty-five. Most people, at present, refuse the test for Huntington's on exactly these grounds: it's too far in the future, there are too many variables, there's no sense being a genetic determinist about a disease associated with aging when there are ten trillion other things to worry about in the next half-century. But Down syndrome is another story altogether: all too many humans, particularly those who've never met, read about, or otherwise been called to imagine people with Down syndrome, are likely to believe that finding out about so "severe" a genetic disorder is tantamount to peeking at the cards in the hand of Fate. What's more, much of the prenatal testing apparatus does indeed fixate on Down syndrome—as if *that* were the one card in Fate's arsenal about which every prospective parent must learn as soon as possible.

In 1995, researchers learned that fetal cells are present (albeit at low levels) in the mother's blood, which means that with polymerase chain reaction technology (PCR), fetal cells can be examined simply by doing a blood test on Mom. This test is different from the triple screen, because the triple screen does not examine fetal cells directly. On one hand this development is unambiguously wonderful; we can simply scoop up a few of the fetus's nucleated erythrocytes, no problem, and do a prenatal cytogenetic evaluation every bit as accurate as amniocentesis—all without sticking that enormous needle into a pregnant woman's belly. And we can do it *early* in the first trimester, even before the fetus is large enough to "see" by means of a sonogram. In fact, if we use FISH (fluorescence in situ hybridization) instead of karyotyping to spot abnormalities in the fetal genes, we can deliver your results even faster, since we won't have to culture the cell line and we can simply watch for the chromosomal material to "light up."

According to the medical abstract that announced this finding, "correct identification of chromosome 21 copy number was made in 65–75 per cent of trisomic cells and in 70–75 per cent of normal disomic cells by using all the tested probes. However, the chromosome 21-specific telometric probe (cos 17F8) showed the best results due to more intense and clearly visible hybridization." If this holds up, then doctors will be able to spot Down syndrome, with high levels of accuracy and without invading the uterus, as soon as fetal cells start showing up in the maternal bloodstream. But what are we to make of this? Is it right? Is it sinister? If we find it daunting that all this clinical exactitude is so preoccupied with that little twenty-first chromosome, then maybe it's worth asking what such a technology can bring in its train. Does this mean that pregnant women will be counseled to abort fetuses with Down syndrome as early as possible? Or will some women refuse the test, for the same reasons they now refuse amniocentesis—not on the basis of the odds against miscarriage but on the conviction that they don't want or need to know about Down syndrome in utero?

The answer to these questions, I think, depends less on advances in medical technology in themselves than on the less precise but more powerful social mechanisms by which we will decide whether a fetus with Down syndrome is to be understood as a blessing, as a curse, or as something more indeterminate. Social mechanisms have more moving parts than any social theorist has yet been able to enumerate, and at the moment it's not clear whether we have a social consensus on Down syndrome, whether we need one, or whether we should actively try to forge one. This much we can say: Once we develop the ability to detect trisomy 21 in the very early stages of pregnancy, prospective parents will then have the potential to make use of that ability in order to prepare for the birth of a disabled child, and they will have the potential to make a decision to abort in the first trimester. Because the first trimester is where many people draw the line on "acceptable" abortions, it's possible that this technology could result in a higher number of abortions of potentially disabled fetuses. This should be a sobering thought. Christine Allison may be wrong to speak of the triple screen in irresponsible terms like "genocide," but it is not at all wrong for any of us to wonder about the ethics of early detection. Yet at the same time, it is not clear what kind of information should be considered mandatory equipment for all parents, nor is it clear that we—whoever "we" are—have the right to expect them to do what "we" think is the right thing with it.

At present, the law seems to allow doctors and parents considerable latitude, and technological advances seem only to increase that latitude still further. But then again, it's often true that legal principles are overridden by social realities—as is the case for millions of American women who have the legal right to abortion but extremely limited access to an abortion provider. It is also true that when a sociomedical apparatus gets powerful and ubiquitous, it can seem to entail its own conclusions even if individual parents and medical practitioners have the largest souls and the best intentions in the world. What else could explain the practice of institutionalizing babies with Down syndrome, except a sociomedical apparatus under which institutionalization was understood as the best of all possible worlds for all concerned, based on the research "evidence"?

It's one thing to leave the parental decisions entirely to the parents; it's another thing to leave the research decisions to the researchers, or the insurance decisions to the insurers, because *those* systemic decisions can significantly constrict parents' options before the parents ever arrive on the scene. In 1995, for instance, *before* the possibility of a FISH-PCR test was announced in the medical journals, the American College of Obstetricians and Gynecologists officially recommended that the "triple screen" for Down syndrome (and other trisomies) be given to all pregnant women regardless of age. Until now, the alphafetoprotein (AFP) test had been the only test so widely recommended; the AFP catches problems far more severe than Down's, namely, neural tube defects, including such lethal anomalies as anencephaly, holoprosencephaly, and einencephaly, but it also yields a high number of false positives. So on one hand, the College's recommendation makes great good sense. If you're going to test, it's better to test accurately than inaccurately, and the triple screen doesn't cost a great deal more than the AFP single screen. But on the other hand, in a society so litigious as ours, the College's recommendation basically makes the triple screen mandatory; parents of "disabled" children could conceivably sue their doctors if they weren't given the test during pregnancy, and then any physician who chose not to administer the test would have to explain why he or she decided not to abide by the profession's official recommendations.

Like everything else about Down syndrome and prenatal testing, this development can have contradictory social effects. If a woman over 35 were given the triple screen and her results were negative, then she might very well forego more expensive tests like amniocentesis and CVS (chorionic villus sampling). That seems all to the good. Yet even the triple screen only identifies Down syndrome around 65 percent of the time: it will still yield a fairly high number of false positives and false negatives, unnecessarily making some women anxious and stressed, or leading them to choose abortion, while other women give birth to babies with Down syndrome after their providers have decisively told them the fetus is normal. How then will the sociomedical apparatus respond to the demands of individual patients, corporate insurers, and advancing technologies? Will the American College of Obstetricians and Gynecologists decide it is necessary to recommend the FISH-PCR universally? In some future decade, will pregnant women be notified in their eighth week that their fetus has Down syndrome, and if so, will they be encouraged, implicitly or explicitly, to abort? Or will abortion be recriminalized by then?

So tangled is the web we weave when once we practice to perceive. Although technologies do not, in and of themselves, impel conclusions, technologies are also inevitably part and product of larger social apparatuses whose sole purpose it is to impel conclusions. Television can amuse or inform; the Internet may be a classroom without walls or the 1990s version of the CB radio. Much depends on how we use them. But we do not "use" telecommunications conglomerates; on the contrary, telecommunications conglomerates set the terms by which we can use their technologies. So it is in the practice of medicine. Should we set our collective sights on the goal of identifying all anomalies detectible in utero? What will count as an "anomaly" worth identifying? What will we do when we have identified an anomaly? Will we attempt a cure in utero if such a thing is feasible? Will we urge parents not to bring children with such anomalies into the world? Or will we set about making the world a more welcoming place for anomalous children? It is in this context that the recommendation of the American College of Obstetricians and Gynecologists is worth examining more closely. Similarly, when the Jones Institute for Reproductive Medicine in Norfolk, Virginia, announced in February 1995 that it would begin screening embryos for

Down syndrome before implanting them in a woman's uterus, it was not unreasonable for people to ask whether this would be a sign of things to come: the Jones Institute had previously screened for Tay-Sachs, but children with Tay-Sachs make up only 1 in 400,000 live births in the United States, and their life expectancy is no more than five years. Down's occurs 500 times as often, and, as institute president Gary D. Hodgen told the *Norfolk Virginian-Pilot*, "one does not see with the same clarity the usefulness of the test . . . to society. But ask an individual couple how willing they are to deal with it."

There is nothing necessarily Faustian about cultivating our collective capacity to identify Down syndrome as soon as possible after fertilization. Maybe most people will understand prenatal testing as the basis for decisions to abort, and maybe some people will understand it as the basis for decisions to prepare. (Apparently, 90 percent choose to abort: only one couple in ten will choose to have a child with Down's if the amniocentesis is positive. But no one knows how many people refuse the test altogether.) Whatever an individual couple might know and whenever they may know it, however, I suspect that there may be *something* wrong about a sociomedical apparatus that devotes so much of its resources to identifying Down syndrome in utero, instead of devoting resources to finding out how to treat Down syndrome symptomatically ex utero. We now know that Down syndrome entails some rather intricate cellular malfunctions and biochemical imbalances; we now know that the brains of infants with Down syndrome develop "normally" up to a point, after which the later developing parts of the brain, such as the hippocampus, develop more slowly and erratically. That means Jamie could be quite good at some cognitive tasks but not others: In his case, he can memorize lists of associated objects but can't generalize from the list, or understand the relation of item to list well enough to perform abstract mental operations like recognizing the shapes of Kentucky or Maine outside the confines of his book of the fifty states. But we don't even know whether any of these idiosyncrasies might affect the way people with Down syndrome synthesize the antibiotics they so often take to treat common infections.

Sometimes the promise is made that for modern medicine, detection is but a prelude to prevention: if we can detect it early, we can fix it. And prevention, we all know, is preferable to treatment. Get to the roots of the disease, not its symptoms. Such is the ethos of modern medicine, and most of the time it's sound and sane. But it's arguable that Down syndrome should not be considered a "disease" in the first place; might we not, therefore, refuse to consider it as something we need to prevent? I have even read pamphlets and medical texts that speak of "curing" Down syndrome, and perhaps there will eventually be some medical researchers willing to suggest that certain genetic anomalies might be corrected in the womb; but the mind boggles at the kind of microscopically subtle and minute biochemical intervention it would take to devise a fetal "correction" for trisomy 21. Unless the "cure" could be administered *before* fertilization, during meiosis, so that all possible chromosomal nondisjunctions were prevented *as they were about to happen*, how might someone go about "fixing" every cell in a developing fetus? How might we go about fixing someone's faulty meiosis in the first place? It is not unheard of for scientists to be so consumed with hubris that they try to remake the world into which they were born—and sometimes they succeed, winning the world's praise or blame. But I doubt whether the technologies of prenatal testing will yield a "cure" for Down syndrome. Genetic engineering may someday allow us to spot and counteract human diseases and disabilities that are caused by a single gene or set of genes; prenatal testing will give prospective parents a wider variety of options and moral quandaries to consider. But the vagaries of meiosis may turn out to be beyond our grasp, just as we cannot now predict, even with the finest biochemical screens, which developing fetuses will go on to experience physical trauma and deliveries that result in birth "defects."

In the meantime, it seems to me that we might do more research into the biochemistry of postnatal humans with Down syndrome. Perhaps all parents of children with Down syndrome, be they pro-life or pro-choice, might sleep a little easier if they knew that Western medicine was more concerned with maximizing the human potential of children born with Down's than with spotting those children before they are born. The technologies themselves may not automatically augur a brave new world without creatures such as Jamie, but when it comes to gauging the larger social apparatus in which the technologies operate, Janet and I simply don't yet know what to think. Either the technologies, from FISH to RU486, could democratize parental decision-making on the ground, or they could give us a medical profession that's as coercive (and insistently well-meaning) as it was in the days when "mongoloids" were institutionalized. So much depends on whether our technologies serve our social desires or our social desires are made to serve our technologies: you can't democratize parental decision making, in this respect or any other, if our medical technologies have already predetermined our options. Whatever the future holds, we suppose that we should all keep our eyes open, whatever shape or color those eyes might be.

It's not merely that I don't have any firm conclusions about the contradictory politics of prenatal testing. I'm also not sure whether I can have any advice for prospective parents who are contemplating what course of action to take when they discover they will bear a "disabled" child. Obviously I can't and don't advocate abortion of fetuses with Down syndrome; indeed, the only argument I have is that such decisions should not be automatic. A fetal diagnosis of Down syndrome should not be understood, either by medical personnel or by parents, as a finding to which abortion is the most logical response. I believe this not only on humanitarian grounds but also as a matter of practicality: unlike Tay-Sachs or trisomy 13, say, Down syndrome is a disability whose effects are too various to predict and often too mild to justify abortion on "quality of life" considerations for the parents and child.

Nonetheless, although this is my belief, it is only my belief. I would not want to see it become something more than belief—something more like a coercive social expectation. There are already plenty of social forces out there telling pregnant women that they may have an abortion only if they agree to be consumed with guilt about it, and I want to do nothing to reinforce those pressures. I believe that no good is achieved by making some forms of childbearing mandatory, even in a matter so close to my heart as this. But by the same token, just as I would deny that I have the right to make other parents feel guilty for aborting a fetus with Down syndrome, so too would I deny that other parents have the right to make Janet and me feel guilty for having Jamie. This is not a "relativist" position: it is based on the ideal of reciprocity. I will not claim right of access to certain areas of your life, so long as you do not claim right of access to equivalent areas of mine. If I do not want to interfere with other people's most intimate decisions, I also want it understood that those of us who do have "disabled" children are not selfish: we are not a corporate

liability, we are not a drain on health care resources, we are not si-
phoning money away from soup kitchens, environmental protection, or job training and day care for single mothers. I know that
when social services and resources are artificially scarce (thanks to
tax cuts, defense buildups, or corporate welfare), scapegoats are
always easy to find, and any unprincipled politician and pundit
can try to pit one underfunded constituency against another. If it
is in my power, I will not let that happen to people like James.

There are, I admit, some days when I am quite convinced that
I should work actively to convince people not to abort fetuses
with Down syndrome, and other days when I am quite convinced
that this would be nothing more than moral arrogance. In my
ideal universe, though, I do have something like a procedure by
which the medical profession would deal with prospective parents
when they've learned that if they choose to carry the pregnancy to
term they will have a child with Down syndrome. To date I've
heard the testimony of two mothers of children with Down syndrome who received their diagnosis toward the end of the second
trimester: one was strongly advised, by her health care professionals, to abort; the other was strongly advised, by *her* health care
professionals, to carry the pregnancy to term. Personally, I'm not
convinced that health care professionals have any business
strongly advising patients to take either course, except when the
mother's life is at risk. In my ideal universe, medical personnel
would follow prenatal testing not so much with "advice" as with
information. The line between advice and information, of course,
is no clearer than the line between conception and birth, but still,
the ideal, I think, would be to give parents as much medical, financial, and social information as they request, as accurately as
our information technologies allow, and (to the greatest extent
possible) turn over the actual decisionmaking to the parents

themselves, who then may very well ask advice from doctors, relatives, and friends.

This sounds hopelessly contentless and wishy-washy, but it's not. There are still plenty of medical practitioners who tell their patients that children with Down syndrome cannot learn; there are plenty of doctors, just as there are plenty of professors, who haven't updated their knowledge of the field in twenty years; and there are plenty of doctors who feel it is their duty, as trained professionals, to tell their patients not only what their condition is but what they'd better do about it. That's not a problem when my own primary physician is telling me to take an antibiotic for a sinus infection, but it *is* a problem when someone's ob-gyn specialist is telling them that X is clearly the right thing to do when you learn that the fetus you're carrying has Down syndrome. Far from being contentless, then, my standards would necessitate a small raft of recommendations and policy guidelines from the American Medical Association and appropriately professional behavior from every working medical professional in the United States. So the problem isn't that my ideal universe is wishy-washy. The problem is that like all ideal universes, it's utopian.

As long as I'm imagining a Utopian States of America, I might as well do it in detail. Upon learning that their child, if born, will be born with Down syndrome, prospective parents would first be given the relevant medical prognoses about congenital defects in the cardiovascular and nervous systems. I give priority to congenital defects because these are the most likely to affect parent and child in the first few years; for some parents, it may be relevant that people with Down syndrome are at higher risk for leukemia and, later, Alzheimer's, but placing great weight on information about a baby's possible health status two to four decades from now seems to me to run afoul of the law of human unpredictability whereby some of us are hit by trains and some of us invent aquamobiles. Then, alongside the information about possible health risks, I'd offer prospective parents the testimony of various families—parents and siblings—of people with Down syndrome, as well as the testimonies of people with Down's themselves. The message: if you choose to have this child, your life may become richer and more wonderful than you can imagine, and the child will grow to be a loving, self-aware, irreplaceable member of the human family. *And* if you choose to have this child, your life may become more arduous and complicated than you can imagine, and you will have to learn some new skills like how to use "parallel talking" to cope with speech delays or how to negotiate with school personnel for on-site occupational therapy. Furthermore, you will be sad. You will be sad often, acutely, and about many things. You will have a completely different set of expectations for your offspring, such that you will be "happy" if he or she manages to live independently or semi-independently as an adult. Like Stevie's mother, you may well wonder why we were put here on this earth, if indeed we were "put" here at all.

The reason you'd need a variety of family testimonies, for those prospective parents who are uncertain about abortion and curious about whether they can cope with a "disabled" child, is simply that people with Down syndrome are individuals. Every bit as needy, wily, surprising, and perverse as any of us, and a little more vulnerable, politically and physically. Members of a group whose identity is written in the biochemical language of the genome, but distinct and idiosyncratic humans nonetheless. It's one thing to hear that there's a one-in-six chance that your baby will be born (six or seven months from now) with spinal anomalies; it's quite another to listen to parents who've guided their children through surgery, or to parents whose children are actually healthier than many nondisabled kids. Janet and I are fond of telling people we dodged all the biggest bullets. When we took him to St. Louis at the age of three for an intensive examination of his cardiovascular and nervous systems, he came back with a clean bill of health; the pediatric cardiologist had turned to his medical student and offered him the chance to check out Jamie's heart, saying, "You can listen if you like—but it's just a beating heart." Meaning, of course, that Jamie would afford the student no chance to learn what a septal defect might sound like in a child with Down syndrome. I think of that moment often, particularly when Jamie is running, swimming, or doubled over with laughter: his little heart is doing just fine, it's just a beating heart. But that's not true of every child with Down's, and it would be irresponsible of us to pretend that Jamie can stand in for all the members of his group merely because he shares a chromosomal nondisjunction with them. All children with Down syndrome have low muscle tone, and all children with Down syndrome will have a more difficult time learning to walk than most people do; some will be born with great determination, some with lousy balance, and some won't feel like walking very much at all. No matter what else they might have in common, they won't all walk in single file.

Our own family testimony is of course unique, which means either that we are identical to everyone else only in our uniqueness or that Tolstoy was quite wrong to suppose that all happy families are alike. We have full-coverage health insurance as well as the assurance that our employers will not fire us for driving up their insurers' premiums. We have Janet's medical expertise, and as college professors, we have extremely flexible work schedules: we usually work sixty hours a week, but most of these take place in our home, and we get to choose *which* sixty hours to work. Our local support services are good, and Jamie has not required extensive surgery or long-term hospitalization. On the other hand, we have no immediate family, either on Janet's side or on mine, living within eight hundred miles of us. We suppose that if there were a few grandparents or aunts within an hour's drive, we could cope with much less flexible work times and manage our child care as well as we do now, and our house would be home to a more extended family. But then maybe Jamie wouldn't be such a seasoned traveler as he is now.

The most important thing about the house into which Jamie was born, however, is that it already contained Nick. Actually, we didn't begin to appreciate what it meant for Jamie to have a five-year-old brother until we met a number of families in the Champaign area whose *first* child was a child with Down's. Not only had we had an introduction to child care before Jamie came along, but we could also rely on Nick to help us watch over the new baby and listen for his monitor. Nick was out of toddler range: he could dress himself (garishly), tie his shoes, and get ready for bed. He no longer engaged in a great deal of potentially dangerous "exploratory" behavior, and we imagined that within a few years we could actually leave the two children alone together long enough to let us cook dinner together. Last but not least, there was only one of Nick. If we'd had to care for Jamie in those first few months while also shepherding a pair of preschoolers or a gaggle of offspring from toddler to young adult, I'm not sure how long we'd have held up under the strain.

We think Jamie was—and is—worth every effort, of course, and we'll say so to any prospective parents who ask, regardless of how their circumstances may differ from ours. But what can we tell the Korean couple who had a child with Down syndrome during the brief time they were at school in the United States and now say they cannot return to Korea with the child because of the social stigma involved? What can we tell the mother in her forties who fears bearing a child with Down syndrome who will likely outlive her, possibly developing Alzheimer's or becoming weak and incontinent years after she's passed away?

It may very well be that Janet and I have nothing to tell them—and nothing in common save for a child with a genetic nondisjunction. But that is not the primary issue with which we (as a couple) or we (as a society) have to struggle. For the question is not whether we (as a society) will recognize the infinite unpredictability of human events, or whether we will understand that there is no single moral calculus that will decide every difficult prenatal case in advance. Some of us will continue to believe that we cannot get along without a single, clear moral standard, and some of us will continue to believe that hard cases make bad law precisely because hard cases demonstrate that moral standards are often inapplicable precisely to the degree they are inflexible. The question, rather, is whether we will maintain a social system that makes allowance for unpredictability, variance, competing moral imperatives, difficult decisions, private decisions, and even perverse decisions. The paradox is that if there is to be a "private" realm in which citizens make decisions about childbearing, decisions that are granted some relative autonomy from state power, then that private realm can only be established publicly; that autonomy from the state can only be granted by the state.

The proposition John Noonan denied must indeed be our foundation: Humanity depends on social recognition, as do all other forms of meaning. Only humans can decide the meaning of a thing, including a word like "human"—and this is true even when humans believe they are doing nothing more or nothing less than interpreting the word of God. We (as a society, as a species) can talk all we want about whether we have a "natural right" to self-determination, or whether fetuses have a "right to life" from the moment of conception, but the simple fact remains that only human cultures can establish and maintain "natural" rights. If it really were self-evident that all humans are created equal and endowed by their Creator with certain inalienable rights such as life, liberty, and the pursuit of happiness, then Thomas Jefferson wouldn't have had to argue the point in the first place, and we (as a nation) wouldn't have had to engage in a war to establish a political entity in which those "self-evident" rights could be enshrined as self-evident.

That's why the debate about abortion and prenatal testing is so vital, so critical for modern democracy; that's why citizens like James compel us to think anew about who and what is "free" in an ostensibly free society. Theocracies and totalitarianisms do not have to worry about the bases of moral and legal authority. In such societies there is little procedural confusion about competing ethical imperatives and little room for debate about whether single moral standards can suffice for all of our difficult cases. If law derives from God or from a sovereign, then we need not deliberate about where our obligations come from or how we might decide how best to align our own lives with the dictates of universal law; all we need to debate is the best method of interpreting the writ of God or the sovereign, and if push comes to shove, severely aberrant interpretations will be handled by the king's (or the Supreme Being's) ministers and representatives. If, however, human law takes its origin and authority from collective social deliberation, then it must acknowledge that justice is fluid and takes the shape of its container. No single writ can dictate in advance the competing rights claims of a ten-week-old fetus with

Down syndrome, a twenty-six-week-old premature infant with multiple organ failure, and an indigent seventy-four-year-old man in a permanent vegetative state. How then to allow for children who do not or cannot walk in single file, and for parents who, however accurately or mistakenly, judge themselves incapable of caring for children with disabilities? How else but to create a "private" legal space in which excruciatingly difficult decisions can be made by those most likely to be affected by them?

It is somewhat misleading, then, to couch the debate in terms of whether there is a "right" to privacy. The issue, instead, is whether our publicly designated private legal spaces will cover lunch counters or uteruses, corporate boardrooms or ob-gyn clinics. This means conceiving of "the private" not as a realm exempt from public morality (as in the libertarian concept of individual privacy) but, instead, as a realm *established by* public morality. Lacking a public and legal concept of "privacy," we would be unable to allow for a world in which one family wants their seventy-four-year-old father to die with dignity rather than remain in a permanent vegetative state whereas another family wants the hospital to do everything possible to keep their brain-dead grandmother "alive"; where one woman decides that she'd better have the child, Down syndrome or no Down syndrome, because she probably won't conceive again, whereas another woman decides she can bear a child with partial trisomy 9 but maybe not a child with Down's. There may be no more important task for democracies than this: to foster and maintain a social and legal consensus that there are some areas of human life in which individuals should be free to apply the rules of social and legal consensus as they see fit. For human forms of social organization, there is no other way to honor hard cases and bad law but for citizens of democracies to grant their fellow citizens a safe haven from political coercion. Sometimes I think there's some deep ethical-linguistic reason that in English, *idiot* and *idiosyncratic* have the same root, *idios*. From the Greek, meaning *private*.

There's a wonderful sense, then, in which the pro-life television ads sponsored by the Arthur S. DeMoss Foundation actually deconstruct themselves: "Life—What a Beautiful Choice." My sentiments exactly. But as Aquinas and Milton taught me, a choice is only a choice if it's a choice.

With Jamie we'd had the luxury of choice many times over. We live in a country where abortion is legal and where we would not be stigmatized for bearing a "disabled" child, so we had quite a broad field in which to decide what kind of prenatal testing we wanted. Then, when he was released from the ICU, we'd exercised our right to refuse the operation that would give Jamie a gastrostomy tube. In retrospect, we're very grateful to have been granted so much autonomy to make the decisions so important to our lives and the lives of our children. But still, when Jamie came home, we felt anything but autonomous. Our infant child was not only medicalized, he was physically *encumbered*. Not yet one month old, not yet eight pounds, he was swathed in a chest strap, wreathed in nasal cannulae, and adorned with a nasal tube. So, too, was our perception of him encumbered by his encumbrances. Just as I felt I had to look at a blood gas machine in order to tell whether Jamie was getting enough oxygen, so too did I feel as if I couldn't detach him from his tubes and straps and hold him to my chest without imperiling his life. I know I did not choose to feel that way, and I also knew I could not choose to demedicalize Jamie simply by force of will.

Every night, we checked his padding, his wires, and the placement of his tubing. Velcro pads held the chest strap in place; the cannula and tube were fixed to Jamie's face with special tape. I know that a person with my name and my neuromuscular map was once practiced at setting and adjusting Jamie's tubes, but there are some memories of that autumn I cannot voluntarily summon up. I've repressed more of the details of those few months than I can possibly retrieve at this distance. But every once in a while, rummaging through the medicine closet for Ace bandages or heating pads, I come across the Hypafix adhesive tape with which we affixed James's feeding tube to the bridge of his nose. It's like discovering evidence of another life, dim but indelible, and you realize that once upon a time you could cope with practically anything. Running a small tube through your baby's nose to his stomach is the worst kind of counterintuitive practice. You have to do it carefully, measuring your length of tubing accurately and listening with a stethoscope to make sure you haven't entered the lung by mistake. Whenever James pulled out his tube, by design or by the random flailing of his arms, we had to do the whole thing over again, in the other nostril this time, lubricating and marking and holding the tube while we fumbled with the world's stickiest tape. It's a four-handed job, and I found it impossible to blame the hospital staff doctors for assuming we wouldn't want to undertake such an enterprise alone.

If you had told me in August 1991—or, for that matter, after an amniocentesis in April 1991—that I'd have to feed my infant by dipping a small plastic tube in K-Y jelly and slipping it into his nose and down his pharynx into his teeny tummy, I'd have told you that I wasn't capable of caring for such a child. But by mid-October, I felt as if I had grown new limbs and new areas of the brain to direct them. Weirdest of all, I was able to accept nasal feedings as part of a routine, using nothing more than the flimsy emotional apparatus I was born with. I was twenty-four when Nick was born, and barely able to take care of myself, let alone a helpless human neonate. For months I shook with terror every time I changed Nick, knowing that if he suddenly learned to roll over and fall off the changing table he might very well die—just as he might die by spasming out of my arms in the middle of the street or by coming upon a kitchen knife just as his brain had gotten organized enough to enable him to reach out and grab things. Nick was two months old before I judged myself capable of taking him for a trip in the car; I packed his baby bag for two hours with every conceivable item and one extra of everything, only to have him throw up and nearly choke on his vomit the minute we arrived at our destination while I shouted for help and fumbled madly with the latch on his car seat. By contrast, I had driven Jamie home while operating his oxygen gauge, maneuvering his oxygen tank, and adjusting his cannula. That alone, I thought, constituted a quantum leap in parental competence. A few weeks later, though, I caught myself thinking about Jamie's nasal tube as if it were a chore on a par with filling out requisition forms in triplicate, and I stopped cold. Where did I get the capacity to deal with *this* as if it were part of my daily life? Where, pray tell, did I get the *chutzpah* to complain when Jamie throws up and makes me feed him another 40 cc by tube?

I will credit myself with this much sense: When I caught myself wondering why and how I was coping with Jamie's vomit and his nasal feedings, I thought about something else. Somehow I knew that if I became too self-aware about how extraordinary my daily child-care routine had become, I would also become incapable of dealing with Jamie's care as if it *were* routine. But I didn't become fully conscious of this knowledge until years later when I saw Bud and Sarah in action, dealing with the daily chores demanded of them by their tiny twins. When James was born, I had had all the benefits of being married to a Ph.D. who was also an R.N.; Bud and Sarah had no medical expertise other than what they had been forced to acquire on the job. I had last seen Bud and Sarah in the fall of 1994, when they were worrying about which design to choose for their birth announcements; by the summer of 1995 they were telling each other about whether their baby might require exploratory surgery—since, after all, his IV had infiltrated, his stoma might be infected, and his creatinine was up over 1.5. I knew from my experience with Jamie that the *worst* thing I could do for Bud and Sarah was to point out to them how much more literate and competent they were in the language of human life than they had been a year ago: One of the reasons they had assimilated a new language and a new form of life so capably was that they had not paused too long to wonder how they'd done it. And I saw in their newfound medical literacy the kind of precarious emotional equilibrium I had once established: *You can do this. You can cope with practically anything.*

I did not establish that equilibrium on my own. Whether it's a consequence or a condition of her competence as a nurse, Janet knows how to forge a schedule out of the clutter of the day. First, she said, we need a chart. Then, she said, you need to understand something about how to deal with neonates who need a helping hand. She proceeded to tell me about a pair of neonatal nurses she had known at Virginia who had competed with each other to keep a baby alive until their shift was over. No absurd heroics, she said, just maintenance work undertaken by two adults until the baby was ready to take care of her vital signs by herself. But they challenged each other to see who could keep the baby alive longer, they proceeded as if engaged in an arm-wrestling marathon, and for the next twelve hours they thought of nothing else.

"So that's what we're going to do," Janet said. "We're going to make a chart, and we're going to see who can get the most milk into Jamie by mouth."

PO, as the medical personnel say: *per orem*. After all, Jamie's nasal tube, like unto a thermonuclear weapon, was there precisely so that we *wouldn't* use it. Each week, a visiting nurse from Diversified Healthcare would set a minimum daily amount for Jamie's milk intake; sometimes the nurse himself would give Jamie a feeding and give us a rest. Whatever Jamie didn't take by bottle would have to go in by tube. You can see the incentive at work here. At first Janet and I were told that we could be satisfied if we got half of Jamie's milk into him *per orem*. The nurse's goal was 120 cc, and we could shoot for around 50 or so. We adjusted to that figure, but only until that extraordinary afternoon when Jamie and I decided that we could do lunch just fine without the tube. We still have that chart today—it speaks to me more immediately than anything else from that time, Jamie's first handprints included—and there it is: On the morning of October 10, 1991, at 8:30, he took 70 cc by bottle and 50 *p.o.*, vomiting back 5 cc. At 9:00, he got 2.5 milliliters of Dimetapp; at 10:30 his heart rate was 146, his respiratory rate 60; at 11:00, his temperature was 97.4, axillary; at noon I gave him Afrin in each nostril. And then, at 12:30, central standard time, the simplest entry to date: under the heading "bottle feed," the notation, *120 cc.*

When Janet came back from teaching, later that afternoon, she looked at the chart in astonishment. "You lucky dog," she said, squinting with mock disdain. "Luck had nothing to do with it," I replied. "All you need is patience and training." The competition was on—but it wasn't for another five full days that we got two consecutive feedings of 120 cc into him. Our chart runs from October 7 right to the end of the month, and even during the breakthrough days of October 15–18, when Jamie took every single feeding *p.o.* (including a gluttonous 165 cc at 7 PM on the 17th), his record is festooned with our desperate attempts to keep him free from infection: the words "naldecon," "amoxil," "erythromycin," "Afrin" line the right side of the chart like a running commentary on the main text of Jamie's first meals. Then came an agonizing week and a half during which we needed to use the nasal tube again on almost every feeding; by this time, James was getting almost coordinated enough to remove the tube at will, which meant that there were some days when Janet and I replaced the tube two or three times. Gradually, though, we got Jamie to bottle-feed; one of Janet's entries on the chart even reads, "30 (breast)," but Jamie's breathing apparatus didn't ever mature enough to let him nurse at the breast with any efficiency. Instead, Janet spent half her waking day with breast pumps, stocking the refrigerator with mother's milk that Jamie would drink either by mouth or by nose.

Early in November we let Jamie go a whole day, and then two, without his nasal tube. Later that month we began to get confident enough to wean him from supplemental oxygen during the night, and slowly but surely we started to see what Jamie's face would look like *sans* tubes. Then, late one weird night after his first week or two of tubelessness, Jamie spoke to us for the first time. It was 2 or 3 A.M., and I was watching *The Abyss* on the VCR while holding a bottle from which Jamie was drinking with great deliberation. I don't remember the movie too well, but I do remember holding a half-full bottle to the light and thinking, *at this rate he'll finish this sometime around dawn*, when suddenly I heard an eerie little wail. I assumed it had come from the TV, but when I looked down I saw my two-month-old Jamie nestled in the crook of my elbow, all tensed up, staring at me with wide, wide eyes and trying to speak: "ooooooooooooooo," he was saying in a thready, raspy voice. "Oooooooooooo." Janet, asleep next to me on the couch, woke up in alarm. "What was that?" she asked.

"That was *him*," I said with a jog of the elbow. "I think he's ooooooooooo-ing."

"Is he hurt? He sounds like he's hurt." Up to this point even Jamie's cries had been soundless, thanks in part to his floppy larynx and his shallow breathing.

"I don't know," I replied. The ooooooooo-ing went on, every bit as eerie and unsettling as when it started. "Maybe space aliens are sending messages through him from Neptune." It wasn't until days later that Janet confessed to me that she'd feared he was dying. But after a few minutes his efforts—and particularly his expressions—were unmistakable: He was saying hello to us, and when we said hello back, he started to smile. He wanted to make something of an opening statement. His muscles weren't ready to pull it off, but his spirit was strong and clear. He was home, in the arms of his proud but profoundly sleepy parents, and he wanted to let them know that he knew it.

CHAPTER THREE

■

Sapping the Strength
of the State

▲

The rest of that winter, as Janet and I say to each other whenever we narrate ourselves to ourselves, was a thrash. Knowing that Jamie's airways were so tiny and fragile that they could be obstructed by even the slightest infection, we washed our hands dozens of times a day, wore masks whenever we felt a sneeze coming on, and made Jamie's visitors go through a similar routine. Our house didn't look exactly like a testing lab for severe biohazards—we didn't wear Mylar suits with scrubbers—but it did boast an impressive array of medical supplies as well as our usual boatload of prescription drugs. And it didn't work. Jamie got one cold after another, and we fought them as if they were plagues. Within weeks he was put on "prophylactic antibiotics"; we thought of the "prophylactic" in this term as an expression of wishful thinking, since Jamie still didn't seem to be warding off bacteria very effectively. I had spent the months before Jamie's birth teaching summer school and going to the gym; by August I was in the best physical shape of my adult life, though I was tired of teaching. By December I had gained twenty-five pounds and was beginning to get weird tinglings in my limbs. Some people eat less when they're stressed; I develop a taste for double cheeseburgers. Janet responded by buying me a pair of rollerblades for Christmas so that I could tool around the neighborhood and perhaps play some roller hockey. On Christmas morning I laced them up eagerly, glided out of the house and down the street, and then tried a short stop the way I had always done on ice skates—by turning the blades sideways and digging in. I wound up with a foot-long scrape along my right thigh and a whole new appreciation of friction.

I had managed to stay on top of my classes, an undergraduate American Lit survey and a graduate seminar on recent African-American literature and literary theory. The undergraduates asked me why I didn't take more time off; I told them that their class was helping me to stay anchored in the real world. Since most of them had been told that college was anything but (or actually antithetical to) the real world, this struck them as either funny or poignant. The graduate students, for their part, almost uniformly trashed the seminar at semester's end, returning me the worst course evaluations I've ever gotten, before or since. Somehow, of all the trials we went through in Jamie's first four months, that one seems the most trivial, and sure enough, it was the hardest to bear. Janet's courses got rave reviews suggesting something close to student ecstasy, as Janet's courses always do, and in early December she flew back to Charlottesville to defend her dissertation. That weekend I decided to see whether Jamie would like some soy milk; that weekend Jamie threw up so often I finally had to bring him into the pediatric clinic.

Jamie threw up a lot. Partly that was because of his laryngomalacia; his reflux valve was hypersensitive, rendering him an infant with a hair-trigger stomach. Partly it was because his gastrointestinal system was immature and, like the rest of his body, developing more slowly than normal. But in this as in so many things he was turning out to differ from Nick in degree rather than in kind. Nick, too, had had trouble keeping his food down when he was a baby, especially when he was wearing new clothes for the first time. With Nick we assumed that vomiting was in fact induced by new clothes; with Jamie, almost any kind of clothes would do.

As we emerged into the new year I began to try to recalibrate my emotional rheostat, knowing I could not go on very much longer with things as they were. I had begun to realize, reluctantly, how angry I was with the course my life had taken, not merely because of Jamie's arrival but, instead, because of what it represented: yet another indefinite, prolonged period of stress, another few months or years of waiting to see whether everything would be all right once we were through with X. For the first six years Janet and I were together, X was graduate school; we used to tell ourselves how interesting it would be to get to know each other someday when we didn't have to work two part-time jobs on top of teaching just to stay afloat. Then when I was hired at Illinois, we thought we were in the clear—but our first year was a shock. Nick's asthma remained dangerous, and Janet and I spent the entire year racing to prepare classes, handing Nick off to each other in the halls because we could only afford day care in the afternoons. We also spent the entire year getting sick. Our next year was much calmer; Nick's asthma came under control, thanks to the invention of nebulized steroids, and then when Janet was hired we had thought our lives were finally going to stabilize. All I'd have to do would be to teach summer school to get ready for the new baby, and then we could settle in, raise our kids, write some books, and teach some classes, the way we thought professors were supposed to do. Now, we were telling ourselves that if we only got through this first winter we would be all right. But we'd told ourselves things like that for so long now that I wasn't sure I could hold on for another year.

Stepping back and putting things in perspective only made them worse. Whenever I remembered how extraordinarily fortunate we'd been, not only as young professors but as humans, all I could feel was guilt. Jamie threw up twice today, Nick had a fever of 102.8, and I had a runny nose under my surgical mask, but my spouse and I had two jobs with flexible hours in a world where thirty thousand children died of starvation yesterday and another thirty thousand American workers were "downsized" so that their CEOs and shareholders could have a little merrier Christmas. I remembered how I had first narrated Jamie the night I came home from the hospital: Upon leaving Janet and Jamie I had stopped at the home of Amanda Anderson and Allen Hance, our colleagues and closest friends at the University of Illinois. Nick had been staying with them for the day. As Amanda and Al poured me a glass of wine and urged me to sit down and relax, I assured them that it was only Down syndrome, nothing serious like Tay-Sachs or cystic fibrosis . . . and then I caught myself, ashamed, saying, "Well, I don't suppose I meant to base my sense of relative well-being on other people's misery." But I found myself doing that for months afterward, and it never stopped infuriating me. The only thing worse, I thought, was the curmudgeonly feeling that still luckier people didn't know how good *they* had it. Nothing else, surely, could account for the irrationality of my initial impulse to be skeptical about amniocentesis. I mean, here we were straining our health and our love for each other in order to fortify Jamie (and his health, and our love for him), and I was thinking that *other people* should forgo amniocentesis lest they enable themselves to avoid situations like ours? It didn't make sense—unless, of course, I was acting out, feeling that if I had to deal with all this, then everyone else would have to, too. I'm glad I wasn't in a position to take my anger and make public policy of it. Indeed, in the end, I'm convinced it was a good thing that my graduate seminar went so badly with my students; it gave me someplace to transfer the anger and frustration that was otherwise free-floating and unmanageable.

However, like Joseph Conrad's Marlowe heading down the Congo into what he thought was the heart of darkness, I found that the manual labor of daily maintenance work was salvific both in its demand for immediate presence of mind and in its capacity for deflection and distraction. There were plenty of things to do. First, our steadfast friend Amanda and I attended "Special Sitters" classes held at the Developmental Services Center so that I could learn to be a "special" parent and she could learn to be an emergency backup person. The purpose of the classes was to teach people health care, psychology, and lifesaving techniques for dealing with moderately-to-severely disabled children; these ranged from young children with seizure disorders to teenagers with severe emotional and behavioral disturbances. Basically, kids much more in jeopardy, and much harder to care for, than Jamie. One of the social workers assigned to our family after Jamie's birth had recommended it to us, and Amanda decided to attend partly out of the goodness of her heart, partly to keep me company, and partly to learn CPR. I was supposed to have learned CPR after Nick was born but hadn't gotten around to it; by the time Nick was a toddler I figured it would be one of those necessary skills I'd never pick up in this life, like ballroom dancing or speaking Spanish or dribbling a basketball with my left hand. Now, though, CPR suddenly assumed the priority it should always have had, and by the end of six weeks Amanda and I were dutifully pounding on the chests of latex dummies, listening for their respirations, and giving them mouth-to-mouth. Thankfully, we have not yet had to practice any of these skills on James.

In one way the Special Sitters classes were self-defeating. They were supposed to train us to work in other people's homes as . . . well, as Special Sitters, but of course we were only training ourselves for ourselves, since neither of us had the spare time available to offer our services to other families for $5 or $6 an hour when we weren't teaching. What almost every parent at the Special Sitters classes needed was *someone else* to be a Special Sitter for their children, but with a few exceptions, most of us were there simply to learn how best to care for our own. In another way, though, the Special Sitters classes were wonderfully effective, not only because they taught me CPR and techniques for dealing with seizures but also because they introduced me to the world of Special Services, the world that twentieth-century capitalist democracies created to tend to the needs of people who would otherwise be ill served either by capitalism or by democracy.

I was particularly impressed with Illinois's provision for "respite care." At the time I was trained as a Special Sitter, the state provided 150 hours per year of respite care to every family with a disabled child. The idea behind the provision is nothing but laudable. To decrease the likelihood of child abuse by overstressed and overwhelmed parents, and (more positively) to create the framework for community networks of care for the disabled, the State of Illinois will provide parents of disabled children with a well-trained babysitter for a certain number of hours per year. In 1991 it was 150; now it's down to 60—since this is among the first programs politicians look to cut when they're trying to find ways to reduce the tax burdens of their wealthiest campaign contributors. But this, for now, is the American version of the African adage that it takes a whole village to raise a child; and though my family has only used it once to date—to help my sister Kathy care for James when Janet, Nick, and I were at the Modern Language Association convention for three days—I remain very impressed that a program like this exists at all. I know how much it must exasperate libertarians, fiscal conservatives, and Social Darwinists to know that some political entities in the United States actually try to make some kind of communal provision for the care of their least able citizens, and I know how vulnerable such provisions are at the end of the American century. For that matter, I know that many social programs benevolent in theory can prove troublesome or harmful in practice: the Department of Children and Family Services, born of the same social impulse that gives us Special Sitters, is notorious in Illinois for its failures—and for the extremely high burnout rate of its workers, who are as routinely faulted for allowing children to remain with abusive parents as for removing children from their natural, albeit abusive, parents. But for all their faults in theory or in practice, programs like these bespeak rather detailed, elastic social contracts between states and their citizens—contracts we need to renegotiate rather than repeal.

At first I was merely grateful that even in a country like the United States, with its relatively weak public sector (compared to most industrialized nations), social services for the disabled took such various and supple forms: Supplemental Security Income for the poor; respite care; speech therapy; physical therapy; occupational therapy. But the more I got involved in Jamie's myriad agencies and appointments, the more I began to examine the liberal social contract that underwrote them. Most liberals—even those who have been duped into denouncing the foundations of liberalism—recognize that this social contract is under assault from the New Right, in its tortured but largely successful effort to delegitimize all forms of "public" ownership and replace the social welfare state with a crazy quilt of economic libertarianism and cultural fascism that sanctifies "private" (that is, corporate) ownership while denying individuals the civil liberty of privacy with regard to reproductive rights and sexual orientation. But few people outside the academic disciplines know that the liberal welfare state is being subjected to impressively severe scrutiny from the cultural left, as well. In the work of social scientists and historians influenced by Michel Foucault, for instance, the palliative social measures devised by capitalist democracies in the late nineteenth century are seen not as instruments of civil liberty but as ever subtler technologies of social control. That's not to say that Foucauldians are convinced that They (those ubiquitous third person plural people) hold the puppet strings to us all, or that the tenor of every social relation depends on who's in power; for Foucauldians, in fact, "power" is not something repressively wielded from above at all but, rather, something *productive*—and pervasive—that informs every realm of social life, from top to bottom. There's a macropolitics of the state and of the military, to be sure, but there's also a micropolitics of the penitentiary—and of the playground, as all of us former schoolchildren should be able to testify.

For Foucault, then, there's no chance of inhabiting some place outside power, any more than there's a chance that we might speak to each other in something other than a language. What that means is that we have to understand human subjectivity not as something that exists in opposition to various social institutions but as something that is made intelligible *by* various social institutions. (Indeed, for "hard-core" Foucauldians, human subjectivity is understood as something like the aftereffect of institutionality: that's the "anti-humanist" aspect of Foucauldian thought.) For instance, a liberal historian would be likely to suppose that discourse about human sexuality was "repressed" in the Victorian era and that the Western understanding of sexuality has become "liberated" since the advent of Freud. Foucault, however, suggests that we have merely exchanged one form of institutional understanding of sexuality for another (from the religious to the medical), and that we have in fact been *compelled* to talk endlessly about our sexualities as if they were the very essences of our beings. Who has compelled us? Well, say the Foucauldians, the discourse has—and to make matters worse and more complicated, we have internalized that discourse, so that we think we are speaking our innermost thoughts when in fact we are only mouthing the words of the latest "discursive formation." What *that* means, if it's true, is that there's no chance of understanding what Down syndrome *really* "is" outside of the spiritual, medical, or philosophical discourses that constitute it. And if *that* is to be believed in its turn, then even the most humane and "reform-minded" of social agencies will necessarily serve to *construct* Down syndrome even as they administer to people *with* Down syndrome. This line of thinking tends to have an ominous ring to it, but lest it sound too paranoid for your average well-meaning bleeding heart liberal, just remember what "institutionalization" might mean to someone with a mentally disabled child. Not every DS parent reads Foucault (or any other revisionist social historian), but every one of us has good reason to be vigilant about *which* social institutions will constitute our children—and why, and (most of all) how.

It is hardly disputable that the new social mechanisms of the nineteenth century—from the census to the reform school—bequeathed us not only a kinder, gentler polity but also an unprecedented science of population surveillance. And remember, that's well *before* the days when anyone with a modem could get hold of your credit record. Of course, sometimes this "surveillance" is indeed benevolent. If people complain about governmental flood or hurricane relief, for instance, it's usually because they want such services to work more effectively, not because they object, on Foucauldian grounds, to an all-seeing technology of "weather management" that makes its soggy citizens into disciplinary custodians of the state. Most people devastated by hurricanes and earthquakes are quite happy, all things considered, to find that the state will help their families huddle together and sleep on standard-issue cots and blankets in the local school gymnasium. One would not want to see large-scale disaster management turned over to a few thousand competing private charities. But then again, sometimes the state's social surveillance does *not* work in the interests of the surveyed, and sometimes governmental programs turn out to be more interested in injecting citizens with plutonium or failing to treat black citizens' syphilis (just to see what will happen) than with finding palliative measures for the brutal inequities born of industrial capitalism. If you have no choice but to live your life by the terms of the social agencies constructed to construct you, this is at least worth worrying about.

Foucauldian thought is routinely denounced, both inside and outside the university, for construing "freedom" as a more insidious form of social control; on this line of thought, totalitarian states are explicitly coercive whereas "open" societies create self-policing subjects who are kept in line partly by the belief that they are free to act as they wish. Like radical-left historians, Foucauldians can manage to see every reform movement as a means of consolidating rather than dispersing the power to control social resources, and they're not always justified in doing so. That's the substantive critique. Then, from people like Camille Paglia, there's the "know-nothing" critique: Foucauldian thought is fancy French theorizing alien to the wholesome American grain of optimism, Deweyan liberalism, and Horatio Alger pluck and initiative. But what's curious about U.S. social services—and the social contract that has so far (barely) sustained them—is that the American tradition is actually so deeply schizophrenic about its social services. On one hand, both liberals and conservatives share a rhetoric of lending a helping hand, being a big brother or a point of light; they differ on the question of whether big brothers or points of light should be sponsored by public funds, but they largely agree that "helping institutions" are instituted to help. Yet, on the other hand, we have a native tradition, stretching from Natty Bumppo to Kirkpatrick Sale, that is extremely skeptical about large forms of social organization, be they public or private. The strange result is that you can find proto- or quasi-Foucauldian attitudes turning up in the academic left, the radical right, and the Unabomber manifesto.

But this is just a new twist on an old tale. The paradox of the American pioneer, as countless cultural historians have noted, is that the figure of the pioneer stands, in this country, as an emblem of society's advance as much as of its repudiation. The pioneer flees the encroaching settlements, but the pioneer also blazes the trail for the interstate highway system. The American social consensus, as a result, is that the individual somehow logically or legally *precedes* "society"—and, curiously enough, every American individual is born into a society that tells them so. (Monty Python once staged an interesting twist on this paradox in the film *Life of Brian*, where a crowd of thousands says in unison, "We're all individuals," except for one timid dissenting voice that says, "Um, I'm not.") America's pioneers, accordingly, can count among their descendants all those ordinary Americans who feared the creation of ZIP codes and the introduction of fluoride in the drinking water, as well as all those civil libertarians alarmed by how effectively the Burger and Rehnquist courts have shredded our Fourth Amendment protections against unreasonable search and seizure. Against the perennial optimist's sense that the social fabric merely needs some repair here and there, American society presents an amazing array of antisocial thought. You can be furious at the profligate Congress or at the devious military; you can believe that the government is withholding information about MIAs or UFOs; you can vent your hatred at either the Bureau of Alcohol, Tobacco and Firearms or at the FBI that gave us COINTELPRO in the 1960s. Either way you cut it, paranoia about "disciplinary society" runs very much in the American grain: neither Earth First nor the Michigan Militia had to read the complete works of Michel Foucault to earn their skepticism about where the social apparatus of the past two centuries has brought us.

The political challenges presented by Foucault and by the New Right were anything but tangential to my experience of Special Sitters class. For one thing, because I happened to be attending Special Sitters class with Amanda, whom I consider one of the keenest contemporary critics of Foucauldian social theory, we often drove back from class talking about whether the social reforms of the Progressive Era represented an extension of the franchise of life, liberty, and happiness or an extension of the machineries of social surveillance. (As it happened, Amanda was working on her critique of Foucault at roughly the same time James was born.) For another thing, my little child was now the *object* of those machineries of social surveillance, and I found it impossible to think of this as anything but benevolent: Big Brother wasn't watching him, after all. On the contrary, a circle of friends was watching *over* him, a circle of friends that also included his big brother.

The question of how to conceive of *contemporary* social relations is at the heart of any historian's work. Either one wants to know how we got here, wherever that is, and thus how the past has conditioned the present; or one wants to be sure one is not simply projecting the attitudes of the present onto the past, reading history backward from the privileged vantage point of knowing how it all turned out. These are abstractions, no doubt, but they're so powerful and pervasive that you can find them at work anywhere, from demonstrations in the streets over whether to celebrate Columbus Day to debates on the Internet over whether J. Langdon Down was a racist for labeling trisomy 21 "mongolism." One of Foucault's unquestioned contributions to historiography is that he focused on untraditional, "everyday" subjects—not the movements of kings and armies, but the histories of madness, of incarceration, of sexuality. How, then, to tell the story of the history of mental retardation? And then how to understand the present tense for mentally retarded children and adults?

Social historians have recently begun to grapple with precisely these questions. In *Inventing the Feeble Mind: A History of Mental Retardation in the United States*, James Trent—who, as it happens, teaches just a few hundred miles down the road from us at Southern Illinois University in Edwardsville—answers these questions in ways that Janet and I have found both powerful and unsettling. The temptation to construe recent history in optimistic terms is clearly overwhelming; there aren't many parents in the country, I wager, who would prefer to have their "disabled" children warehoused in buildings unfit for animals, slowly starved, or beaten. Special Sitters is undoubtedly an advance over the mental hospitals of the 1940s, in any terms you care to name. But in tracing his long, catastrophic narrative of alienation, institutionalization, pathologization, abuse, sterilization, neglect, rescue, and, again, abuse, Trent avoids the temptation to tell a tale of gradual triumph. You can't fix history, he knows, and what's more, you can't change the place it's left you in; all you can do is locate troubling patterns.

The "retarded" start off, in Trent's account, as the unmolested feeble-minded individuals of the eighteenth century—we know them today as "fools" and "village idiots"—before being redefined as members of new subgroups, *imbeciles* and *idiots,* in the nineteenth century, whereupon they were championed by French educator and social reformer Edward Seguin. Seguin's plan was to create special institutions for the education and training of the "feeble-minded"; later in the century, the supervisors who were now running those institutions decided that the retarded inmates should work for their keep within the institutions (the mildly retarded being responsible for the more severely retarded, and so on). Before long, the institutions had developed a self-perpetuating logic of their own, complete with a permanent crust of administrators and new technologies of personnel management. By the twentieth century, the "feeble-minded" had become constructed as a class of civic menaces who were routinely sterilized, and by mid-century they were officially classed as "mental deficients" and packed by the thousands into vast, hellish state-run caverns.

The consensus behind this treatment of the feeble-minded was decidedly bipartisan. Modern liberals especially should note that it was Oliver Wendell Holmes who wrote the landmark Supreme Court decision in *Buck* v. *Bell* (1927), declaring involuntary sterilization to be constitutional. Everything about that decision, from its origin to its effects, is rotten beyond belief. The case involved a seventeen-year-old Virginia girl, Carrie Buck, who, in 1924, was raped by a local Charlottesville man. Her foster parents responded by committing Carrie to the Virginia Colony for Epileptics and the Feebleminded. Three years earlier, her mother, Emma, had been committed and labeled "retarded" as well, as was the baby girl, Vivian, to whom Carrie eventually gave birth as a result of the rape. All this took place in a decade when eugenics swept the country from the Ku Klux Klan to the Supreme Court, when states held "good breeding" contests for prize families, when Congress passed stringent anti-immigration laws barring the inferior races of Southern and Eastern Europe from migrating to these shores. It was the 1920s, and no one was very interested in distinguishing between "retarded" persons and those who were merely emotionally disturbed—as the result of rape, for instance. For Carrie Buck did indeed have enough good sense to be disturbed by her rape, just as she was disturbed to learn that she was bearing a child, just as she was disturbed again when the child was taken from her by state custodians. Ms. Buck was sterilized by the Commonwealth of Virginia in a surgical procedure about which her medical caretakers lied to her. Medical professionals in Virginia and across the nation decided that the Buck case would not only test the constitutionality of state sterilization laws but also provide them with the rationale for implementing much broader sterilization policies, and so actively sought Supreme Court review of their actions. Writing for the majority, the sage and "liberal" Justice Holmes wrote,

> We have seen more than once that the public welfare may call upon the best citizens for their lives. It would be strange if it could not call upon those who already sap the strength of

the state for these lesser sacrifices, often not felt to be such by those concerned, in order to prevent our being swamped with incompetence. It is better for all the world, if instead of waiting to execute degenerate offspring for crime, or to let them starve for their imbecility, society can prevent those who are manifestly unfit from continuing their kind. The principle that sustains compulsory vaccination is broad enough to cover cutting the Fallopian tubes. . . . Three generations of imbeciles is enough.

Holmes was smart enough, however, to add a crucial caveat to his decision. If sterilization were truly to serve the social good, it would have to be applied as widely as possible. "However it might be if this reasoning were applied generally," he wrote, "it fails when it is confined to the small number who are in the institutions named and is not applied to the multitude." Holmes's reasoning is worth revisiting in the era of *The Bell Curve*, which can stand as another eloquent warning about what might happen if "we" (the smart people) are overrun with incompetence. The state can call its citizens to war, so it would be strange if it could not also call its citizens to war against the feeble-minded. Forced sterilization is after all so much slighter a sacrifice than death, even if, as Holmes briefly admits in a fine display of imaginative sympathy, the sterilized don't always think so. (Or is he saying that the imbeciles don't even know they're making "sacrifices"?) And you know what? The effects of the court's decision were immediate. Sterilization saved thousands of taxpayer dollars, or so it was said, because there were fewer imbeciles sapping the strength of the state. The American Association on Mental Deficiency applauded the trend and insisted that all training for the care of the "feeble-minded" should include information about sterilization. Then, in 1933, a newly elected German regime noted that the United States had not only legalized but legitimized sterilization. Henceforth, it was not merely tolerable but a positive social good. The rest, as they say, is history. Or, as Trent notes, "In 1934, officials of the Third Reich began what would eventually be the sterilization of four hundred thousand Germans, or one in every one hundred citizens." In the United States, in the meantime, Vivian Buck died at the tender age of eight. As Robert Hayman has recently pointed out, no national leaders took note of Vivian's death, just as no one had taken note when, in her final year of grade school, she made the honor roll.

But time marches on, even if it leaves behind a whole mess of feeble people who stumble or toddle or can't keep up and are sent to the showers for their incompetence. In the 1940s and 1950s, as sterilization fell out of favor and lawmakers began to rethink the consequences of eugenics as national policy, prominent people like Pearl Buck and Dale Evans Rogers wrote books about their "afflicted" children; by 1962, the climate of opinion had changed sufficiently to allow President Kennedy to make public his sister Rosemary's mental retardation. Since then, American social attitudes toward retardation have improved in many ways. Most people no longer believe that a congenital disability is the parents' "fault," and most know that anyone—paupers and presidents alike—can have a mentally disabled person in the family. Community mental health facilities are common and accessible; Special Olympics is a household word; people with Down syndrome are nationally known actors, speakers, and authors. Yet, as Trent reminds us, there is still so much that hasn't changed a bit. In the late 1960s, California governor Ronald Reagan, defending the inhumane conditions of his state's mental hospitals, called them "the biggest hotel chain in the state"; in 1972, the atrocities uncovered at New York's Willowbrook State School for the Mentally Disabled seared the public imagination and gave new life to exposé journalism; and even today, "feeble-minded" persons are often verbally and physically abused by their institutional custodians, while compassionate, capable workers in "special services" have their municipal jobs yanked out from under them by the latest craze for "less government." Even the "corrective deinstitutionalization" (an interesting term from a Foucauldian perspective) of the late 1970s has leached into the travails of poverty and homelessness in the 1980s and 1990s. State mental hospitals were supposed to release their patients into supervised homes and community centers, but there were so few homes and centers— and so little enthusiasm for building more of them—that institutions wound up simply dumping their inmates onto city streets to fend for themselves.

This is where Jamie comes in. But is there any room for him in this history? In one sense, Jamie is nothing more than Foucault fodder, one among millions of humans whose institutionally defined and manufactured "otherness" (disease, madness, perversion) underwrites the fiction that the rest of us are sane, rational, autonomous individuals. If that's the case, then Trent is right to cast a pall over the past twenty-five years of "reform": In the end, the mechanisms of social control will always run over the small bodies in their path. As if that weren't enough, there's also the Foucauldian question that has hamstrung the humanities for the past decade: Is it wrong to *speak for* others, to assume that one can *represent* the interests of another in a faithful and transparent way? How can one be an advocate for the mentally retarded while believing that institutions never die and that every act of representation is also an act of usurpation? Is there no way to have faith in Camelot, in Special Olympics, in Advocacy?

Janet and I have been over these questions many times, from the moment we were introduced to Champaign's Developmental Services Center, where Jamie got his first screenings and I got my training in CPR and Special Sitting, to the months in 1994 when we were writing a joint review of Trent's book (during which we hashed out a lot of the discussion in the preceding pages). We've learned that whatever we may believe about the history of madness, sexuality, incarceration, or mental retardation, we find it emotionally and intellectually impossible to be Foucauldians about the present. We *have* to act, for both theoretical and practical reasons, in the belief that these agencies can benefit our child, even as the sorry history of institutionalization weighs on our brains like a nightmare. To act in any other way, to indict all such institutions across the board, would be to consign Jamie to the kind of self-fulfilling prophecy that follows from unearned cynicism: *We know they can't help, so why bother?* It would be hard to imagine a more irresponsible attitude toward his life's prospects.

Whatever anyone might say about the relations between subjects and discourses, we've had the benefit of seeing Jamie's agents face to face. They *are* agents: they are defined by their agency (in both senses), and James is their agentless object, the name repeated a thousand times in the eight-inch stack of medical prognoses, cognitive evaluations, and assorted therapy reports that constitute the subject known as James Lyon Bérubé. But they also happen to be our neighbors and friends. Rita Huddle, Jamie's first speech therapist at DSC, is also the mother of two of Nick's friends in tae kwon do class, where we run into her regularly; Nancy Yeagle, his first occupational therapist, is also the mother of one of his first playmates at day care as well as the spouse of the chef at a local Italian restaurant Jamie's quite fond of. And Sara Jane Annin, his case worker, is not only a friend and confidante, but the mother of *two* children with Down syndrome—one of whom, Daniel, dictated to her (at the age of five) a remarkable narrative on the origin of the Easter Bunny: When Christ was crucified, all the world was sad. Everyone left. But the bunnies stayed, because they were not afraid. So Jesus told the bunnies that they were right not to be afraid, and that it would henceforth be their task to bring cheer to children on Easter Sunday. Sara Jane showed us the book, complete with her illustrations of Daniel's story. We thought it was the most incisive explanation we'd ever heard for the interdependence of Christ and the Easter Bunny. We also thought the illustrations were beautiful. We didn't worry too much at the time about how to construe the history of social systems and social services.

Perhaps there are good reasons why "institutionality" looks different in a small town like Champaign or Urbana than in a world capital like Paris or London or New York. God bless us, every one.

Before Jamie received speech or occupational therapy, he had to get physical therapy. Because we'd ruled out the option of cutting his tight neck muscles and resewing them, we had thereby taken on a second task alongside the nasal feedings: correcting Jamie's torticollis by doing daily neck stretches. At first we took Jamie to see a local masseuse and deep-tissue therapist named Bjorg Holte, who had been recommended to us by all our many friends who suffer from lower back pain. Bjorg rubbed Jamie's little body with almond oil, played some spacy ambient music (he loved this, and it relaxed us quite effectively, too), and worked on his neck for an hour at a time. James was also assigned a physical therapist by our HMO, which refused to recognize Bjorg as a real person for insurance purposes. (This was all right with us: we could only afford a few visits to Bjorg, but we didn't expect that an HMO would offer us any referrals to a brilliant deep-tissue therapist who plays ambient music and all.) We had heard that "early intervention" techniques worked best if they intervened early, so we began making all the appointments we could manage, and we tried to learn a few massage techniques to use at home. We even bought almond oil and searched record stores for the same tape that had so caught Jamie's infant attention at Bjorg's. We never found the tape, but we did get a small jar of the oil, and its rich, piquant almond smell lingered over us all that winter and all the next spring.

The oil was the only nice thing about our nightly Jamie-massages; the rest was . . . a thrash. Each evening after Jamie's bath, we laid him out on the kitchen table, still wrapped in his hooded bath towel, with a soft quilt and crib sheet under him. Then we tortured him for as long as we could stand his frenzied protests and dry, voiceless screams. Our goal was literally to stretch his neck muscles on the left side, and for the first few months, that meant holding his head at mid-point or tilted to the right while massaging and kneading the muscle connecting his clavicle to his skull. The first report from the orthopedic surgeon reads: *The patient's head is tilted toward the right. His ear is toward the left shoulder. That would be a classic torticollis. Gentle stretching of the sternocleidomastoid on the left is important.* In those days you could hardly get Jamie's head to the midpoint; stretching him any further simply caused him too much pain for him—or us—to bear. We tried to make sure he slept only on his right side so that his head wouldn't develop a rest position so severely tilted toward his left shoulder, and we eventually bought him that $100 piece of foam. But we soon came to dread those massages. Jamie loved playing with us, loved trying to reach for us, loved watching the black-and-white figures on his mobile, loved looking up at us while he ate as much as he could *p.o.* But he strenuously resisted having his neck mashed on, and we began to wonder if he would develop a fear and hatred of the smell of almond oil.

At six months he was finally sitting up—but only with help. At the advice of one of his DSC therapists, Janet had made a special "sitting box" for Jamie: a large cardboard box, covered on all sides with contact paper, in which we could prop Jamie in a corner and support him with a small table at his chest. The thing looked like a parent's clumsy contribution to the set of the school play, and our descriptions of Jamie's sitting box made it sound more like imprisonment than like therapy, but Jamie loved it. In his box, with his table, he could reach for objects without any danger of falling over—and we watched intently as his nervous system gradually got itself organized enough to enable him to reach for objects. We found that we were falling into what we now call the "developmental trap": on the one hand, we didn't want to measure Jamie against "normal" children, so we tried not to be anxious about when he reached (or wasn't reaching) important developmental milestones (like reaching). But on the other hand, we had no other scale to go by than that of "normal" children. Jamie's delays had to be calibrated as delays by reference to *something*, and we didn't want to be lulled into not doing enough for him.

Amanda calls this the Dialectic of Down, but it might as well be called the dialectic of disability. Anyone with any kind of "delayed" child knows how irrelevant and how indispensable are the standard charts of "normal" child development. It wasn't long before we realized that this paradox would be with us for the rest of our lives. We were free of the impulse to "rush" Jamie, to teach him integral calculus at the age of five and read *Ulysses* at eight; we had no desire to make him one of those "better babies," no regrets for not playing him Mozart's *Jupiter Symphony* in the womb, no urge to fight to get him into the designer kindergarten of our choice. But we knew we couldn't allow ourselves to be complacent, either. Jamie had hypotonia; he would take the path of least resistance. He appeared to be developing some Jamie-version of the sweet disposition universally (and mistakenly) attributed to all children with Down syndrome; he would not mind if we stopped taking him to physical therapy and allowed him to reach for objects only from a prone position. Yet we would be doing him a horrible disservice if we didn't try to see what his mental and physical potential *was*, the better to help him reach it. At the same time, we didn't want to overreach. We would have to push him without pushing him.

It wasn't clear, either, how much stress his neck would take. His first X-rays, dating from his days in the hospital, were somewhat inconclusive. It looked as if his first cervical vertebra (C1) was fused to the skull, the third (C3) was connected to the first, and the second (C2) was kind of hanging out in between. His assessment at birth was inconclusive: *There is a bony mass above C2 which may represent an ossification center for the odontoid. The lateral masses of C1 are not visualized. The C1 posterior elements move with the occipital bone of the skull with flexion rather than remaining in normal alignment with the cervical spine. This may represent a fusion anomaly with the calvarium.* But his bones weren't finished developing yet, of course, and there was no way to know whether "aggressive" physical therapy on his neck muscles would further damage his spine. "It's like he just got zapped in the neck," Janet would say. The torticollis was one thing, the vertebral anomalies were another, and the laryngomalacia was a third. None was the cause of the other: One was muscular, one was skeletal, one was respiratory. His heart emerged unscathed, but he got zapped in the neck. Worse, Janet began to believe that she had been the cause of the torticollis. If only she hadn't spent so much time sitting at the computer writing her dissertation, she thought, he wouldn't have wound up with a bent neck. Of course, this was nonsense, and everyone told her so, from her doctors to her spouse. But I felt a pang of retroactive guilt nonetheless. Long before we knew anything was wrong with James, I had urged Janet to write as much of the dissertation as possible before the pregnancy was too advanced. At the time, I was thinking only of stress. One does not want to be finishing a dissertation, preparing a semester's courses, and getting ready to give birth all at the same time. Or so I've heard. Now Janet was thinking that *she'd* zapped Jamie.

His neck, in turn, affected his appearance, and his appearance affected our expectations of other people's expectations of him. As long as Jamie's only problem was a head tilt, he merely looked more thoughtful than most infants, but underneath the surface and the surface appearance, his tight neck muscles started to affect his facial muscles and even the bones they covered, giving him a marked facial asymmetry that seemed, each week, to be getting worse. The asymmetry isn't easy to describe; it wasn't simply that he had one crinkly ear and one normal ear. It was as if the features on the left side of his face had a different vanishing point than the features on his right, as if they were drawn on a different plane. He even had less cheek on the left, and his left eye was looking more almond-shaped than his right. We eventually learned that his asymmetry wasn't just a matter of looks; if left uncorrected, it could further delay his walking, by further delaying his ability to stand, by further delaying his ability to center himself. But even as a cosmetic matter it concerned us. Jamie would be judged first by his appearance, and up to this point, one couldn't tell from a casual glance that he had Down syndrome. We didn't expect him to look like any other child with Down's, of course; but we also didn't want him to look too "normal," lest people expect too much of him. We also didn't want him to be more asymmetrical than he already was just because we got lazy.

Otherwise, his vertebrae seemed to be holding up just fine for now, but it was clear that in other respects he had entered a new phase of evaluation. From now on it would no longer be a clear-cut question of being whole or broken, requiring surgery on his spine or heart. Now it would be a muddier matter of charting his progress, determining his delays, and then determining whether we could do anything *about* his delays. It was weird enough to think that we could help reshape the bones of his face by massaging his neck, but it was all the weirder to think that we could enhance his ability to sit or walk or eat two years from now just by doing a few exercises with him today. How do you begin to make sense of the information that—although we can't be sure—your seven-month-old infant may only have the cognitive capacity of a five month old? What does that *mean*? And what if, at seven months, he turned out to have the cognitive capacity of a six month old but only the physical capacity of a three month old who couldn't yet roll over? How would this affect his development in his eighth month? Even as Janet and I disdained the very idea of asking such absurd questions about Jamie's development, as if humans could be cut into uniform four-week slices and weighed, there were days when we were sure we thought about nothing else.

I don't want to give the impression that I remember everything I thought at the time; as with Jamie's nasal tube feedings, it's when I try to recall those days that I realize how much I don't recall. For instance, when my mother visited us during that first year, she was amazed to find that Janet and I were wearing tiny bells on our chests, wound around our necks on pieces of string. One of our therapists, we explained, had told us to wear these bells and ring them whenever Jamie smiled, and we did so, as much out of a sense of duty as out of a sense of fun. But three years later, as I began to try to record what that first year was like, it was my mother who said, "I hope you'll say something about the bells." "What bells?" I asked. I had forgotten that we'd worn those bells, and even after my mother had reminded me of them, I could not remember what their purpose was. "I thought that was very impressive," she said. "You were stimulating his facial responses. You were very excited about it." Well, I replied, that *is* pretty impressive, but it would be even more impressive to me if I could remember it.

But thanks for the memories, wherever they may have come from. One day Janet and I went to a local restaurant and found ourselves mumbling about how we remembered Jamie's time in the NICU, and then mumbling about how strange it was that we'd each remembered the same thing, seemingly unbidden. Only after a puzzling half-hour did we realize that the restaurant's bathrooms used the same red, sweet, pungent liquid soap with which we'd scrubbed ourselves each time we entered the ICU. HibiClens, it's called, and it brought back memories of breathing tubes, dim fluorescent lights, and disposable scrubbing sponges. Voluntary memory can take you only so far before involuntary memory does the rest—or so my voluntary memory of Marcel Proust's *Remembrance of Things Past* tells me: "When from a long-distant past nothing subsists . . . taste and smell alone, more fragile but more enduring, more unsubstantial, more persistent, more faithful, remain poised a long time, like souls, remembering, waiting, hoping, amid the ruins of all the rest; and bear unflinchingly, in the tiny and almost impalpable drop of their essence, the vast structure of recollection." Taste and smell, perhaps, the smell of sweet red HibiClens or almond oil or fresh NICU linen, but also touch and sound: the feel of a disposable sponge, the sense of the oil oozing into your fingertips, the sound of those tiny bells, the sound of my mother's voice, the sound of my mother's voice telling me of those bells.

Finally we began taking Jamie to physical therapists who worked for our HMO. Now he had an appointment for speech and occupational therapy once a week at DSC, on Mondays, physical therapy across town on Wednesdays, and an occasional session with Bjorg whenever she could fit us in. We settled into that schedule for a while, only to have it interrupted when the HMO physical therapists moved to another city or into private practice. This was going to be something of a *leitmotif* for Jamie's first therapists. No sooner did he get to know them than they opened a private practice, and we knew we wouldn't be able to afford anything like that for quite some time. In the meantime, our HMO was footing the $120-an-hour bill for James's physical therapy once a week, and his $100-an-hour sessions at DSC were picked up by the State of Illinois by means of some budgetary process more complicated than gene splicing. Jamie qualified for the DSC Early Childhood Program until he was three, at which point he became the rough equivalent of a disabled adult under Illinois law and was no longer eligible for children's services. Over the next few years, as the state began defunding many of its social services for children, we were asked to contribute a fee toward Jamie's DSC therapy; the DSC staff was embarrassingly apologetic about this, but we saw no reason not to go along. Since Illinois has a punitive flat state income tax, we figured that lower-income Illinoisians had already paid for enough of our social services, and there was nothing wrong with applying a means test to the parents of "special needs" children. Fortunately for us, we could afford it. But back when Jamie was still under a year old, our state services and our private health insurance were keeping him stocked with therapists for as long as HMOs and DSCs could keep their therapists on staff. It wasn't until Jamie entered public school, two years later, that we began to understand what *that* economic process entails for the social contracts we'd signed so far.

Actually, it turned out to be an extraordinary stroke of fortune that James's first physical therapists left when they did. The therapists themselves were fine, but not terribly aggressive with Jamie, who was a very difficult child to work with—so young, so loose-limbed and low-toned, so vulnerable in the neck. He didn't take much to them; as one prefers back rubs to calisthenics, so did Jamie prefer massages to neck stretches. Then, our HMO decided to reassign us to a therapist who had just arrived in town from Israel and who was working at the HMO nursing home but had done primary training with disabled infants. So if we would agree to drive Jamie to weekly appointments at the nursing home on the *other* other side of town, we could have him seen by a woman named Ofra Tandoor, who was already reputed to be a miracle worker. That was fine by us, not least because Jamie's visits to the nursing home were much remarked upon by the residents. And as for Ofra—Ofra simply changed his life.

Ofra's first evaluation of James was not encouraging. *Precaution: potential for instability at C1-C2 interface. Head is held at 45° left. Elevation of the shoulder. No part of the neck is visible. Left trunk shorter than right and difficult to elongate.* My first impression of her was that she didn't like me very much; she seemed abrupt, even curt. She was far more aggressive with Jamie than his earlier therapists had been, particularly when it came to hands-on neck and trunk stretches, and Jamie spent much of his first hour with her howling as wildly as he could with his hoarse screams. When I timidly mentioned that we were uneasy about his cervical vertebrae, she shot a look at me and said she knew about his neck and was trying to work the muscles first. Then, she said, we could determine how stable his neck was by finding out what exercises he could and couldn't do. This sounded backward to me, but what did I know? All I knew was that Jamie was screaming.

Well, so much for first impressions. It wasn't for another year that Jamie could get through an hour of therapy with Ofra without crying at some point, but over the next few months we began to see dramatic improvement in practically everything; we even began to hope that Jamie would be able to stand by the time he visited both sets of grandparents in late August. Ofra's manner wasn't soothing, but if all therapists were as gifted as she was, I could learn to do without soothing. At each of Jamie's appointments she showed us how everything about Jamie was connected to everything else: In order to get his neck and head straight enough to allow him to center himself and (eventually) walk, for instance, we would have to do many things, not least of which would be the task of inducing him to move food around with equal facility in both sides of his mouth. I remember Ofra teaching me mouth exercises to do with Jamie. After I had gotten them down, more or less, I turned to her, puzzled, and said that Jamie was already doing mouth exercises for speech therapy. How could mouth exercises help him *walk*? Ofra replied at some length, explaining that his mouth muscles had everything to do with his neck muscles (stretching one would help him stretch the other), and the more we could combat his asymmetry on a number of fronts at once, the better our chances of having his muscle groups help each other in the job of getting him to sit up unassisted and gradually to stand. So the sooner he could learn to eat with both sides of his mouth, the sooner he'd stand and walk, and standing and walking, in turn, would help teach him any number of new cognitive skills as he became more adept at exploring his environment. His eating would affect his walking would affect his learning, and even his crying for an hour would help expand his lungs: the jaw bone was connected to the leg bone was connected to the lungs was connected to the heart was connected to the brain. The physical affects the mental affects the physical. I suppose that's what it means to be an organism.

It wasn't just Jamie's asymmetry we were dealing with, either; it was also his low muscle tone, which in this case was exacerbated by his mother's admirable but eerie loose-jointedness—a trait she passed on, with fine impartiality, to both Nick and James, even though James really didn't need it. Thus, when Jamie finally did learn to sit up, he did so by lying flat on his stomach, swinging his legs out at an impossible angle from the hip until his feet almost touched his ears, and then pushing himself up into a sitting position as if his legs were two thirds of a tripod. I would have been satisfied with this, but Ofra wasn't: she was duly amazed at his rubbery pretzelness but alarmed that his trunk muscles were too weak to let him push himself to a sit from the side. "No," she would say, smiling, in heavily accented English, "thees ees very bad. You see"—suddenly pushing Jamie over onto his side, to his surprise and mine—"he can sit up but he ees not stable. We must make him balance like thees." Whereupon she made Jamie bring both his legs around to the same side, placing his hands on the opposite side of his legs, and urging him to push himself up with his arms and tighten his trunk muscles. So his trunk would be centered, his legs would be extended slightly to his right, and he would be set in a leaning position with his arms holding him up on the left. Jamie didn't see the point of this, since he was being asked to sit up by the same person who'd just pushed him down for sitting up, but gradually he learned to do things the right way. I was thrilled. Ofra wasn't. "Look," she said, setting Jamie's arms on the other side of his legs, "he can push heemself up from the left side but not from the right. If he does not do it from the right hees chest will tilt his body even more over," pushing him down again for emphasis.

On to the trunk muscles, then. This meant rolling out the enormous green rubber ball Ofra used for her adult therapy sessions and making Jamie sit on top of the ball while she brought first one arm and then the other down to his side, insisting that he keep his balance. Jamie wailed. As his gross motor skills grew by leaps and bounds (well, not leaps, not yet), Ofra started honing in on his fine motor skills: picking up objects in a pincers grip between thumb and index instead of palming; stringing beads; picking up poker chips from the floor. Jamie wailed. And so it went for month after month. Jamie got straighter and stronger, and soon Ofra's youngest client was sitting up on his own.

Even at this age—Jamie was still under a year old—it was clear how vividly our little boy responded to encouragement and praise. When he reached for things in his sitting box or when he sat up on his own, we were delighted: sometimes we ooohed and aaahed, sometimes we clapped, sometimes we told him he was doing great work. Nick was, and still is, his chief cheerleader. Watching his delight in watching Jamie's progress quickly became, for me, one of the primary delights of being alive, and it was clear that Jamie felt more or less the same way. As did Janet.

A complicated kind of symbiosis, built on a relationship that was growing central to Jamie: As far as he was concerned, his big brother was the coolest organism on the planet, and anything he could do to delight Nick must clearly be good in itself. Often Jamie would wait specifically for Nick's reaction—to a noise, to a toy, to his efforts to sit up—but it was better still when Nick noticed his little brother before his little brother noticed him. "Mom! Dad!" Nick would cry with delight. "Jamie reached for his bottle and got it all the way to his mouth!" For his part, whenever he heard something like this, Jamie broke into a broad, silly smile—and stopped concentrating on what he was doing for a second, which meant that Nick or Janet or I occasionally knocked him over with applause. He would push himself to a sit, we would cheer, he would smile and fall down. But it was clear that whether he'd inherited it from us or chemically synthesized it on his own, Jamie had a love of praise that was serving him well in his efforts to develop physically.

We almost never succumbed to the temptation to compare his milestones with Nick's. I can still recall Nick's first attempts to reach objects (he tried to pick the letters off the cover of Jorge Luis Borges' *Labyrinths*), and I can remember that Janet and I, as dutiful and stunned first-time parents, wrote down the precise day Nick first rolled over, sat up, ate solid food, pulled himself to a stand, spoke, read the letters *F* and *M*, and cleaned his room without being told (actually, we're still waiting to record that last item). Before Jamie was born, I was afraid that we'd be too jaded, as second-time-around parents, to be stunned enough by our child's development or dutiful enough to keep any records of his growth. There's a wonderful Dave Barry bit that sets out this dynamic in a few choice words. The first baby's album looks something like this:

January 5—Today Rupert is exactly one and a half weeks old!
He weighs 8 pounds, 3.587 ounces, up 2.342 ounces from yesterday!
He had two poopy-diapers today, but definitely not as runny as the
ones he had January 3! Also not quite so greenish!

And so on. By the time these people have their *second* baby,
they're sick of albums. Oh, they try to slap something together, but it's obvious that their hearts aren't really in it:

1966–74—Byron was born and is now in the second grade.

I wondered, upon first reading Dave Barry's book on babies the
summer before James was born, whether in fact our first entry on
him would be dated 1999. I remembered sheepishly that when
Janet had gotten home from her doctor's appointment back in
late February and had said, beaming, "I have some news," I had
failed even to remember why she'd gone to the doctor in the first
place.

But now everything was changed, changed utterly: Jamie's
milestones were every bit as amazing and (as our friends and family learned, to their delight or dismay) as narratable as were
Nick's, and the remarkable thing about them was that Jamie not
only reached them more slowly but progressed with them more
slowly as well. With Nick, developmental milestones were fairly
discrete: One day he learned to reach and grasp, the next day we
had to put away every sharp object in the house, as Nick grabbed
keys, pens, and ears of corn with infant abandon. Jamie, by contrast, was not only slower but *elaborately* slower. For many weeks
after he grasped his first toy, he acted as if he were relearning
grasping, a little more efficiently each time. In his sitting box or
in the walker that had once been Nick's, he would settle himself

comfortably, then look to us for a plaything. In his walker he was especially comic: we would place a doll or a set of plastic rings or a rattle on the tray in front of his chest, and after gazing at it for a moment Jamie would widen his eyes with delight and throw both his arms back and then up over his head before bringing them down, carefully, to the object, queasily calibrating his hands' arrival as if he were landing a helicopter on rough terrain. "World's worst predator," we said, imagining how long a cheetah would survive in the wild if it gasped and threw its paws into the air every time a gazelle happened to land at its feet. But Jamie was also telegraphing his delight to all of us, and once when I watched him go through one of his rituals of "surprise and grab," I imagined that we could see all his teeny neurons firing in order, just that much more slowly, telling him as they cleared a brand-new pathway through the brain, *This is something you like. Get it.* The arms and hands took their orders, rotated into place, and began the difficult process of Manual Retrieval. Whereupon his parents would say, "Jamie get it!" Get it?

We marveled at his ability to marvel. Like all infants, he hadn't yet distinguished the accidental from the essential elements of toys—that is, he was every bit as interested by the handle or the plastic-molded sides of the Busy Box as he was by its spinning color wheel or its tiny bell. Every parent knows the phenomenon; up to a certain point, the child is no less interested in the wrapping paper than in the birthday present inside. Pedestrian as this observation might be, it contains within it a philosophical question that's been fairly central to the history of Western thought: What are the essential properties of a thing, the elements without which the thing cannot be the thing it is, and what are the accidental properties, the options, the peripheral add-ons? Every table may have legs (usually four, sometimes three, occasionally more, sometimes only one), but how is it that every table is not made of wood? There's the kernel, and then there's the husk: Which would *you* rather eat? Well, if you're eight months old, or even eighteen months old, these questions don't make a great deal of sense. The kernel's fun, and the husk is fun, too. Young children think, well, I'll get to the birthday present part—I really *like* Ernie and Bert dolls, you know—but I also want to spend some quality time with this colorful paper with all the triangles and numbers on it, too.

Jamie, like Nick before him, immersed himself in the *gestalt* of objects before getting down to arcane medieval disputes about the philosophical status of "essence" and "accident." When he liked a toy, he liked everything about it—and he liked his links of plastic rings most of all. He couldn't connect them yet, because he wasn't coordinated enough to hold one ring while grasping another in a pincers grip, finding the loop, and attaching the second ring to the first. But he could *dis*connect them; he could disconnect them violently, which was still more fun; he could swing them about; he could pick them up from the middle or from the ends—and he could play with them for five, ten, even fifteen minutes at a time. We marveled as our child marveled. You never know which one of the shower presents is going to be so integral a part of your child's early psychic life. One afternoon I asked Janet why it was that Jamie loved his rings so much. "I've wondered that myself," she said. No surprise there. We were sharing a brain. "I think it's because he feels so . . . *competent* with his rings." That sounded right. And the more competent he feels, we knew, the more he feels encouraged to get better.

The same held true for his attempts to sit. We could see how hard he was trying, and, as Ofra once told us, he would have to try twice as hard to do the things other children could do and it might take him twice as long. In these struggles, Ofra said, we should exploit Jamie's love of praise as much as possible. There would be nothing wrong with this. Jamie's desires were still identical to his needs, and his parents would be applauding him not for scoring touchdowns or identifying the capital of Nigeria but for fundamental physical achievements he *should* be encouraged to take pride in. Positive reinforcement with none of the guilty aftertaste.

And then we got the results of his first hearing test.

> *Pt seen for hearing evaluation per Dr. Davison. Pt's father reports that James has had ~6 infections over the winter. Dad reports that pt turns his head toward sound and recognizes parents' voices. Pt has Downs Syndrome.*
>
> *Test results: Sound field measures revealed responses to speech stimuli at 60 dBHz and possibly at 45 dBHz. Child was not responsive to warbled tone stimuli. Imp.: moderate-moderately severe hearing loss, possibly totally conductive, possibly mixed in nature. Child seemed to lose interest in task so it is recommended that his hearing be reassessed in 3 mos to determine if these responses are accurate.*

Moderate to moderately severe hearing loss. Possibly totally conductive, possibly mixed. Reassess in three months. Then, if they couldn't get "accurate" measurements in three months, they'd have to sedate Jamie and test his hearing neurologically, to see whether his problems were in his ears or in the brain itself. It might be correctable. It might not. I longed for the decisiveness of his physical therapy: either he could sit or he couldn't, either he could chew on his left side or he couldn't.

I wasn't even sure *this* test was accurate. I had told the audiologists that Jamie had had many ear infections over the winter, which was perfectly true, but I had also assured them that he could hear me call his name *in a whisper* from across the room. That information, I noted, was registered in the report only as "recognizes parents' voices." And Jamie's performance on the test was far less impressive than my narrative of him. He and I were placed in a small, dark, square room, and James was asked to respond to sounds emitted from one of two speakers located in opposite corners. "Uh-oh! Uh-oh! James!" the audiologist would call, her voice channeled into channel one or channel two, and if Jamie turned in the right direction, a small box would light up and an electric monkey (on the right) or an elephant (on the left) would do a little mechanical jig. Well, first of all, Jamie didn't respond to the voice half the time because it wasn't one of his parents' voices. Second, we rarely called him "James," and we never said "uh-oh." Third, he turned half the time simply to see the elephant and/or monkey, and not because he heard a voice. So the way I figured it, the test had both false negatives and false positives. This made it an inaccurate test, and I very politely explained to the audiologists why I thought so.

They were understanding. After all, Pt. was so young, it was difficult to read his responses, and we'd know better in three months or so. They were also quite sure that he had a pretty serious hearing loss and that I wouldn't help anything by pretending it wasn't there. They said so very politely, too.

I came home very depressed, and very worried. All the praise in the world wouldn't help Jamie if he couldn't hear it. Didn't he already have enough strikes against him? His speech would come slowly enough as it was. His tongue wasn't terribly thick, but since all his facial and nasal and oral passages were so narrow, it was still pretty thick in comparison to the oral cavity in which it resided. And it would take him so much longer to *understand* human language, never mind to replicate it. His trunk muscles were so weak that he couldn't get very deep breaths, which meant, possibly, that once he began talking he wouldn't be able to say too many words at once. On top of all this he would have to compensate for a moderate to moderately severe hearing loss? I began to cry. It just wasn't fair. Two years earlier, in August 1990, while showering and generally getting ready to teach my first graduate seminar, I somehow managed to put a Q-tip through my eardrum. I was cleaning my ears when I felt something like an insect bite on my left side, so I left the Q-tip dangling from my right ear as I slapped my rib cage with my right hand—and then suddenly spasmed in such a way as to jerk my right shoulder up and (but of course) directly into the Q-tip, driving it into the middle ear, past the tympanum, and . . . and I collapsed with the pain. I managed to call Amanda and Al, who drove me to the emergency room, and I even managed to meet my seminar later that day, too. But I had lost much of the hearing in my right ear, and I would stay that way for two months. It was excruciating. What was weirder was that my temporary hearing loss now mirrored Janet's *permanent* hearing loss in *her* left ear; for two months we were completely alike in that we could only hear each other talking in bed if our good ears were up. Since I habitually mumble and since Janet's hearing loss is mild to moderate, the most common word in our household is inevitably *WHAT?* Now Jamie would grow up in the *WHAT?* house with a greater hearing loss than we could imagine. I just couldn't bear the thought.

When I got home and broke the news to Janet, she was silent a long time, as I thought she'd be. "Of course, I don't think it's as bad as the test says," I added. "I mean, I know he can recognize our voices below 45 decibels, and some of the stimuli they gave him *I* could barely hear. So we don't know. Sure, he probably has some hearing loss. We knew that, what with all his ear infections. But I know that test wasn't the last word. His hearing isn't as bad as all that." I listened to my own words. They sounded hollow and forced, sure enough, as if I were trying to convince myself by talking. But I wasn't. I *believed* this. It was *true*. I could prove it. I could ring a bell at God knows what decibel level, or rattle his plastic links, and Jamie and I would begin to play a mute game the intricacy of which none of this afternoon's audiologists could begin to fathom. But none of it would dispel my sadness, or Janet's. She was near tears herself.

"It's so funny. I've been thinking all day," she said, haltingly, "about whether he'll ever have a life like other kids. I mean, who's going to come to *his* birthday parties?"

I had to admit that that question hadn't yet occurred to me, either on that day or on any other.

■

CHAPTER FOUR

Walking the Talk

▲

Janet has a less mediated relation to sadness than I do. Her sadness seems purer, less diluted than mine, which is almost inevitably tinged with things like anger or fear or aggravation. It is rare that I experience the kind of sadness I felt at the amusement park in Old Orchard Beach, a free-floating sadness with no ulterior purpose and no plan for remediation. When I think of what this country might be like today if Robert Kennedy had been elected president in 1968 in place of Richard Nixon, or when I am wounded in matters of the heart, my grief tends to take root in rage and stay there; when I am saddened that all is not and will not be well with Jamie, my grief bypasses anger at agentless entities like chromosomes and quickly defaults into fear for his future. Perhaps this inability to deal with grief head on is inscribed somewhere in my own chromosomes, but I have reason to believe it's a trait I learned when Nick was young. In his first forty months on the planet, Nick was hospitalized for severe asthma no fewer than three times; the first time, in June 1988, the admitting physician thought—not without reason—that we would lose him. Janet and I were helpless, of course. Or so we thought. The second time Nick was hospitalized, I was called upon to restrain him physically while a resident pediatrician tried vainly for half an hour to start an intravenous line in his arm. Only some years later, when I succumbed to food poisoning and was given my very own IV during hospitalization, did I understand viscerally how painful it is to have someone root around the underside of your wrist with a big needle. But even in 1988 I knew better than to get angry at allergens, so whenever I came anywhere near grief about Nick's asthma, I worried about the years ahead, instead.

With Jamie there was plenty of future to worry about. Not long after he was born, I took my first look at a magazine called *Exceptional Parent*, which addresses the concerns of parents of children with various kinds of physical and mental disabilities. Amid the poignant but numbing ads for monitors, electric wheelchairs, and prosthetic devices, I found a "problems" column, where parents could turn for advice and (perhaps) comfort. The problem to which this particular column was devoted happened to be that of a man in his sixties who could no longer support his adult son with disabilities because he lived in an area whose social services had been eviscerated. He couldn't pick up and take his job elsewhere at his age, nor could he supplement his child's needs from the meager savings that job had made possible over the past couple of decades. What was he to do? I thought this was a fairly compelling question. More than this, I knew at once that this man's dilemma was the future I feared more than any other—the scenario to which I defaulted whenever I felt anything like grief or disappointment about James. What could this magazine tell me to allay my fears, to help me convert mere sadness into something productive and protective for my child?

Unfortunately, the magazine could tell me nothing. The man was offered counseling and Prozac—even though Prozac wouldn't do anything to alter the social dispensation in which this man and his son found themselves trapped, any more than it enhances the skills of the incompetent drivers who populate our roads and surround my car at just those moments when I have to rush to pick up or drop off a child.

So even though Janet responded to Jamie's hearing test with a question about his future, I knew she was speaking in terms rather different from mine. The question of who would come to his birthday parties was really a question about who he was and who he would be acknowledged to be; it was not the kind of question that could be laid to rest later that year, when, on September 16, 1992, his first birthday party was attended by about twenty of our colleagues and their children. For my part, I sat through Jamie's hearing test and wanted to pick apart its assumptions and protocols; Janet, less inclined to deflection, got the results and was saddened. But that's not to say that Janet's ability to realize sadness *as* sadness, before it becomes something else, disables her from reflecting on Jamie's prospects or on the general question of What Is to Be Done. On the contrary, I think, it helps her gauge (much better than I do) the middle distance between Jamie's next developmental evaluation and the social landscape he'll confront when his parents are over sixty. Then, when Janet's capacity for unadulterated sadness meets my capacity to convert grief to worry, we ask ourselves: How can we guide him through childhood, knowing it will be a childhood so unlike that of his brother, his peers, and even his fellow humans with Down syndrome? Once we know his hearing—or his birthday party—is in jeopardy, what obligations must we assume along with the burden of that knowledge?

In at least one respect I turned out to be right in the short run: Jamie's hearing *wasn't* as bad as that test suggested. It now seems mild to moderate, in one ear and borderline normal in the other—though the lines between "moderate to severe," "moderate," "mild to moderate," "mild," "borderline to mild," and "borderline normal" are every bit as fuzzy as those terms suggest. Yet his hearing is compromised nonetheless, and now, over three years later, Janet and I debate with each other and with his speech therapists the pros and cons of fitting him with hearing aids. Our goal is the same now as it was then: to keep his expressive language skills somewhere within shouting range of his receptive language skills. For like almost all toddlers, James understands much, much more than he can say. It seems a shame to try so hard to violate that condition, especially since most humans above the age of four, myself included, are so emphatically at the other end of the spectrum, forever talking in egregious excess of our understanding. In Jamie's case, we became afraid that at some point during his second or third year of life he would simply give up on trying to talk, since his speech production apparatus had so many strikes against it from the outset: not merely the mental disabilities entailed by Down's, but the floppy larynx that gave him his hoarse voice and an inability to monitor his airflow the way we do when we scream, whisper, or sing.

I used to say of Nick, when he was just under a year old, that he had distinctly emerged into a personhood complete with idiosyncrasies, preferences, and moods, but wasn't a full partner yet until he began to talk—at which point we were going to brace ourselves for his adolescence. With James, however, we did no such joking. Once we acquired the dimmest idea of how much he understood, we'd have lent him our tongues just to be able to promote him to full partner immediately. At the same time, we rejoiced every time Jamie showed us he knew what we were talking about. From what we hear, that's not an uncommon reaction

among parents of children with Down syndrome. In an essay ti-
tled "A Vision of the Future," Emily Perl Kingsley tells the story
of how she talked to her infant Jason incessantly, without any real
faith that he could take it in, until she received her first ambigu-
ous shadow of a sign that her words might mean something to
her baby. Curiously enough, that first shadow of a sign came
when Jason was four months old—again, not bad for a human,
though terribly delayed by the standard of any other primate
baby. Having been told by a doctor that maybe some extra stimulation wouldn't be a bad thing for Jason, Kingsley decided to give
his advice a chance:

In the interest of having maximum stimulation and color
and input, we tore down the old, bland, pastel-colored baby
wallpaper we had originally chosen and replaced it with wallpaper that had huge, brilliant, red and purple flowers. I kept
saying to him, over and over, "See the flower, see the flower."
Frankly, I didn't know what else to say. Then one day, when
he was about four months old, I said, again, "See the flower,"
and he turned and put his little hand right in the middle of a
big red flower. Now, I don't know whether this was totally accidental, whether he was just stretching, but to me, it was a
message. It seemed to me as if he had internalized what I had
been saying to him all these months and he was saying to me,
"Yeah, Mom, I get it already. I know this is a flower. Let's go
on to something else, huh?"

In any case, I went crazy. I jumped up and down and I
started to cry and I ran to the phone and I called up Charles
and I said, "This kid can learn! There's something in there!
This is not a vegetable! This is a person! This is a person who
can learn!" And that was the first day that, emotionally, I

made the commitment to my own child. Up to that point, I was "going through the motions." But that was the day when I started to recognize that perhaps my son was a human being. Perhaps he was a person and an individual.

It's because Emily and Jason Kingsley had that moment in 1974 that Janet and I could start with the assumption that Jamie would learn as much as he could of whatever we threw at him; it's because other parents showed us how responsive their children were that we could expect Jamie to learn about flowers and colors, how to wash his hands and find his shoes when asked. But speech is another order of magnitude altogether. Rats, horses, and chimps can learn a range of mundane and impressive tasks—from flower identifying to shoe finding—with a little operant conditioning and a decent trainer; only humans learn to produce whole clauses, sentences, and paragraphs of babble. Humans with Down syndrome regularly learn to do that, too, but not always, and not always efficiently. A fine biochemical interference produces annoying static in their neural nets, and minute distortions of their vocal and breathing apparatuses make the physical work of speaking more complicated than anything Demosthenes might have imagined when he first decided to stuff his mouth with extra speech impediments.

More than anything, we wanted Jamie to walk that walk and talk that talk. We knew his progress toward those goals would be analogous to the process by which he seized toys from his walker; every step would be prolonged and arduous, every triumph precious and magnified. Our fond hopes that he would be able to stand by the time we took our first family vacation in August 1992, when he was still eleven months old, turned out to be merely fond hopes. Janet and I fulfilled one of our promises to each other, by ferrying Nick and Jamie from Illinois to Virginia to Connecticut to Maine; we learned how much our younger child flourished amid an extended family keen to make much of him; we found that our mini station wagon could cover five thousand miles laden with enough gear to get T. E. Lawrence across the Arabian peninsula on foot; and we introduced Jamie to the beaches and waves he will doubtless always love. But our longings alone were far from enough to get him to stand on his own.

Even as we were trying to "rush" him, knowing that our efforts had nothing to do with status, reflected glory, or the college of his choice, we felt torn—and Janet, feeling both contradiction and sadness more acutely than I, registered the strain more viscerally as well. One crisp autumn afternoon, as I was combing through the random wreckage of one of our storage cabinets, I chanced upon a palm-sized tape recorder I had long forgotten. With this tiny device I had once recorded Nick's first attempts at words, his uncontrolled giggling at the difference between his big bear (bass voice) and little bear (falsetto), his insistence on chirping, "doo dah, doo dah," during my delicately nuanced version of "Camptown Races." The very touch of the machine reminded me that when Nick began to talk fluently (thereby advancing to full partner in the family firm) and, at the age of two, demanded to know what the tape recorder was called, I had foolishly told him it was "complicated"; dutifully, he called the tape recorder a *complicated* for many months until I finally decided it was time to introduce him to the vagaries of parental miscommunication. I pressed "play." Out came a squeaky voice singsonging *doo dah, doo dah*, asking for juice, erupting at *POP!* goes the weasel. I was transfixed: my little Nick, captured on tape at the threshold of language. Within a few months after *doo dah, doo dah*, he would be asking us the names of all the spices in the spice

rack; a few months after that he would be making up his first toddler puns—taking off his socks and pointing first to a teddy bear
and then to his toes, saying, "bare feet!" or asking what kind of
animal he was and, responding to the information that he was a
little human, shouting, "I'm a little *cumin*! Ha ha ha ha!" Once
that baby Nicholas found out what fun he could have with words,
he wasted no time romping through every kind of miscue he
could find—no matter how complicated.

I played the tape for Janet. After less than a minute she began
to tear up, and then to cry. "Shut it off," she said, "I can't bear it."
I was stunned. Here was our Nick, preserved for us as no photograph could preserve him, captured and rescued from a time
when we could afford no videocamera to track his every step: but
here also was our Nick, no older then than Jamie was when I
found the tape recorder—fourteen or fifteen months—darting off
on embryonic verbal acrobatics his little brother couldn't even
imagine. All that night, Janet wondered what we'd gotten into,
whether we could bear not only the obligations but the sense of
never fulfilling them, not only the disappointments but the probability that the future would always contain the possibility of further disappointment. I remembered how a harmless verse from a
lullaby had once stopped her cold: *You will grow up big and strong,
sleepy little baby.* Janet had sung that to James one evening until
her voice caught on "big and strong," whereupon she realized
that she had no assurance at all that her little baby would grow
up big and strong. I tried vainly, as I had tried that earlier night,
to remind her that we'd told each other we wouldn't compare
Jamie to Nick, that all bets were off, that we would have no anxieties about whether he was "keeping up" or "falling behind." But
I couldn't redo the way our tape had played out: We had one
gifted child and one retarded child, a pair of offspring on the op-

posite plains of the bell curve, and sometimes the statistical mountain of "normalcy" separating them would simply be too formidable for us to scale or ignore.

"Sometimes," Janet said, "sometimes I wish he could always stay just this age." But wasn't all our sorrow predicated on our anxieties about his developmental delays? Weren't we consumed by the obligation to discover which delays could be countered and to counter them? Wasn't it our job to promote our Jamie, to help make him a walkin' talkin' rootin' tootin' toddler? "Absolutely," Janet replied, but before her sadness became anxiety or fear, it was also sadness: "But if he were always one year old, he'd never have his little heart broken. He'd never be turned down for a date. He'd never learn that other children might make fun of him. And he'd always have us to make him laugh."

I disagreed with Janet completely, but I didn't say anything. Janet and I can sometimes be gratuitously contentious people. When the mood is wrong, we can argue about wallpaper, computer settings, scheduling conflicts, brands of seltzer, or the position of the driver's seat in the car. In another life we'd be tenacious lawyers, exhausting negotiators. Once we had an all-afternoon argument about whether some student's letter of recommendation would arrive too late. You know, the really important stuff. But James's arrival changed the terms of our disagreements entirely. For one thing, we've never argued about him—not about his development, his therapies, his health, his schools, his skills, or his medicines. He's much too important to argue about, and he's made us realize that Nick always was, too. So when we're crabby, we don't crab about the kids. We crab about serious matters instead, like the fact that Janet drives with the car seat absurdly far forward for a woman who's five foot eight.

So I didn't even tell Janet what I was thinking—namely, that Jamie would only get happier and more competent in the next few years, that adolescence was a million years away, that he'd always have us to make him laugh no matter what. For what would be the point of trying to talk Janet out of sadness instead of simply rubbing her shoulders? Besides, I knew I had heard similar sentiments before, somewhere in one of the underread books of the Western canon. In fact, I had even gone so far as to assign them and teach them, when I asked a class to read William Edward Burghardt Du Bois's *The Souls of Black Folk* in its entirety:

> No bitter meanness now shall sicken his baby heart till it die a living death, no taunt shall madden his happy boyhood.... Well sped, my boy, before the world had dubbed your ambition insolence, had held your ideals unattainable, and taught you to cringe and bow. Better far this nameless void that stops my life than a sea of sorrows for you.
>
> Idle words: he might have borne his burden more bravely than we,—aye, and found it lighter too, some day; for surely, surely this is not the end.

So wrote a brilliant and courageous man of the passing of his firstborn, refusing himself even the consolation of thinking that his son, dead at the age of eighteen months, had at least escaped the sentence of growing up amid a venomous, murderous racism that may well have claimed his life at a later date. However much Janet and I fear other people's irrational fears, however much we fear that Jamie will be ostracized or simply laughed at, we do not fear that he will be lynched or beaten by police. Still, we have some general idea of what it means for parents to try to weigh their hope of social progress against the comforts of their child's infantile innocence.

Much of Jamie's second year settled into routine. We hired a young woman to sit with him in the afternoons; we smoothed out his weekly appointments for speech therapy and physical therapy, bought him therapy devices disguised as balls and toys; we juggled his schedule, Nick's, and ours. In the midst of our juggling, we tried to keep our composure as some joker threw us a bowling ball or a chainsaw to juggle as well. There were papers to grade, committee crises to defuse, essays to write . . . and through it all, our children continued to play host to a dizzying variety of pesty microorganisms. I began to let my students in on my growing conviction that human children were really complex biochemical devices for the propagation of viruses; there was one prolonged, blistering winter when the wind chills hit seventy below and the temperature stayed in the twenties until the middle of April, during which I began every class by declaiming the name of a European city that lay *north* of Champaign-Urbana yet was fifty degrees warmer, all thanks to the gentle zephyrs borne over the Iberian peninsula by the Atlantic Gulf Stream. "That's *our* Gulf Stream," I told my classes. "We built it, we own it, it's ours. Why should Naples and Monaco reap all the benefit?" Some mornings I careered madly from drugstore to drugstore, looking for the 80 mg acetaminophen suppositories that would bring Jamie's fever down, finding only 120 mg sizes we would have to cut into thirds. Some days we would take Jamie and Nick for tag-team visits to the pediatric clinic—Jamie for strep and Nick for an elusive bowel disorder—and spend the better part of a day shlepping our charges from X-ray to ear-nose-throat to the waiting room of the blood lab and back. To this day I cannot spend more than an hour or two with James or Nick at the doctor's without coming home and eating two meals on top of one another. And I know there were days I felt I couldn't take any more of this. If someone didn't arrive at my doorstep and whisk me away to my private Caribbean island I would surely put my hand through a pane of glass before too long. But even the most hectic routine can become routine, and we rarely forgot to remember that we had work schedules of almost infinite elasticity to accommodate even the most inopportune microorganism, parent-teacher conference, or rescheduled therapy appointment.

Amanda took to calling us "bumper cars" for the harum-scarum way we traveled around town and through our lives. But our bumper-cars mode of existence was not without its fringe benefits. I learned to work extremely quickly in short bursts, never knowing when I would next be interrupted by a phone call from Nick's school or a shout from the babysitter as Jamie threw up his lunch; Janet, clearly something more than human, excited in her colleagues and students those most powerful of Aristotelian emotions, pity and terror. We were exempt from, sublimely indifferent to, the minor neuroses and unfathomable territorialisms of everyday academic life, and we had some of the best excuses we knew of—no less valuable for being real—for fatigue, tardiness, or general discombobulation. We were learning that for almost all the waking day, the task of raising Jamie would be different in degree, not in kind, from the task of raising Nick. We would have to help him feed himself for a good while longer, and we couldn't expect him to memorize the spice rack; but even as we crashed our bumper cars up one street and down another, our Jamie was gradually emerging, like a slowly developing Polaroid of a child, into a vivid and indelible creature with a sense of humor and a set of preferences all his own—to go along with his singular fingerprints and his raft of microorganisms.

Every so often the routine fell apart: Jamie was hospitalized overnight for croup; I was invited to Brazil by the United States Information Agency, two weeks of seminars on American litera-ture on three weeks' notice; we bought a house. For Janet's birthday I had bought a pair of tickets to see a bunch of twen-tysomething bands touring through central Illinois, and once I'd purchased the tickets I told Amanda that I knew I would bring some awful disease down upon my children, for almost every time Janet and I planned a Big Night Out to hear some music, one of our kids fell ill. Sure enough, *that* was when Jamie developed the high fever and scary barking cough of croup; that was the night Jamie was hospitalized. We gave the tickets to a neighbor and hunkered down for a night of breathing treatments, hospital food, and four-hour sleeping shifts. *Please don't let him develop asthma*, we whispered into the night. *Nick-quality asthma, in his little airways, would just be too much for him. Please just give him a few years to get bigger before our lousy genes start compromising his respiratory system.* But dawn came early, Jamie's fever broke, the twentysome-thing bands left town, and by mid-afternoon he was released from the hospital on a new round of medications, returning home clingy and tired but safe. No wheezing, no barking, no asthma. When we bought our new house that summer, we tried to cush-ion the disruptive effects of the move as best we could, hedging his keen—and growing—sensitivity to domestic disorder. After a solid week of familiarizing himself with what was always referred to as "Jamie's house," though, he began to settle in with obvious delight at his new room, his carpeted stairs (stairs! a wholly new item on the sociophysical landscape!), and his great big playroom in the split-level basement.

He loved being sung to; he especially loved a song that went, *I*

*love my rooster, my rooster loves me, I feed my rooster 'neath the bayberry
tree*, with further verses for a dog, a cat, and a lamb, along with
their characteristic noises (*my little lambie says baa, baa*), and on
one car trip he compelled us to play the song on his lullabies tape
maybe ten or twelve times in a row. My friend Larry Gallagher
gave me a tape of Nick Drake's music, Nick Drake being an early
1970s British folkster with a gravelly, soulful voice and a mon-
strous, eventually fatal case of depression, and Jamie focused on
one of his uncharacteristically bouncy, upbeat tunes called "Hazy
Jane II." It quickly became the first song—of many—to which
Jamie danced. Of course, since he wasn't standing yet, he wasn't
really dancing. But he was clearly bopping back and forth, up and
down in his car seat or his high chair, and only to Nick Drake.
When Larry learned that "Hazy Jane II" had inspired Jamie to
dance, he said, "That's the first song that got him dancing, huh?
Well, that must be his essential whiteness coming out." But that
explanation wouldn't suffice to explain Jamie's growing eclecti-
cism, his increasingly passionate love for lullabies, Raffi, Nick
Drake, Bob Marley and the Wailers, Patsy Cline, and B. B. King
(whom he latched onto a good while later, when he could ask for
B. B. by name).

As he got ever closer to standing and walking, his love of
music helped him no less than two other crucial loves—his love
of praise, and his love of Nick. All children are thrilled when they
first learn they can have some physical effect on the world, and
every child I've ever met is thrilled when the effect they have on
the world makes other people happy, particularly the people who
feed, clothe, hold, and sing to them. But something about Jamie's
delight was different in degree, not in kind, from the delight
we'd seen from Nick. Doubtless that had something to do with
Nick himself, who greeted Jamie's every attempt to stand with an
enthusiasm at once extravagant and altogether sincere. We have a

videotape—dating from the time we were first given a camcorder by Janet's parents, complete with the implicit charge, *capture our grandchildren*—of Jamie pulling his rubbery body to a stand on a kitchen chair. In the background Janet is making supper, and the other parent, having chopped the onions, has obviously run to get the camcorder. Jamie's efforts are as technically incompetent as his first efforts to sit up: using his hyperflexibility to compensate for his hypotonia, he propels himself upward bowleggedly instead of coming up from a squat (which his stomach and thigh muscles can't manage). As he stands clutching the seat of the chair, he looks up at Nick, who's applauding open-mouthed and saying, "so good! so good! standing UP!" with all the emphasis a seven year old can bring to speech. Jamie is beaming. And for a second, maybe two seconds, maybe even three, he tries, tottering, to stay up even as he takes his hands off the chair. Nick gasps and cheers; Jamie shudders with delight—and crashes onto the floor, laughing, to begin the attempt once again. It's all right here in the video archive, and nothing could be clearer: Although Jamie's muscles are so much weaker than his will, his love for his brother, and his love of his brother's love, is literally changing what his body can do.

When Nick was still under a year old, I read a book that opened by attacking my idea of what language was and how we use it. In fact, it opens by quoting one of the major autobiographies in the Western tradition, in which Augustine writes of how he learned to talk as a child:

> When they (my elders) named some object, and accord-
> ingly moved toward something, I saw this and I grasped that

the thing was called by the sound they uttered when they meant to point it out. Their intention was shown by their bodily movements, as it were the natural language of all peoples: the expression of the face, the play of the eyes, the movement of other parts of the body, and the tone of voice which expresses our state of mind in seeking, having, rejecting, or avoiding something. Thus, as I heard words repeatedly used in their proper places in various sentences, I gradually learnt to understand what objects they signified; and after I had trained my mouth to form these signs, I used them to express my own desires.

Then the book proceeds to repudiate Augustine's account:

These words, it seems to me, give us a particular picture of the essence of human language. It is this: the individual words in language name objects—sentences are combinations of such names.—In this picture of language we find the roots of the following idea: Every word has a meaning. This meaning is correlated with the word. It is the object for which the word stands.

Augustine does not speak of there being any difference between kinds of word. If you describe the learning of language in this way you are, I believe, thinking primarily of nouns like "table," "chair," "bread," and of people's names, and only secondarily of the names of certain actions and properties; and of the remaining kinds of word as something that will take care of itself. . . .

. . . That philosophical concept of meaning has its place in a primitive idea of the way language functions. But one can say that it is the idea of a language more primitive than ours.

So begins Ludwig Wittgenstein's *Philosophical Investigations*, and so began my introduction to "antifoundationalist" philosophy and literary theory in the mid- to late 1980s. Wittgenstein will go on to argue that words accrue their meanings not by their reference to objects but by way of their use in the language as a whole—or, as he calls it, a "language-game," a *sprachspiel*. In other words, "table" ordinarily refers to a table, unless we start arguing about whether *that* thing over there, the thing you call a "table," isn't really a desk. Then what does "terrorist" refer to, or "freedom fighter," or "however," or "over," or "love," or "yow"? The only reason we get suckered into asking questions like these, Wittgenstein suggests, is that we are held captive by the picture painted for us by people like Augustine and Plato. We should think of words and their functions, instead, the way we think about pieces in chess: What matters is not the shape of the piece or its "intrinsic" physical properties but the way it is moved according to the rules of the game. A bolt or a flower could "stand for" (that is, *be*) the queen, just as we could, in principle, call banks "tables" and Central American leftists "freedom fighters" tomorrow. The results might be temporarily confusing (did you say the *flower* can move in all directions without limit?), but they would not violate the rules by which language and chess are "played." "Philosophy," Wittgenstein famously declares, "is a battle against the bewitchment of our intelligence by means of language," and the bewitchment of which he wanted to cure us was precisely the sense that language use consists of giving "ostensive definitions" whereby people point to objects and say their names. See the flower, see the flower.

This is all very well and good, and it served me adequately as an introduction to a "pragmatist" theory of language that got me out of thinking fruitlessly about the relation between words and things (since I could hardly think in such terms except when I was thinking about nouns and proper names), but Nick soon showed me that however sound Wittgenstein might be in principle, the unfashionable Saint Augustine actually had the advantage in practice. Over the space of a couple of months, Nick acquired not only "object constancy"—that is, the understanding that objects persisted even when he couldn't see them, and the concomitant ability to remember where the crackers were even after his parents had hidden the box—but object *reference* as well. He couldn't talk, couldn't do much more than babble random syllables and phonemes to see which ones might get a response (*dadada* more than *glyphkthl*, for instance), but I could walk into his room as he woke up from his nap, see him quickly pull himself to a stand, and ask him where the *window* was, whereupon he would point to a window, just like Augustine said. Where's the painting? There's the painting. Where's your crib? There's your crib. And your feet, and your tummy, and your books. The ostensive definitions seemed to be working just fine, thank you.

Then something weird started to happen. It was clear that Nick knew the names of objects and was waiting, in Augustine's words, to train his mouth to say them; but one day I learned that for his purposes, anything hanging on a wall was a "painting," even if it was a mirror or a calendar. Anything round was a ball. But the large picture window in the living room wasn't yet a window, and my feet weren't feet.

It took only one mute conversation to correct those last two misunderstandings on Nick's part, but I knew I had caught my child doing something fascinating. What was his principle of organization? Why did he extend "ball" to all round things but not "window" to all transparent panes of glass set in walls? How, for that matter, could he organize nouns and their "ostensive definitions" into discrete groups in the first place?

What Nick was doing, working his way down the road to language, was something the child developmental psychologists call "overextension." Philosopher W. V. O. Quine calls it "the scandal of induction": Somehow, the child generalizes wildly on the basis of very little evidence. Inductive reasoning involves just that kind of expansion; from the specific, one surmises the general. What's *scandalous* about the way we learn language, though, is how little evidence we require for induction—and how successful most of our attempts turn out to be. Somehow, we surmise that the name we're learning applies not just to the thing before our eyes but to a whole class of objects similar to the thing.

How do we manage to intuit those classes of objects? Are there Archetypal Objects lying behind each individual object— say, a perfect Ball of which all earthly balls are but the shadow and copy? At the dawn of Western philosophy, Plato decided that there were indeed such archetypal objects, and he called them "ideas." Now that I had come to a fresh appreciation of old Augustine, my next lesson would come from Plato himself, the philosopher against or under whose influence every Western thinker has labored, right down to Wittgenstein. Indeed, the reason Wittgenstein's thought is called "antifoundationalist" is that it is primarily anti-*Platonic*. Here's why. You see a bed, then another bed, then another. They all differ in important respects: size, comfort, color, materials, cost, layaway plan. But they are all, somehow, beds. How absurd it would be to call each object by a different name, yet we somehow understand that the difference among beds is a difference *within* a larger category, not a difference among individual objects named Lucille, Long Tall Sally, and Peggy Sue. Likewise, there's a difference between a line drive home run that just barely clears the left field foul pole at 320 feet and a behemoth blast that lands in the upper deck behind center field, but in some sense they're both home runs. How is that? Plato answered this question like so: every bed, like every home run, participates in a general *idea* of bedness (or whatever), such that we recognize all beds as inaccurate copies of the perfect, primeval Bed—the "idea" of bed. Wittgenstein thinks this is mysticist nonsense. It's a bed if we sleep on it, and it's a home run if the rules of baseball say so, regardless of whether it was an impressive or a lame home run, end of question. The meaning of the word *is* its use in the language. As far as groups are concerned, Wittgenstein is downright unsettling: Objects in groups need not share every "essential" feature in common, any more than there is something essential that every game shares, something that makes it a "game." Rather, objects in groups share "family resemblances"—a particularly telling phrase for parents of children with genetic anomalies—and these family resemblances form a kind of rope whose continuity is made up of similar but discontinuous threads:

I can think of no better expression to characterize these similarities than "family resemblances"; for the various resemblances between members of a family: build, features, color of eyes, gait, temperament, etc. etc. overlap and criss-cross in the same way.—And I shall say: "games" form a family.

And for instance the kinds of number [that is, the varieties of groups—M.B.] form a family in the same way. . . . And we extend our concept of number as in spinning a thread we twist fibre on fibre. And the strength of the thread does not reside in the fact that some one fibre runs through its whole length, but in the overlapping of many fibres.

I know that my family—my progenitors as well as my progeny—form something more or less like a group. And I know that I couldn't get around in the world without Wittgenstein's sense of "family resemblances," without which, I think, we get trapped in the dangerous Platonist game of looking for the essential, fundamental common elements linking all games, or all black Americans, or all Western philosophers. But here, too, in one important respect, Wittgenstein seems bested by his predecessors. The reason Nick labeled all wall hangings "pictures" was that he was making a general guess about what my word could mean. At one extreme, it could mean "the unique thing right there on that wall, the one his brilliant aunt Todd painted," and at the other extreme, it could mean "all colorful things." Nick opened with a bid somewhere in the middle, opting for "all colorful things hanging on a wall." Perhaps, as I had once heard in a class on literary theory, Plato didn't mean his idea of "ideas" as a kind of dogma—as if every object had to be an instance of the Ideal Object of Its Kind, all beds imperfectly referring to the Ideal Bed that existed only in the mind of the Creator. (You can see how easy it was for this interpretation of Plato to be picked up and remodeled by Christian philosophy in later centuries.) Maybe Plato was just offering the Western world's first theorization of "groupness," so that there would be some general philosophical ground for lumping things into groups and calling them by the same name. In which case, Plato wouldn't look all that different from Wittgenstein after all: *Things that serve functions more or less like these, we will call beds; people who behave more or less in such-and-such a way in relation to law, we will call terrorists.* Even if they don't partake of the ideal Idea of "terrorist," by their deeds we shall know them. By this reasoning, Plato didn't intend the doctrine of Ideas to be taken literally; his presentation of them, through his dialogues' creation of the character of Socrates, was somewhat ironic; he was just providing people with a way to counter the arguments of the pre-Socratics and the sophists, who had no way of conceptualizing groupness in any fashion whatsoever.

I don't buy this revisionist-Plato argument, myself, though I do think it's quite plausible that Plato's account of the Ideas was a response to pre-Socratic theories of identity and perception. Actually, it's probably not a good idea to make Plato look more like Wittgenstein; the difference between Platonic and anti-Platonic theories of language are quite dramatic and account for a great deal of contemporary debate in the humanities and social sciences. In its simplest form, the difference can be framed like so: Does language *reflect* "reality," or, rather, does language *create* "reality"? Anyone who's read my discussion of "mongoloids" and "developmental delays" back in Chapter 1 probably knows by now that I don't side with the extreme version of either position, since I believe instead that language is *itself* an integral part of the reality that we humans know. But if you want a more vivid sense of what's at stake in the debate, think of Descartes's founding principle: *cogito ergo sum*. I think therefore I am—perhaps the most famous pronouncement in the Western philosophical tradition. It wasn't just a declaration, either; it was a statement of method as well. Descartes started from the premise that he should doubt the existence of everything his mind and his senses told him—the existence of the world, of God, of other people, of himself. But then, he reasoned, *someone* has to be doing the doubting, and that person has to be me. *Cogito ergo sum*.

Hold on a second, though. Where did those *words* come from? How come, when Descartes doubted everything, there were still Latin verb forms for him to fall back on? One contemporary philosopher has remarked, appropriately, that Descartes doubted everything except the existence of the French and Latin languages, which, in the end, were the only things worth doubting. It's a rather overly dramatic claim, but its point is quite valid: Latin already contains an "I." It's built right into every verb: *cogito, sum.* You can't provide an "objective" philosophical grounding of the individual by speaking Latin. That's cheating. In other words, Descartes might not have discovered anything important about the nature of individual thought; he might simply have filled in the appropriate blank that Latin provided for him. If you compare Latin to a language like Ewe (spoken chiefly in Togo and Ghana), in which there are no such first person singular verb constructions, then you'll probably agree that if Descartes had spoken Ewe back in the early seventeenth century, he'd have had to come up with a founding principle other than "I think therefore I am."

The implications of this are hard to overstate. If the validity of basic philosophical principles depends, in a substantial sense, on the language they're spoken in, then isn't language something more than just a medium for thought? Doesn't it *shape* our thoughts in material, indelible ways? At this point, the difference between Platonists and anti-Platonists can be framed in another way: The Platonists contend that we speak language, and (some of) the anti-Platonists, especially the French poststructuralists of the 1960s and 1970s, contend instead that *language speaks us.* So far, so good. But then the Platonists have a question in response. Granted, language influences and even constrains thought. Yet how do you explain the fact that the vast majority of the world's kajillion languages *do*, after all, contain first person singular words, pronouns, and verb forms? Might not the ancient Romans have devised a language with words like *cogito* and *sum* because it gave them a convenient way to acknowledge all those occasions on which we might need or desire to speak as individual selves? That may be so, reply the anti-Platonists; nonetheless, the fact remains that anyone acquiring a language has to learn how *it* speaks *them*: English-speaking children have to be taught to say "I." It's a social-linguistic convention, like calling round bouncy things "balls." We say, "It is raining," and no one asks us, "What is?" The French say, "I have hunger," and no one asks, "Where?" Well into his second year, in fact, Nick persisted in saying "take him" to his parents whenever he wanted to be picked up. "No, no, take *me*," we said to him, to which he answered, logically enough, "take *you*." So in the end, there's a very strong sense in which we humans speak language; it doesn't speak us. Latin didn't drop from the sky; language-using humans devised it somehow. That's how language works. *We* use *it*—except when we're actually *learning* a language (as we always are), in which case it feels like it's the other way around.

Very well, you say, but then how do we ordinary humans learn to conceive of groups like "paintings" and "beds" and "terrorists" without taking course after course in the history of Western philosophy? Good question. Here's how psycholinguist Steven Pinker, author of *The Language Instinct: How the Mind Creates Language*, explains the scandal of induction:

There is one more reason we should stand in awe of the simple act of learning a word. The logician W.V.O. Quine asks us to imagine a linguist studying a newly discovered tribe. A rabbit scurries by, and a native shouts, "Gavagai!" What does *gavagai* mean? Logically speaking, it needn't be "rabbit." It could refer to that particular rabbit (Flopsy, for example). It could mean any furry thing, any mammal, or any member of that species of rabbit (say, *Oryctolagus cuniculus*), or

any member of that variety of that species (say, chinchilla rabbit). It could mean scurrying rabbit, scurrying thing, rabbit
plus the ground it scurries upon, or scurrying in general. It
could mean footprint-maker, or habitat for rabbit-fleas. It
could mean the top half of a rabbit, or rabbit-meat-on-the-
hoof, or possessor of at least one rabbit's foot. It could mean
anything that is either a rabbit or a Buick. It could mean collection of undetached rabbit parts, or "Lo! Rabbithood
again!," or "It rabbiteth," analogous to "It raineth."

Oddly, Pinker never supposes that *gavagai* could be an imperative: Get your slingshot! Look alive! Run, you fool! But his point
is clear, clear enough to allow me to test it on my subjects at
home. When I read Pinker's book in 1995, when Nick was nine
and Jamie about to turn four, I decided to ask Nick how a baby
might decide to apply the word "painting" to every colorful thing
hanging on a wall (he liked the "Lo! rabbithood again!" every bit
as much as I did). We sifted through Pinker's options. Some
seemed silly, some seemed plausible, and some ("top half of a rabbit") seemed like guesses no sane infant would dare to make. In
the end, Nick said, the guess that "rabbit" meant, more or less,
"all animals that look and move pretty much like this" was simply a safe bet: you'd be closer to the mark than if you'd assumed it
applied to all animals—or, at the other extreme, just to this one
Peter Cottontail.

I told Nick that was a great answer. For if the baby turned out
to be wrong—if moons and circles turned out to be something
other than "ball"—he or she would have a fairly minor conceptual
adjustment to make. Think of all the recalibration our befuddled
brains would have to do if we thought "bed" meant "thing in the
middle of mommy and daddy's room" and "window" was a syn-

onym for "Big Bird"! The scandal of induction is that our first guesses are so close to the mark, so well tailored to understanding clusters of nouns and the verbs that might do things to them. As Pinker puts it,

> In an important sense, there really are things and kinds of things and actions out there in the world, and our mind is designed to find them and to label them with words. That important sense is Darwin's. It's a jungle out there, and the organism designed to make successful predictions about what is going to happen next will leave behind more babies designed just like it. Slicing space-time into objects and actions is an eminently sensible way to make predictions given the way the world is put together. Conceiving of an extent of solid matter as a thing—that is, giving a single mentalese name to all its parts—invites the prediction that those parts will continue to occupy some region of space and will move as a unit. And for many portions of the world, that prediction is correct. Look away, and the rabbit still exists; lift the rabbit by the scruff of the neck, and the rabbit's foot and the rabbit ears come along for the ride.

Thus it is, as Pinker later suggests, that organisms tend to learn to survive when they learn to tell their offspring, "Don't tease the sabertooth." But Pinker's own deft language begs a question: If humans are organisms "designed to make successful predictions about what is going to happen," then who or what did the designing behind that passive verb?

What the hammer? What the chain?
In what furnace was thy brain?

What the anvil? what dread grasp
Dare its deadly terrors clasp?

Nick was ten or eleven months old when he first began to point to objects and understand them as members of groups. Jamie was almost twice that age. But suddenly, as we flipped through his baby books, Jamie began to plug into the nouns and proper names. Chicken Little, Henny Penny, Cocky Locky, Goosey Poosey. These were not names of chickens, hens, cocks, or geese in general. Nor were words like "Ernie," "Bert," "Cookie Monster," "mommy," "daddy," or "Nick." But, now, *cat*—Jamie knew that was a much broader term, a capacious lexical item that covered not only the animal owned by our neighbors but also the creature who frightened a little mouse under the chair. And speaking of which: *mouse, chair, animal, frightened.* . . .

His speech therapist, his physical therapist, and his occupational therapist agreed: Jamie was beginning to get a sense of what his family members were talking about. You could ask him where the ball was, and he would get it; you could put three tiny plastic Muppets in front of him and say, "Jamie, please give me Ernie," and he would dutifully hand you the Ernie figure. The apparatus was definitely in place, and until Jamie could train his mouth to catch up with his mind, our task was quite clear. If we wanted him to keep communicating verbally despite his oral motor delays, if we wanted him not to give up on the idea of language, then we would have to teach him to sign.

The ASL sign for "play" is wonderfully expressive: both hands held out with pinkies and thumbs extended, the other three fingers cupped into the palm, both wrists spinning to and fro in simple harmonic motion. To make the sign for "more," hold your fingers out, straight and close together; bending your hands, place your thumbs on your index or middle fingertips; tap your hands together at the fingertips a few times, front and center. For "book," bring your hands together, flat, front and center, and then hinge and open them as if they mimed the opening of a book. "Milk" is two fists chugging up and down, like milking a cow; "work" is rather similar, one fist tapping on top of the other; "good" brings your right hand, open, from your lips to your open left hand, held in front of you at chest level; "thank you" brings your open right hand out from your heart. Jamie and his family learned many more signs than these, but these alone sufficed for a great deal of conversation. *More* came to signal practically anything having to do with desire, like, *Let's keep doing this*, or *Please, oh please*, or *This was a really good idea*. *Milk* sometimes doubled for *juice*, and both were occasionally indicated by *bottle* or *drink*. And all of Jamie's signs were clear and unmistakable, save for the ones he tried to make up every now and then, manual hieroglyphics whose meanings we will never fathom—with two exceptions: *dancing*, a gentle swaying of his upper body back and forth, and *loud,* thumbs pressed to cheeks and fingers spread wide on either side of his face.

He learned his signs from watching us and his teachers, of course. That wasn't surprising. What *was* surprising was how much mental work his signs bespoke. If Steven Pinker and Noam Chomsky are right, then ordinary children are truly performing dazzling tasks every time they pick up another trick in the language game—and they're doing it because they're hard-wired to do it, as the language-producing areas of the human brain ignite and take off. Learning ASL, however, is somewhat more difficult: every bit as impressive cognitively, with some physical mimicry and hand-eye coordination thrown in for good measure. Not that Janet and I underestimate the human vocal apparatus; quite the contrary. We know very well what kind of orchestration and genius it takes to produce modulated meaningful sounds. We've walked Jamie slowly through every stage of vocalization, compensating for his larynx, his tongue, his hypotonia, his weak chest; and we've introduced him to all the women on Janet's side of the family, each one of whom has a beautiful and supple singing voice. But every time I read one of those precious, tedious descriptions of how marvelous are the faculties of major league ballplayers who make bewilderingly complex mind-body decisions in fractions of a second, I think, well, who wouldn't want to hit .340 and make six quintillion dollars a year—but god*damn*, you should have seen my Jamie learning English and ASL.

Teaching him the sign for *play*, in other words, involved our giving him a complicated kind of "ostensive definition." First we would play with Jamie. He liked that. And if "play" entailed picking up small objects with a pincer grip (instead of palming them) or stacking blocks, then "play" was therapy, too. Jamie also liked that. Then we would say, "play." And then we would make little whirligigs of our hands. Jamie *loved* that. He watched our gestures, he smiled, he tried to make them too, knowing that signing for "play" was now an integral part of *doing* "play," as if his block stacking were incomplete without this silent color commentary. And his laughter: There was no surer sign that he had learned something than when he doubled over with delight at the introduction of a new word, motif, or therapy device disguised as a toy. Say the word, sign the word, do the word—whether the word referred to a thing, like "milk" or *gavagai*, or an action, like "play," or a staple of basic courtesy, like "thank you." The word, the thing, the action or thing. Sometimes I imagine that Jamie will grow up and write his own *Confessions*, in which he'll say of our efforts in those early lessons, "Their intention was shown by their bodily movements, as it were the natural language of all peoples: the expression of the face, the play of the eyes, the movement of other parts of the body, and the tone of voice which expresses our state of mind in seeking, having, rejecting, or avoiding something." But, then again, the bodily movements we were showing him were anything *but* the natural language of all peoples: modern signing, for all its potential universality, has only existed for a couple of generations.

It is now customary for speech therapists to "prescribe" signing for language-delayed children. But 'twas not always so, and even today some of the strange old prejudices remain. Chief among these is the fear that learning to sign will somehow *prevent* young children from learning to talk, as though language acquisition were a zero-sum game: if they spend all that neural energy learning signs, they'll have nothing left over for learning the words. Nothing could be further from the truth. ASL isn't a crutch for deaf children; it's a language for deaf and hearing children alike, and nothing prevents children from learning one language on top of another—or one language *because of* another. Those hearing children who learn to sign as a kind of tide-me-over measure turn out only to be hungrier for speech when their bodies finally allow them to produce it. They know what it is to communicate verbally, they know their parents, siblings, and friends do it, and they know that by signing they've become a player in the language game as well. When they learn to speak, they have two languages at their command; sure enough, if none of their interlocutors can sign, then their signing becomes vestigial. Janet and I know we've forgotten many signs once Jamie learned to produce their words instead, but Jamie will probably always say "thank you" while holding his hand to his heart. And why not? Isn't that gesture, proffered along with his hoarse "thank you," so much more expressive of his thanks? Don't we all talk with our hands, except that most of us don't do it so systematically? For me, one of the unsung triumphs of Spike Lee's *Do the Right Thing* was that Lee had plumbed one of the "essential" similarities underlying the Italian- and African-American cultures of Brooklyn: There isn't a character in the film who can get through a sentence without talking with his or her hands—with the *whole* hands, that is, from the shoulders on down. Jamie's version of the talk is much the same, and though he's now been signing off and on for over two years, it's still all his own. Hold up two fingers with your right hand. Then take that hand and make the "play" sign, this time rotating the hand just in front of your forehead. Jamie will gladly repeat what you've just said, and he knows very well how it applies to him: *too silly*.

Oddly, the sign for "silly" can also be the sign for "foolish," depending on how it's inflected, depending on the conversational context. Yet in Middle English, six or seven hundred years ago, "silly" was a synonym for "innocent." Surely that etymology resonates for Jamie, or for any child whose silliness is but a function of his or her innocence; surely Jamie's insistence on stacking a plastic duck on top of a block is *silly* rather than *foolish*, and surely he stacked the duck and turned to you with a mischievous grin because he knew he was mixing objects in a *silly* way. But every so often when I've told James that he is indeed too silly, I've had to reassure a therapist or two that I don't mean to insult him by calling him "foolish," and that Jamie understands my sign not as a rebuke but as a manual version of the wry smile by which it is usually accompanied. The meaning of the word is its use in the language, after all. It's not rare that I speak ironically or ambiguously to my children, and it's not rare that they respond in kind. This has caused many an onlooker to give us a hairy eyeball. What astonishes me, though, is that children seem hard-wired not merely for language but for irony. Where, or how, might we find the region of the brain responsible for *that*? When Nick started full-time day care in Champaign, five years ago, I became a local celebrity among his schoolmates because when one of them asked what I had eaten for breakfast, I said distractedly, "Um, sneakers." This brought about such hilarity that I was asked about my breakfasts on a daily basis, and Nick's four-year-old classmates weren't satisfied until I had exceeded my previous report somehow. Best of all, they liked the deadpan delivery that went awry. When asked about my breakfast, I would have to roll my eyes, think, and carefully enumerate . . . let's see . . . cereal, toast, coffee, juice . . . the tension mounted, the children began to cluster around me . . . and *basketballs*, whereupon they erupted into a cacophony that would not subside until I challenged them all to a game of *who can be the quietest?* and turned them over to their regularly scheduled teachers. I'm perfectly willing to believe we humans have a language "instinct" and that it expresses itself as elegantly in ASL as in spoken English. But I wonder whether our innate capacity for language comes complete with an innate capacity for language *abuse*, like irony—a capacity that allowed my four-year-old Nick to roll *his* eyes at his classmates and complain that his daddy was, as everyone could tell, *too silly*. In those days, we didn't know how to sign.

Unfortunately, even apparently well-educated people often make the mistake of thinking that ASL is a crude derivative of English, capable only of the kind of "speech" once popularly attributed to native American Indians: *Me go out now. Me got many friend. You happy mommy*. Even in the pages of our national newsweeklies you can find columnists inveighing against the use of signing, as if cultural recognition and acceptance of ASL constituted a fatal capitulation to political correctness, one more victory for the PC Reign of Terror blighting our fair land. I've read arguments from people who desperately want to be considered "liberals" yet also want to prevent ASL speakers from competing in school debates and to deny foreign language credit to hearing students who learn ASL. The assumption is always the same: Not only is ASL not a "real" language, it *prevents people from learning* real language. Why, if the deaf and the hearing-impaired would only learn to speak, they wouldn't be trapped in that hand-jive pseudo-talk that *we* mainstream people can't understand. Fortunately, there was no one in our house or in our immediate circle who felt that way. On the contrary, our immediate circle contained a number of people who were fluent ASL speakers, including one woman who's a licensed ASL teacher. When she heard that Jamie had learned a few rudimentary signs, she started to greet him, whenever they met, with a series of signs too rapid and complicated for me to follow—and Jamie just lit up, eagerly watching her every move, trying to imitate even the signs I was sure he didn't understand.

Just as Nick had coached his brother to stand, to walk, and to play catch, so too did he practice signing with James, speaking along with his signs, breaking down individual words for James syllable by syllable. Sometimes he tried to get Jamie to say "ball" while signing *ball*: "b, b, ball," Nick would say dutifully, stressing consonants whenever possible. Sometimes he tried to get Jamie to say preposterous things well beyond his capacity, like "the . . . fish . . . is . . . in . . . the . . . microwave," syllable by syllable, consonant by consonant. So far this second approach hasn't worked very well, though we try not to discourage Nick from giving free language lessons whenever the mood strikes him. To this day, none of us knows the ASL for "microwave."

What Jamie couldn't sign and couldn't say, he could point to—and nothing expanded his repertoire of ostensive definitions so quickly as his books. He was a bibliophile from the minute he learned to turn pages, which, all else being unequal, was remarkably early: He could turn pages before he could use a pincer grip on small objects. Much to the delight and amazement of his DSC therapists, he could "orient" books—that is, turn them right side up—long before he knew up from down in any other context. In that respect, at least, he was definitely born in the right house. Books about animals or the alphabet or colors or numbers or maybe Sesame Street characters were his favorites, until this eclectic group was joined by books about trucks and trains, whereupon the whole batch was superseded by Maurice Sendak's classic *Where the Wild Things Are*, surely a Great Book by any standard. Jamie began by identifying with Max (this was quite clear not only from the frequency with which he pointed to Max but also from the vigorous way he nodded when I asked him if he was like Max)—and then, in one of those "oscillations" described by reader-response criticism and feminist film theory, switched over to identifying with the wild things themselves, roaring his terrible roar and showing his terrible claws.

At first I thought his objects in books were simply more stable, more manageable for him than the objects in the rest of the world; he could expand his pointing vocabulary so much more easily by marking out the world as a text and vice versa. Nick had done the same thing, albeit faster. In fact, Nick demonstrated very early on that he could *memorize* his books, even if we'd only read them to him two or three times. Whenever I would care-lessly get a word wrong or nod off, wearily, in the middle of the narrative (thus provoking the question of just who was reading a bedtime story to whom), Nick would correct me, indignantly, for even the most minor infractions—like substituting *take* for *lead* in the crucial sentence, "but wicked Foxy Woxy did not lead them to the palace." Jamie was beginning to reveal the same for-midable memory, signing for "hush" just before we turned the page and encountered the quiet old lady whispering hush in *Goodnight Moon*, pointing out the little bunny's bookcase and signing for "books" even though the bunny's books are (mysteri-ously) never mentioned in the written text. If his books could help him compensate for everything else that stood in the way of his learning, great. But despite his silence, Jamie was every bit as present in ordinary conversation as he was when he had his wild things laid out in front of him—as we learned one afternoon when, in the middle of a discussion of whether Nick should play baseball, we looked over and saw Jamie following every word he could, pointing to Nick and signing for "ball."

Still, his physical barriers were excruciating to us. The light in his large, deep eyes, the smile that somehow involved his whole body, his charming and helpless laughter—all this told us he was ready to play and to talk about it, too. But all the books in the world could not, of themselves, expand his range of consonants or strengthen his control over his tongue. That was Ofra's job, and Rita and Sara Jane's, and ours. He introduced himself to English phonemes carefully and conservatively, opening with *g* and *k*, the guttural back-of-the-throat consonants he found most congenial to his floppy speech apparatus. Our task, then, was to get him to produce front-of-mouth sounds like *b*, *m*, and *p*. We cast our net as widely as we could. We walked him through the alphabet, not by letter but by sound, starting with the relatively easy ones—*ba, ba, ba, da, da, da, fa, fa, fa, ma, ma, ma, pa, pa, pa*, and so on (actually, *fa* is no slouch). We got right in his face, about eight inches away from his nose—I liked to go through this routine right after changing his diaper—so he'd know that this would be an exercise in mutual cueing. I would give him a close-up look at how the mouth makes consonants and cue him to imitate whatever I did. In return, I'd imitate whatever *he* did, so he could see how it looked on somebody else. Jamie could play this game for over five minutes, particularly when we were putting on his pajamas at bedtime, and by the time we got to *za, za, za*, we had a fair idea of how many consonants' sounds he could make. Five. On a good day, maybe six or seven. I recalled how I'd felt in Brazil, with my knowledge of Portuguese confined to a handful of guidebook phrases and my halting, inadequate French of no use whatsoever. Every day I came back to my hotel exhausted from the effort of trying to talk with cabbies, sales clerks, and wait staff, so much so that I began to feel the language barrier as a physical force, constricting my chest and confounding my tongue. My makeshift signs weren't any good, either. On my first foray into a hardware store in São Paulo, I tried to make whatever gestures would indicate my need for a three-pronged adapter and apparently gave a salesman the idea that I was interested in forming a *ménage à trois*. By that standard, Jamie was doing much better than I. But he still had a longer way to go.

We made our progress reports periodically to Ofra, Rita, and Sara Jane, who gave us exercises for James. Remember, they said, he isn't hearing all those consonants; for some of them, he's faking it by mimicking your mouth movements. So for *m*, we would hum, and place his hands on our lips so he could feel the vibrations; for *b*, we would get in his face even more aggressively, and mold his mouth with our fingers; for *l*, we would give him small chunks of bread in the left side of his mouth—still the smaller side of his face—and see if he could bring the bread to midpoint. This last exercise didn't produce any *la, la, la's*, but it did get his tongue warmed up for omnidirectional palate movement. As he slowly made his way through the language into which he'd been born, he began to pick up more of the basics, and we began to wonder what his first word would be.

Just before his second birthday, he acquired an *l*; his little *lalalalala*'s were exquisite, and he was so proud of them that he made them at all hours, for the most capricious reasons. But his first word, when it came late that summer, had nothing to do with his lalalalatest consonant acquisition; it was something more impressive—and more useful, too, if my similar experience in Brazil was any guide.

Oops.

The first word I'd heard on Brazilian soil was *desculpe*, pardon me, from an Asian woman who'd twice rammed my Achilles tendon with her luggage cart; and sure enough, it was the first word I uttered, too. It's not a bad idea, I decided, if you're new to the territory, to enter the language by way of its apologies. But Jamie, as it happened, had other ideas. His "oops," aside from manifesting a final double consonant both vastly impressive and occasionally messy, was an index of every kind of miscue, whether it was a real mistake, like dropping the toast, or whether it was just too silly, like a tower of blocks falling down with a crash. It even gave rise to a new stanza in one of his lullabies, right after the stanza about the lamb:

I love my Jamie, my Jamie loves me,
I feed my Jamie 'neath the bayberry tree.

My little Jamie goes oops, oops,
My little lambie goes baa, baa,
My little kitty cat goes meow, meow. . . .

You get the idea.

Best of all, "oops" turned out to be the device by which Jamie
tracked his own progress toward walking. His physical therapy
sessions remained thrash-laden, as Ofra began to get more ambitious with his trunk muscles. The image I recall most is of a
shirtless James on top of a green rubber ball maybe two feet in di-
ameter, Ofra trying to get him to support his trunk without leaning on his arms. Jamie would extend a hand onto the ball to
stabilize himself, Ofra would sweep it away. Howling, Jamie
would repel, arching his back to keep himself from falling face
first onto the ball. After a few minutes of this his face would turn
red, or purple, or mottled with screaming, and inevitably I
protested that he wasn't strong enough, that he'd spiral into
bronchospasm. Ofra was solicitous but firm with me as well as
with Jamie. "Let him yell, it is goot for heem," she admonished
me. "His lungs need to expand. His chest needs to expand. He ees
stronger than you think." But when Jamie was clearly tired, Ofra
adjusted her routine and gave him small-motor tasks and bread in
the left side of his mouth. She was determined: He would walk by
the age of two, because he could—as long as he had the strength
and the confidence to get up and stay up. Once he was up, he
could go explore and learn, by getting things for himself—
though I knew this meant he could also learn about the mysteri-
ous things his parents put on tables, like knives and glasses
of water. Yet his walking would make possible his further cognitive development, assuming he didn't run into kitchen knives
first.

Just before he turned two, he took his first steps. Like his first consonants, they were dramatic, hard-won, and few in number. Up to this point he had been scooting around by sitting up and swiveling his legs around his hips, shimmying forward and sideways and describing a kind of curlicue motion around the floor. Now, he would push himself to a stand, and, with his mother or father waiting no more than an adult arm's length away, gingerly raise his right foot, swing his hips awkwardly, and plant the foot a few inches forward. Sometimes he followed through on the left foot as well, but for his earliest steps, he used the left as his base of operations, like the still point of a compass. Needless to say, he didn't travel far. But for now, he didn't need to. At the end of his steps, he would practically fall into his mother's waiting arms, there to be showered with hugs and praise—no small incentive for longer walks, when Janet set him down a few *more* feet away this time, saying, "Again!" and holding out her arms to catch him.

How thrilled he was to find himself capable of walking, and how thrilled he was to *see* himself walking, toddling a few steps in the kitchen, dancing tentatively in front of the black-glass oven door that gave him back a clear reflection of himself. As for his parents, well, after our two years of effort, we hardly had time to be thrilled enough, because no sooner did he learn to walk than we got a phone call informing us that there was an open spot in the Toddler I class at First United Methodist day care. FUM was the place Nick had gone back when his daddy was eating sneakers and basketballs; it's a wonderful place for young children, and they were eager to take on their first "disabled" child—so much so that they helped us arrange with Jamie's therapists at DSC for special "in-service" classes on children with disabilities. We knew many of the staff, of course, thanks to Nick, and we knew it was time for Jamie to get out and see other children. We just didn't know if he was ready.

Take his walking, for instance. Toddler I consisted of children eighteen to twenty-four months old, so Jamie wouldn't be alone in not knowing how to use a potty, but every other child in the class was capable of making FUM's daily walks to the park three blocks away, or the fire station around the corner. As of Jamie's first day at FUM, he had taken all of seven steps consecutively, from the living room couch to the end of the coffee table, and we had treated that accomplishment as if he'd completed his first marathon. How could he handle the morning and afternoon walks to the park when he couldn't yet make it out of a room on his own? Olga and Marcia, the Toddler I teachers, assured us that they could accommodate James easily. Toddler I went to the park in two groups, each of whom walked alongside a small wagon. When Jamie got tired, he could simply ride *in* the wagon. "Okay," we said, skeptically, "but for a while he'll probably be riding in the wagon almost the whole way." That was fine, replied Olga and Marcia. Just you watch, they said, and by the spring he'll be a full partner.

We went home and typed up a three-page introduction to James, from his signs to his eating habits to his unstable verte-brae, closing our letter by saying that in an emergency, one of us would always be available either at home or at the English building, that we loved our Jamie passionately and wanted him to have the best life possible, and that we were grateful to FUM for including him in Toddler I, because we knew it would get him off to a great start. But still we had our doubts—not about FUM but about James. His social and cognitive skills were clearly advanced enough for the Toddler I group, but his physical skills placed him closer to the entry level of Infant II, twelve to eighteen months.

We even had a guilty sense that we shouldn't be putting James in day care at all. Just as many parents, most of them mothers, are made to feel guilty for working full time to cover for the decline in American workers' wages (and the concomitant explosion in executive wages), so too did we wonder whether we were abdicating our responsibility to make every waking hour with James into one-on-one developmental therapy. He had only just learned to toddle, let alone Toddle I, and he had but one word at his disposal, vastly useful though it might be. Was it right for us to think about day care, or should we wait another year?

That question got itself answered more quickly than we had imagined possible. Within weeks, Jamie was walking across rooms, picking up new words, and memorizing new finger-plays and songs. Every time he reached a new walking milestone, Olga and Marcia relayed it to us the minute we showed up in the afternoon: he made it all the way down the hall; he made it all the way down the hall and out to the front door; he made it all the way *to the corner*. Something important was happening here, and even though we knew how much Nick had meant to Jamie's development, we had sadly underestimated its potential: Jamie was *modeling*. It was one thing for him to see his parents walking, or his big brother, or other children on TV; it was quite another for him to be playing in a room alongside a dozen humans his size who could obviously amble around for toys with much greater facility than he. Toddler I was not quite a Hobbesian state of nature, mind you; there was no brutal competition for playthings in which the race went always to the swift. Quite the contrary. Jamie's classmates saw to it that he was always part of the gang, they encouraged him to walk and talk and interact, and they even gave him a nickname. Because he was "Jamie B.," to distinguish him from a little girl named Jamie L., and because most of Tod-

dler I couldn't say "Jamie B.," he soon became "B." And from
what we saw and heard, B. had plenty of friends, some of whom
had a faint idea that he was "special," and some of whom simply
liked him because he was nice. In return, Jamie taught the whole
class his new sounds: how to moo like a cow, bark like a dog, baa
like a sheep, hoo like an owl, cluck like a hen (great tongue exercise), and roar like a wild thing (a Toddler I favorite). The only
drawback, we found, was that Jamie now knew songs and routines of which his parents were ignorant, as I learned one night
while singing James to sleep, when Jamie suddenly sat up in my
arms and put both his arms over his head in a circle. Something
about the sunshine? Jamie shook his head and made the sign
more emphatically, tapping his hands together. I was at a loss,
and, agonizingly, told him so. For his part, he couldn't believe
how obtuse his daddy had become: *Hands in circle over head, dad,
hands in circle over head!! What part of "hands in circle over head"
don't you understand?*

The next morning when I dropped him off at FUM, I asked
Marcia if she knew what Jamie's sign meant, and she said, "Oh,
yes, that's Mister Moon."

O Mister Moon, Moon, bright and shiny moon,
    (hands in circle over head)
Hiding behind the trees,
    (fingers in front of face)
I want to look at you with my big telescope,
    (two cupped hands to the right eye)
You look so close I could lasso you with a rope.
    (swinging motion with right arm)
O Mister Moon, Moon, bright and shiny moon,
    (hands in circle over head)

Won't you please shine down on, please shine down on, please shine
   down on me,
      (hands from sky to shoulders each time)
O Mister Moooooooon. . . .
      (wiggling hands to and fro)

And there was "Hurry, Hurry, Find the Fire Truck," too, not to mention "Five Little Monkeys." I made sure to get a copy of the lyrics to these, so his parents wouldn't be so woefully behind the curve.

But the lesson for the day was pretty clear: Jamie would not grow up on his own, any more than you or I did. He would construct his sense of self by routing it through the actions and reactions of others, and they would help him become Jamie—just as he would eventually learn to feed himself by emulating other children, particularly one young child named Ellen who visited his house, sat in his high chair, and wolfed down everything that didn't move, all of which impressed Jamie more than he could say. He would become an individual little human, and perhaps someday he would even achieve the kind of individual autonomy that's been prized in the Western world, since the eighteenth century or thereabouts, as the philosophical foundation for political and ethical action, but he would achieve these things partly by modeling, partly with a little help from his friends. If he were to walk and talk like the rest of the semi-autonomous individuals in his peer groups, at age two or at twenty-two, he would need a lot of support. He would realize his individual potential only by leaning on our mutual human interdependence—just like everyone else, only a bit more so.

By the time Jamie started walking and talking, we knew how much his newfound independence depended on his dependence on others. He had a creative and sympathetic primary physician from the moment he was born—Donald Davison, who performed that first tracheoscopy, watched him through his first precarious weeks, guided him through season after season of colds and ear infections, wrote meticulously detailed reports and referrals, and never failed to tell him when he was doing just *great*. He had Ofra Tandoor, he had Sara Jane Annin, he had Rita Huddle and Nancy Yeagle, all of whom collectively hauled him up onto his own two feet, as the saying goes, giving him two good legs to stand on. Just before Ofra returned to Israel, Jamie gave her a little surprise: a fine-motor skill even she didn't think him capable of. Here's the church, and here's the steeple, open the doors, and see all the people. And now all those people included Olga, Marcia, and his twelve playmates at First United Methodist, the ones with whom he walked to the park twice every day, weather permitting.

By December, he was another child. Our videotapes of the holidays capture him strolling around the house confidently, chasing Nick, taking his first stabs at walking up the stairs. By the next spring, he could make it to the park and back, most of the time. His gait was halting and inelegant, for he walked with a wide base that only another year of physical therapy would diminish: His torso was still quite weak, and he compensated for the weakness by splaying his legs widely, like a tripod without a third leg. It would be some time before he could center his feet under his shoulders, and a longer time still before he would be stable enough to think about running. But he was walking, he was making the sign for walking, and he was even trying to *say* "walking," the all-important present participle. Then one April evening we saw him on the local news. There was a story about the legal status of gay and lesbian couples who wanted to adopt children, and for some reason, the news illustrated this story by using some stock kid footage taken in Champaign's West Side Park, where the FUM toddlers were toddling around alongside their wagons. For a few seconds, the camera focused on Jamie alone, pushing from the back of the first wagon. Janet and I snapped to attention: Our Jamie was on television, walking through the park. What did this mean? He wasn't up for adoption; no couples, gay or straight, were applying to be his caretakers; he was just a generic Child in the background, unwittingly illustrating a news story about children and parenting. After we thought about it for a few minutes, we decided we couldn't be more pleased. Not only was our idiosyncratic Jamie an autonomous individual creature, but also, for a few brief seconds, he had become representative of children in general. At least in that respect, we thought, the local news had gotten the story pretty much exactly right.

■

CHAPTER FIVE

Bragging and Rights

▲

In November 1995, a story went out over the AP newswire about a young man named Luke Zimmerman, a 5-foot-4, 130-pound tailback for the Beverly Hills High School football team. According to the story, Luke has only been in for four plays all season and has never touched the ball but is acknowledged as a leader and an inspiration to his teammates. Luke is sixteen, and he has Down syndrome; his story is one of many, but simply because he is indelibly a member of a group, his own story necessarily stands in for all people with Down syndrome. In that respect, Luke, like Jamie, both is and is not an individual, both is and is not like everyone else. At the very least, his life and his story serve as testimony to what people with Down syndrome can achieve; their achievements, in turn, affect the perceptions of the nondisabled population; and the perceptions of the nondisabled population can have an enormous impact on what people with Down syndrome can achieve. It's something of a shock, then, when you find that the fourth paragraph of the AP story contains the information that "Down syndrome children usually never develop beyond age eight mentally." That one sentence—mistaken, erroneous, misleading—unfortunately frames Luke and all that he might potentially signify. *He's changing people's expectations, sure, but there are limits to what he can know, and* we *know precisely what those limits are.* One parent of a child with Down's reacted to this story with an aplomb that deflected his outrage: Since most newspapers are pitched at a third-grade reading level, he noted, even Luke's "peak" mental age should serve him just fine for reading stories off the AP wire.

For my part, I sometimes feel cornered by talking about Jamie's intelligence, as if the burden of proof is on me, official spokesman on his behalf. It's not unlike the feeling I had some years ago when I was first looking for an academic job and university hiring committees quizzed me about one of the subjects of my dissertation, the forgotten African-American poet Melvin Tolson. "Sure he's interesting," people would say, "and sure, we've neglected the work of any number of black poets, and sure, we know how variable 'aesthetic value' can be, and sure, you've written two hundred very compelling pages about him, but look, the bottom line is this. We just want to know, between you and us— *Is he any good?*" This time the question is different on the surface—*How smart is he, honestly?* or, *In the end, aren't you disappointed to have a retarded child?*—but underneath there's the same subtext: *Do we really have to give this person our full attention?* And underneath that: *Why should we? After all, the burden of proof is yours. Say all you want about the variability of aesthetic judgment or the multiplicity of human intelligences, but let's get to the bottom line and let's do it now. Is this person sufficiently similar to the people we already value?*

I've been taking intelligence tests for as long as I can remember. My parents tell me that when they scheduled my first test, at four, they simply wanted to know if I should be placed in "gifted" classes, since I was reading flashcards within six hours after emerging from the womb, or something like that. Thirty years later, looking back over my permanent record, I draw three lessons from my history as an SAT brat: one, that I grew up in a house that valued measurable forms of intelligence; two, that I learned very early on how to do well in intelligence tests; three, that this self-referential form of knowledge has served me very well in a culture that sorts its citizens by means of intelligence and aptitude tests. By the time I was seventeen I regarded my tests more or less as high-grade versions of the *New York Times* crossword puzzle. Like the crossword puzzle, the tests were very reliable, which meant that individual test takers tended to produce the same results over time. (Whether the tests are "valid" as well as reliable—that is, whether they test something worth testing—is a question that will not be resolved by mere human inquiry.) But like crossword puzzles, the tests seemed to value the kind of knowledge that was specific to test taking—and I was the kind of child who clearly lacked some practical forms of intelligence, like a sense of when to wear a coat, or a sense of how to comport yourself in a manner that would lead people to invite you back for dinner. Thus, I was admitted to an Ivy League university regardless of the fact that I had the social skills of a frog. In retrospect, the narrowness of my tests seems to pose a serious ethical problem. Imagine the outcry if we allocated admissions to elite colleges on the basis of whether high school students knew how to use crossword-staple words like *stoa*, *oleo*, and *alar*. (The very fact that SAT preparation courses boost their students' scores is evidence that the tests are measuring something other than "scholastic aptitude" in a pure sense.) Or if college admissions seem too mundane, imagine a society and a testing system that undervalues the interpersonal skills of its prospective doctors and lawyers.

So by the time I became a parent, I was more than ready to

cast a cold eye on intelligence testing. Yet our first child turned up "gifted." Like every other American child, he's tested anew every year; unlike most other American children, he places somewhere in the top 1–5 percent of test takers nationwide. Jamie's first official test, at age two, pegged his IQ somewhere in the low to mid-60s—but the test also suggested such a wide "scatter" of talents and abilities that we were advised not to put our trust in numerical accuracy. We were told that some of his skills were "age-appropriate," some "near normal," some significantly delayed . . . and that besides, IQ tests aren't very accurate until the age of five or thereabouts (which is why many researchers claim that IQ can be strongly influenced by "early intervention" and programs like Head Start). We didn't think too much of this, but then, we didn't think that we'd ever run up against people who would weigh our Jamie in the balance of an IQ test and find him expendable. We thought that most people knew that intelligence comes in many forms and many guises. Developmental psychologist Howard Gardner describes seven intelligences—linguistic, logical-mathematical, interpersonal, intrapersonal, spatial, musical, and bodily-kinesthetic—only two of which are currently tested (on the verbal and mathematical sections of the SAT, of course). We could chart Jamie's development on all seven scales, if need be, but we usually don't expect to go to such lengths just to make a case for his intelligence.

Still, how smart is he, really? To answer this question is to play with a stacked deck, since Jamie's "smartness" isn't really the most important thing about him. But every once in a while parents of "disabled" children have to do some bragging, partly to remind themselves of how much their kids have accomplished, and partly to get the rest of the world to readjust its expectations of our children. We want those expectations adjusted upward, of course, and we hope our children make the news for their *abilities* rather than their disabilities. But more than this, we want some-day to live in a world where the achievements of people with dis-abilities are so widely recognized and so universally lauded that they're practically a regular feature in the news. So, on occasion, we brag.

When James turned three, he became ineligible for further DSC treatment; from this point on, he was referred to Illinois' public school system and assigned to a school commensurate with his needs. First, then, Jamie's teachers, therapists, and parents had to hash out what that phrase might mean: *commensurate with his needs*. In order for our school district to assess Jamie's needs and abilities, they had to give him an intelligence test. Jamie wouldn't take the test without me by his side, so while Janet talked to a speech pathologist in the next room, Jamie took his test as I looked over his shoulder. Three or four people adminis-tered the test. I dutifully reported to them that Jamie knew the names of colors and could count to ten; each of these talents placed him well within the range of "normal" three year olds. The test proceeded somewhat oddly. Jamie's testers wanted to make sure he wasn't giving them false positives, so they held up an 8 and asked him, "Is this a 4?" Jamie, being a complaisant soul, seemed to accede to this absurd question. I grew alarmed. Nei-ther Janet nor I had ever asked him trick questions, questions to which the answer was an obvious *no*. For now, Jamie was willing to call an 8 a 4 if he thought that was part of the game. It wasn't until some months later that he learned how hilarious it is to be deliberately facetious, bamboozling the adults by claiming that his name is Rick, that he's ten years old, or that goats and horses ride on the school bus.

So with all the sincerity and good will in the world, he correctly identified objects like triangles, fish, and trees; he even flagged "flag," a word I didn't know he knew. But it was clear that the test wasn't capturing—that is, wasn't *re-presenting*—a workable idea of Jamie's smarts. So I intervened. I explained that we never, never asked him whether an 8 was a 4. We knew that he knew the single-digit integers by their shape, not by their order, such that he could name a 5 regardless of whether it followed a 4 or a 9. What's more, we'd found that he understood the *concepts* embedded in these numbers, such that he could look at three objects and say "three." But most important, I explained, Jamie's intelligence has very little to do with what he can say. Let me give you an example, I said. I have recently found that Jamie will sometimes shrug his shoulders, turn both palms upward, and say "B? B?" in a quizzical voice. Only after a week or so of this did I realize what kind of iceberg lay under the water. Although my little boy couldn't voice the entire thought, he was saying, *Where can it be? Where can it be?* And the reason I know *that* is that he says "B" on only two occasions. One is when I'm scrambling around the house looking for my keys, my wallet, or my coat. The other is when I circle back down the same aisle in the supermarket, turning the cart 180 degrees and heading back in the opposite direction. Somehow, Jamie knows when I'm looking for something. His eyes catch something in my eyes, or his eyes catch the cereal boxes floating past him in reverse order, and he knows: *Something must be found. I know that Daddy is looking for something. I want to let Daddy know that I know he is looking for something. Where can it be?*

What he couldn't say, Jamie had compressed into a phoneme, into a letter. He knew he couldn't hand me the thing, whatever it was, but he knew he could bond with me, verbally, as a fellow searcher. *I know what you're thinking*, he says. *Where can it be? Let's find this thing, Dad.* He only says this in context, when it's appropriate: never when we're eating dinner, but *always* when we need to know the location of keys, wallets, or the spaghetti sauces in aisle 3. Now tell me, I charged Jamie's testers, tell me of the "intelligence" test that can record a form of human intelligence as specific as this.

Jamie's had his unsolicited breakthrough moments, too, just as Nick did. With Nick, it was the morning he opened his Dr. Seuss ABC, pointed to an F, and said, "F." He was just over a year old. Jamie was three when he offered us his version of this trick, but when Jamie spoke up, it was to say "Georgia" and "Hawaii" as he flipped through Nick's book of the fifty states. By that point in his life, Jamie had learned that he could astonish his parents and therapists every now and then—by walking up a stair or two, by clasping his hands into *here's the church, and here's the steeple*, or by riding a toddler bike down the hallway—and sure enough, when Janet and I turned to Jamie on the dining room floor and shrieked, "*What did you say?*" he replied with a sly, bird-eating grin that said, *Ha! you didn't know I'd been memorizing the states, did you?*

The moment was especially weird because Nick, too, has been a map maven since the age of three. Janet's childhood was relatively map-free, but I remember that when I was little, I filled page after page of scrap paper with the minute cartographic details of imaginary lands. Is it possible that Janet and I bequeathed to both our children a fondness for geography, or that there is a dominant mapmaking allele for which I alone am responsible? I suppose it's more likely that Jamie was emulating his big brother the map maven. For that matter, you could explain his predilections for states by noting that our house is festooned with maps, regardless of whether our genomes are festooned with mapmaking alleles. Still, Jamie shares many, many quirks with his brother, and this is one of them: the desire—and, just as important, the capacity—to memorize and reproduce entire lists of objects, like states.

But Jamie is not quite Nick's equal. By the time Nick was four, he could not only name all the states in the book, but he could identify them by shape *outside* the book as well, sometimes even if he'd only seen part of the shape. Jamie could claim no such uncanny proficiency. After he'd more or less memorized the archive, he still couldn't recognize the states outside the states book. In other words, Jamie could apparently catalog and retrieve raw information nearly as well as his brother, and there was no doubt that he had a remarkable memory by any standard; but he couldn't abstract that information or reflect on it at whatever the next conceptual level might be, the level at which humans are able to manipulate odd shapes like Georgia mentally.

"So he was just memorizing the book," one of my friends once said. "He didn't really learn the names of the states."

Well, I replied, that happens to be an *extremely* interesting question. When, in fact, can we say that we have "learned" something, and when are we merely relying on short-term memory? Memory by itself is no big thing; even chickens can learn to hit a lever to get a pellet. But if memory is one of the preconditions for the possibility of intelligent thought, and if "intelligent" people tend also to be efficient storers and retrievers of information, then memory and intelligence must be at once inextricable and distinct. The question is, When has your memory led you *past* memory? How do we know when an item has passed from the mind's holding area to the long-term storage bin? If you've ever tied your shoes without thinking about it, then you've learned something and made it automatic, almost as if you'd turned over the thinking to your fingers so that your brain could go about something else. At some point in that process, your memory hooked up with a series of other cognitive processes, such that although you may know how to tie your shoes, you're not likely to say, "I *remember* how to tie my shoes." But what had Jamie learned by reading Nick's states book? Had he in fact learned something about distinctive shapes and names, or had he merely learned to memorize a series of items?

Well, just ask any child. When Nick was two, he could recognize the red sign saying **BEST** outside our local Best store in Charlottesville, Virginia, but he couldn't read "best" if it were on the page just like so. Jamie knows how to recognize—and say— "EXIT" when it's on an exit sign, and what's more, when I say, "'exit' means we go. . . ," he dutifully says, "Out!" and points out the nearest door. Still, he can't yet read "exit" when I write it on the page. Conversely, he can't read "taco," but he's never failed to spot a Taco Bell sign and (shortly thereafter) to propose that we eat some tacos. So for now, he's a good consumer but a poor critic. In this, I suspect, he is not alone.

He can read the entire alphabet, and he even knows all the sounds the letters make. But the only words he can read consistently are "Jamie" and "James," and after we spell out the latter version, he almost always says, "two lines," since = is his symbol in his day care class. James =. Every child has a symbol next to his or her name; James' just happens to be =, and he even calls it his "symbol." He can't say "s" very well unless he's imitating a snake, so it sounds more like "timbo" when he tries it. Most of his classmates, who are a year younger than James, can speak with far greater fluency than he can, though most of them can't read, either. None of those classmates can count to forty the way Jamie can, even if he does sometimes omit "fifteen" or say "twenty-ten"

for thirty. And few children in his class have Jamie's sense of the-
atricality or mock ventriloquism: one of Jamie's favorite games,
for instance, is to play "two monkeys" with a hand puppet that
looks like a toucan. First the bird sings the song about how one
little monkey fell out of bed, then the bird falls over, and then the
bird gets back up, shaking his head, whereupon a giggling Jamie
says, "Wait a minute! *That's* not right," mimicking the way the
bird once said (with my voice), "Wait a minute! *That's* not right,
the *bird* doesn't fall out of bed!" These days, Jamie's version of
this game is more intricate. Puppet or no puppet, Jamie pretends
that *he's* operating the toucan, and though his classmates can't see
the imaginary bird, they do see Jamie wagging his hand back and
forth, saying, "Wait a minute! *That's* not right," whenever he sees
something comically out of the ordinary. In other words, my kid's
not that good at abstract thinking, but he's got a great memory,
he's a whiz at counting, and he's got a great ear for slapstick. So
perhaps my James Two Lines is, in some respects, the equal of his
classmates after all. He knows all their names, and he knows all
their symbols, too: you can ask him about Nykesha's symbol, and
he will say "X," and he'll be right. You can ask him who his
teachers are, and he can tell you. He's learned that information,
he's memorized it, but most important, in both a personal and a
philosophical sense, he *understands* it.

One of the reasons I like Ludwig Wittgenstein so much is that he
asks such crabby questions and addresses them in so particularly
unphilosophic a fashion. You'll be rolling along, reading about
games and lines and family resemblances, and all of a sudden, he
turns on you and says, "When are you really reading and not just
memorizing?" Or if that seems too simple, how about, "What

does it mean to 'understand' something?" Can you understand something for just a second, or is "understanding" something more tenacious, not quite permanent—something more like a mental state? Wittgenstein writes:

> "Understanding a word": a state. But a *mental* state?—Depression, excitement, pain, are called mental states. Carry out a grammatical investigation as follows: we say
>> "He was depressed the whole day."
>> "He was in great excitement the whole day."
>> "He has been in continuous pain since yesterday."—
>> We also say "Since yesterday I have understood this word."
> "Continuously," though?—To be sure, one can speak of an interruption of understanding. But in what cases? Compare: "When did your pains get less?" and "When did you stop understanding that word?"

Part of Wittgenstein's point, obvious though it may seem, is that we really can understand something about understanding merely by looking closely at the way we talk about it. *Look at the way your language game is played*, Wittgenstein tells us, *and you'll learn what you need to know about the players.* Certainly, we know there's a difference between memorizing a states book and "understanding" it, just as there's a difference between being able to recognize a sign and being able to read. And certainly, few humans say things like "You know what? I understood the word all day."

But you know what? Children say things like that all the time—partly because they're learning new words every couple of hours or so, and partly because, along with new words, they're slowly learning the rules of their language game. They don't yet know better than to say, "I understood the word all day." Indeed, any number of toddlers might find that a perfectly reasonable rendition of the facts. But they can't say exactly when they stopped memorizing and started understanding, any more than they know not to say "It felled me" when they fall off a chair or "Mommy, do you have a penis?" in a crowded shoe store. The first mistake, obvious but arcane, involves knowing transitive from intransitive verb forms in English; the second mistake is more social than grammatical, and more embarrassing—as Janet learned when two-year-old Nick blurted it out one afternoon in a crowded shoe store.

I know that when I was a child I memorized words long before I could "read" them. I wasn't really reading the word *grandmother* on my flash cards; the word was too long and confusing. But I knew it was the card for "grandmother" nonetheless, in part because it had a picture of an elderly woman in a rocking chair, and in part because I knew the longest word on my flash cards would always be "grandmother." I kept up the pretense because I was rewarded for it: my "reading" dazzled the adults in the room, especially my grandmother. I eventually learned the word and continued using it long after I had any living grandmothers to apply it to. Yet it would be a mistake to think that memorization is merely a temporary stage we pass through on the way to real knowledge. It *is* that, but it isn't *only* that. Your memory has enabled you to learn X, but even when you thoroughly understand X (or you say you do), you still need to draw on the skills that helped you learn X in the first place. It is impossible, for example, to master irregular verb forms or irregular plural nouns in English except by memorizing them: I have one goose, two geese, I haved one moose, two meese.

So no, Jamie can't read yet, and I'm not sure how fluent his reading will be, when it comes. Nor can I predict how well his reading will translate into speech. His speech therapy is still largely a series of exercises in trying to get him to expose more of the iceberg lying underneath his words. His therapists try "expansion," trying to get him to move from one word to two, from two words to three, but for James, the transition from one word to two was about as momentous and difficult as the planet's transition from one-celled to two-celled life. *That* transition took anywhere between one and two billion years; James's was somewhat quicker. But only somewhat. Every time we got him to expand, he would contract again, knowing that saying "car" would be sufficient to distinguish a car from his other toys and that "green" would be sufficient to distinguish a green car from twenty other cars. It follows, then, that one would never need to say something so prolix as "green car."

Sometimes the thought below the surface was larger and more elaborate than I could imagine. One Friday afternoon I picked Jamie up from day care only to have him greet me with "Pizza!" "You want to get a pizza," I said, to chortles from James. Then came what seemed to be a non sequitur. "Heidi," he added, naming his favorite babysitter. "Oh, *I* see," I laughed. "You want Heidi to come *and* you want to get a pizza." It was as if he'd had the entire evening planned—Heidi, pizza, maybe a movie, then back to his place for a few drinks. I hadn't expected adolescence to arrive so soon, or to express itself in only two words.

Terri McKenzie, his in-school therapist, makes videotapes of Jamie and shows us how to "parallel talk" while he plays, and reminds us to limit the number of questions we ask him. "Parallel talking" is another term for running commentary: *You are playing with blocks. You put the red block on top.* This not only describes Jamie's actions for him but also lets him know that his actions can be made into a narrative. The general idea is to let Jamie learn the language by hearing it, not by asking him questions; questions often do nothing but confuse him, just as they would confuse anyone trying to learn a new language. Similarly, just as we have to learn to foster his receptive abilities, he has to learn to enhance his expressive abilities. While Terri works on parallel talking, then, Jamie Smith, his HMO therapist, does oral exercises and tries to get a string of five morphemes from him. *Bears go running*: that's a bear, a plural, a verb, another verb, and a present-participle ending. Five morphemes. James usually cuts it down to three or four. Yet he clearly understands what a present participle is for. When he's asked, "What is the bear doing?" he brightly says, "running," or "sleeping," or "playing," depending on what the bear is in fact doing. He's learned an important grammatical rule, I think—or maybe he's just memorized it.

I'm not being facetious. For two sessions, Jamie the HMO therapist worked on getting Jamie the HMO client to say possessive *s*. She advised me to ask Jamie questions the answers to which were possessives, such as "Whose feet are these?" *Jamie's*! or "Whose bed are you in?" *Nick's*! But Jamie dropped the project after one of James's audiology tests was forwarded to her. The test showed that James's hearing loss was preventing him from hearing sibilants like *s*, *f*, and *th*, so there was no point, clearly, in getting him to produce possessive esses. "But he's been doing it," I noted, turning to James and saying, "Whose feet are these?" "Jamie't," Jamie promptly replied, doing his usual substitution of *t* for a hard *s*. He couldn't hear it distinctly, and he couldn't produce it correctly, either, but he'd learned a grammatical rule—or so I thought. Jamie the therapist suggested he might be learning the possessive, maybe, but then again, he might just be imitating it.

Now, *wait* a minute. *That's* not right. How can Jamie "imitate" a possessive *s*? Jamie can't tie his shoes, nor can he plausibly pretend he's tying *my* shoes—though this does not stop him from trying. Let's put that another way. If James doesn't really "know" possessive *s*, then what does it mean to be able to imitate something you can't do? And where's Wittgenstein when I need him?

It's not that I want Jamie to learn "proper grammar"; when he's bigger he can split all the infinitives he wants and end every sentence with every preposition he can think of. It's just that I want other people to·treat him as a full partner, and I want his therapists to know everything he knows but can't say. Grammar gets a bad rap. Most people associate it with phonics, pointers, incomprehensible regulations, discipline, hair buns, and bizarre mnemonic devices they'll never remember. But you can go a long way when you know how to produce a grammar—especially if you can't say too many words at once. One day just after Jamie had turned three, he and I were doing a Sesame Street song he likes, a cool, jazzy number sung by Telly Monster and Elmo as they illustrate the difference between heavy and light. Elmo carries a feather, and Telly, being something of a sad sack, gets to carry around a load of bricks that eventually gets the better of him at the end of the third verse. Elmo opens the song:

> *Elmo and Telly proudly invite*
> *You to watch a demonstration of heavy and light.*
> *Pay attention so you get it right,*
> *'Cause Telly's is heavy, and Elmo's is light!*

A few hours later that afternoon, when I asked Jamie to carry his plate to the sink, he told me it was heavy, whereupon I not only took the plate from him but also asked him, "Who carries what is heavy?" This was a trick. Indeed, Janet often accuses me, and rightly so, of uttering contextless phrases that refer implicitly to conversations conducted days or years earlier—driving down the road and suddenly saying, "and another thing about Chernobyl. . . ," picking up from where we'd left off in 1986. But Jamie knew perfectly well what I meant. He cocked his head and thought hard: *Who carries what is heavy?* I had never even asked him a "who" question with a "what" in it before.

After a second Jamie said, "Telly."

He'd understood the lesson Elmo and Telly had taught him, and he'd correctly applied it to his heavy plate; but more than this, he could pick up the lesson as a sentence and toss it around with his mental grammar, too. Proud as I was, I merely said to James, calm and smiling, "That's right. Telly carries what is heavy." Then I told the story to Janet, Nick, and pretty near everyone who'd ever met Jamie—especially his speech therapists.

Yet all this is still rote memorization; maybe even a bright chimp could learn to point to Telly, memorize states, and ask to stop at Taco Bell. Perhaps, then, a better measure of Jamie is his ability to figure out things all on his own, unprompted by either of his prodding parents. There was the time Jamie piped up from the back seat and said "Kate, Kate"—not the stuff of genius, perhaps, but clear evidence that he knew we were heading north on North Lincoln Avenue, along the route he and I took every Tuesday to see Kate Garth, the physical therapist who'd taken over Jamie's care when Ofra Tandoor returned to Israel. But even then, so what? Maybe Jamie, like that Benjy at the end of *The Sound and the Fury*, had merely memorized the passing landmarks. Jamie likes routines; they reinforce his memories, and his memories are all the more useful when they're reinforced. But Benjy can't stand it when his routine goes awry. When his servant, Luster, leads the carriage the wrong way on Benjy's Sunday trip to the Compson graveyard, Benjy begins to howl, full of sound and fury: "Bellow on bellow, his voice mounted, with scarce interval for breath. There was more than astonishment in it, it was horror; shock; agony eyeless, tongueless; just sound." Not until the carriage swings around does Benjy hush, "his eyes . . . empty and blue and serene again as cornice and façade flowed smoothly once more from left to right, post and tree, window and doorway and signboard each in its ordered place." So goes the novel's famous but enigmatic conclusion: an experimental narrative about decay and dissolution ends with an image of order trivial to us but crucial to Benjy, the novel's least competent narrator. Here, apparently, the adult Benjy has memorized something about order but hasn't quite understood it. Jamie, too, knew the sequence of turns, fences, open fields, gas stations, and road signs that led to Kate, Kate, Kate. But imagine my astonishment when one day I came off the interstate heading *south* on North Lincoln (something I almost never do), only to hear my three-year-old peep, "Kate." *He hadn't merely memorized a sequence. He knew exactly where he was*, almost as if he had stored a visual map of the environs as seen from above.

Of course, most of us humans learn to do this, as Wittgenstein might say, without thinking about it (unless we say, "I remembered the directions all day"). But not all of us, not even those of us with forty-six chromosomes, can do it so efficiently, so smoothly. Some of us careen around town as if we'd been blindfolded and spun around three times. As it happens, Jamie's mother has almost no spatial orientation to speak of and habitually refers to herself as the Wandering Goy. She also finds it difficult to operate a computer by using a mouse, partly because she can't coordinate the movement of the mouse with the location of the cursor on the screen, but Jamie finds the mouse the most natural thing in the world—as we discovered one afternoon when we entered the playroom to find that Jamie had seated himself at the computer, exited from Nick's "Civilization" game, and clicked on the correct icon for "Millie's Math House" instead.

Then there was the morning Jamie spotted Nancy Yeagle's car in the parking lot. Had we planned this as an experiment it couldn't have been more controlled: Janet and Jamie arrived early one day to his weekly occupational therapy appointment with Nancy. After a few minutes, Nancy drove up in a nondescript cream-colored Subaru, and when she got out of the car, Jamie recognized her, saying, "Mincy, Mincy." As far as we can tell, that was the first time he saw Nancy in her car. The therapy session lasted half an hour, and then Jamie went to day care. Nancy's son Langston goes to the same day care at FUM. That afternoon, when Janet retrieved Jamie from FUM, they walked out into the gathering dusk, and as they entered the parking lot, Jamie said "Mincy" and pointed to her car, a generic cream-colored Subaru recognizable only because Nancy had emerged from it earlier in the day.

I thought that was pretty damn smart. Almost as memorable as the day he found me sleeping on the couch, toddled across the floor, and got a blanket to cover me. When Janet told me about this, I was just floored. *Empathy*. Doesn't that count as a form of intelligence, too? Janet and I disagreed on this one. I insisted that Jamie was seeing to my needs as I would to his. He had learned reciprocity, and he was physically mature enough to do something about it. Janet said he was just imitating something he'd seen other empathetic people do. I still think Janet's wrong, but even if she's right, then James's is an accomplishment worth pondering: Along with imitating a possessive *s* he couldn't hear, it

would seem, he had also learned to imitate a virtue he didn't possess.

These days, we find we're more vigilant about reporting Jamie's
cognitive development than about recording his physical
progress, and for good reason: In a tangible sense, his physical
progress reports itself. For a long time after James became capable of walking up and down stairs, our major concern was to get
him doing those standard kid activities—running and jumping.
Before too long he managed to break into a fast walk, swing his
left arm, and say, "Running!" Before too long he began punctuat-
ing his most emphatic no's with small jumps. This made Jamie
all the cuter, and it made physical therapy all the easier, because
when we had to teach him how to raise a ball over his head (trunk
muscles) or stand on one foot and kick (quadriceps), we were able
to do PT by disguising it as basketball and soccer. So it will be
when he learns to dress himself and use the toilet: the record of
those accomplishments will be fairly visible. His mental abilities,
however, rarely manifest themselves on their own. He doesn't talk
to strangers about who carries what is heavy, and he's often quite
difficult to understand even when he does say clever things. A
year ago he was saying something that sounded like "tree" when
he wanted to watch Sesame Street; last week he turned to me
while we were playing downstairs and said, "Daddy be right
back." Since I wasn't going anywhere and told him so, he had to
gesture upstairs repeatedly and say, "peanut butter jelly" and
"Daddy do it" before I understood that he was ordering me to
leave the room, to make him a peanut butter and jelly sandwich,
and to be right back. I did no such thing, of course, since he's not
allowed to eat in the playroom, but I immediately made a mental

note to relate this little peroration to his speech therapists at my first opportunity. Sometimes Jamie cannot represent himself; he must be represented.

In fact, our representations of him are crucial—even legally necessary—to his education and social development. When it comes time to draw up his annual IEP, we have to consult with his teachers and therapists to determine how he can best receive a FAPE in the LRE under IDEA. We also had to learn a whole new alphabet. But I suppose that goes without saying.

In 1975, Congress passed Public Law 94-142, the Education for All Handicapped Children Act; in 1990 the law was renamed the Individuals with Disabilities Education Act, or IDEA. As the term "handicapped" has gradually dropped out of our official lexicon of disability, we update the names of our laws even when we don't change their content. Sometimes we even change the name and keep the acronym, as when Champaign's Department of Services for Crippled Children became the Department of Specialized Care for Children. For some people, the new terminology sounds merely like euphemism; to some people it sounds too politically correct; to some people it sounds like the soul of sense. A rose by any other name might smell as sweet and yet have different social connotations. Under IDEA, all "children with disabilities" are entitled to a "free appropriate public education" (FAPE) in the "least restrictive environment" (LRE); accordingly, to "the maximum extent appropriate," children with disabilities must be educated alongside their nondisabled peers. The law explicitly requires that "special classes, special schooling or other removal of children with disabilities from the regular educational environment occurs only when the nature or the severity of the disability is such that education in regular classes with the use of supplementary aids and services cannot be achieved satisfactorily." I'm not quoting all this material to be pedantic. Every word here is freighted with ore—and contested anew in lawsuit upon lawsuit. What *is* the least restrictive environment, or the maximum extent appropriate? What is a free appropriate education, and who's supposed to be "satisfied" when education in regular classes "cannot be achieved satisfactorily"? Even the most basic terms call out for further definition. "Children with disabilities," for instance, names a more restricted group than "individuals with handicaps," who are covered by Section 504 of the Rehabilitation Act of 1973. If you flip through Volume 20, Section 1401 of the United States Code, you'll find that for the purposes of IDEA, "The term 'children with disabilities' means children . . . with mental retardation, hearing impairments including deafness, speech or language impairments, visual impairments including blindness, serious emotional disturbance, orthopedic impairments, autism, traumatic brain injury, other health impairments, or specific learning disabilities . . . who by reason thereof need special education and related services." "Individuals with handicaps," by contrast, covers adults as well as kids with epilepsy, AIDS, or other "health impairments" that affect their lives but don't necessarily affect their placement in school.

Thanks to IDEA, disabled American children are now federally entitled to free transportation and all other services necessary to their schooling, including speech pathology, counseling, occupational and physical therapy, and even "medical services . . . for diagnostic and evaluation purposes only." But according to Eileen Ordover and Kathleen Boundy, disability attorneys with the Center for Law and Education, "It is not always easy (or possible or even reasonable) to separate 'education' from 'treatment' or 'educational' needs from health or 'medical' ones." And whether children will actually receive the services they need in the way they need them—that depends on how knowledgeable and energetic their advocates are. Federal law sets the general standard, but the states and localities fill in the blanks, defining "appropriate education" and "least restrictive environment" as they see fit. The clause on medical services is particularly troublesome; it's not clear whether it applies only to services provided by physicians— or, for that matter, whether "diagnostic and evaluation purposes" can be distinguished from educational purposes at all.

This is how it's all supposed to work. Under IDEA, each "disabled" child gets, at age three and annually thereafter until age eighteen, a written Individualized Education Plan (IEP); in September 1994, Jamie got his first one. The IEP is devised by a multidisciplinary team of evaluators, and schools have to follow your kid's program or risk losing their IDEA funding. IEPs can sometimes be contentious, but most of the time they're exercises in cooperation. Parents can and should advocate for services, and school officials can and should listen to and negotiate with parents' evaluations of their children's needs. In fact, parents can accomplish a great deal—and send an important signal to their children's teachers and therapists—simply by coming to an IEP fully prepared and informed about their options. To be fully prepared, a parent needs most of all to have assessed their child's strengths and weaknesses, so as to be able to report on the child's progress and suggest courses of action. For instance, Jamie wasn't assigned an in-school occupational therapist at first. When it came time to update his IEP, though, we reported that Jamie had a lot of trouble with gross motor skills like putting on pants and fine motor skills like using scissors. We didn't think he needed physical therapy, we thought his speech therapy with Terri was doing him wonders, and we thought occupational therapy would help him acquire some basic classroom skills. Jamie's teachers agreed—and informed us that although he had difficulty with some tasks involving spatial relations, he was just astonishingly competent at using the mouse to operate the classroom computer.

There's lots of wiggle room in the IDEA, but the law's not infinitely plastic. You can't place a child in a separate school if a special classroom in a regular school would serve the child better, nor can you place a child in a segregated special class in regular school if participation in regular classrooms would serve the child better. The purpose of the IEP, then, is to determine the child's needs and to balance these against the resources and interests of the school district. In 1982, the Supreme Court case of *Board of Education of Hendrick Hudson School District* v. *Rowley* held that children with disabilities (in this case, an eight-year-old deaf girl, Ann Rowley) would be expected to perform at grade level if they were included in regular classrooms; but in 1989, the Fifth Circuit Court of Appeals loosened this standard, holding in *Daniel R. R.* v. *State Board of Education* that school curricula could be modified to some extent if modification would accommodate a student with disabilities. In the case at hand, however, the court decided that Daniel, a six year old with Down syndrome, would be better off in a "special needs" classroom because he required so much attention as to disrupt the rest of the class. Still, in the wake of the *Daniel R. R.* decision, including disabled children in regular classrooms is considered the option of choice. Only if inclusion doesn't work can children be placed in different classes or schools. The *Daniel R. R.* test is comprehensive enough to have been persuasive in other jurisdictions, partly because it offers four criteria for determining a child's most appropriate placement: the educational benefit to the child; the nonacademic benefits to the child; the potential disruption to the classroom; and the cost of the placement with all necessary supplementary aids and services. As lawyer and disability rights advocate Barbara Ebenstein has summarized the policy implications of the case, "The school district must make reasonable efforts to accommodate the child in a regular classroom—not 'mere token gestures'—but if the child cannot be placed in a regular classroom, the school district should integrate the child into regular school activities whenever possible."

Just as there's a significant legal difference between "children with disabilities" and "individuals with handicaps," so too is there a difference between "mainstreaming" and "inclusion." "Mainstreaming" refers to the policies that were clearly progressive in the political context of the 1970s—namely, separate special ed classes where disabled children can receive the "special" attention they need. People who fought for "mainstreaming" are therefore sometimes baffled by the proponents of "full inclusion," who call for all disabled children to be educated with their nondisabled peers in regular classes. Just as "regular" parents and teachers fear that inclusion will distract schools from teaching their "regular" students, then, the people who fought for mainstreaming fear that inclusion will deprive disabled students of the "special" services they fought for twenty years ago. But much of the time, the differences between mainstreaming and inclusion aren't as stark as all that. According to the *Daniel R. R.* decision, for instance, an individual child may very well be assigned both a special ed and a regular classroom, as circumstances dictate. To make matters even more terminologically complicated, nonspecialists such as parents, politicians, and journalists often use the two terms interchangeably. On the whole, though, one can say that current policy trends favor inclusion first, mainstreaming next, and segregated classrooms or special schools only if the first two options don't work.

In fact, a federal district court in New Jersey has recently held, in *Oberti* v. *Board of Education of the Borough of Clementon School District* (1992), that the *Daniel R. R.* case requires schools to attempt inclusion before exploring other alternatives, even if the child in question can't master any grade-appropriate curriculum. Rafael Oberti, an eight year old with Down syndrome, couldn't do third-grade work, but the court, relying on the testimony of educators, suggested that he could make use of "a variety of accommodations including a resource room, curriculum modification, and 'parallel instruction,'" which, according to Ebenstein, "would permit Rafael to work on an activity beneficial to him while the rest of the class worked on a different activity." "Parallel instruction" is a fairly capacious term and can take as many forms as there are children; in one fifth-grade classroom, for instance, while most of the children are taking a reading test, a student with disabilities is working on the classroom newsletter along with children who have already mastered the test material. It makes good sense, especially when you remember that there are no laws stipulating that all children in a given classroom have to be engaged in the same activity.

Still, decisions like *Daniel R. R.* and *Oberti* may strike many people as strange. After all, if the disabled are to be included in regular classrooms, what purpose does inclusion serve for children who just can't do the work? It's a good question, but so far it hasn't received too many good answers. Instead, American conservatives have started a cottage industry of complaint, charging that "inclusion" saps resources from "normal" and "gifted" students—and worse, that it bespeaks the further erosion of American public education. In his latest book, *Dumbing Down Our Kids*, education critic Charles Sykes characterizes the IDEA as follows: "From the beginning," he writes, "social and political considerations were placed at the forefront, while concerns about the impact on classroom order and educational quality were shoved into the background." Never mind the fact that this is false on its face, as a review of the case law will show. What's ironic here is that "social considerations" and "educational quality" are tendentiously *opposed* to each other by Sykes, even though IDEA was written and passed precisely in the belief that educational quality should be one of our primary social considerations. Yet Sykes's argument is not anomalous. From what I've seen, very few of the political opponents of inclusion have done any real homework on the matter. The debate so far offers less evidence of the dumbing down of public education than of the dumbing down of right-wing cultural criticism.

The conservatives' basic argument runs like this: Resources are finite, as is the patience and training of teachers, and the inclusion of disabled children in regular classrooms will only prevent "normal" kids from getting the services *they* need. For doesn't justice demand we attend to tomorrow's leaders before we attend to a cohort of children who—with luck—may end up flipping burgers or pushing brooms?

This line of argument involves a couple of assumptions worth a closer look. First, it assumes a correlation between a person's level of academic success and his or her social and material value. The smartest people succeed (whatever that means), and the average and below-average wind up in the "service" industries required by the smart folks. This is the kind of story some wealthy people tell themselves all the time, but one wonders whether it can withstand the light of day. After all, many bright children go on to relatively low-paying jobs in university philosophy or anthropology departments, for instance, while bullies and dunderheads go on to run the country. Second, the argument suggests that we should concentrate our educational resources on those

best equipped to use them—but it defines "educational resources" as narrowly as possible, as if our schools exist only to enhance children's verbal and mathematical abilities. Third, the
argument assumes that education is a zero-sum game, where the
benefits that accrue to student X necessarily require that student
Y be harmed; one is led to think that the entire class is somehow
irreparably damaged if its average IQ is dragged down by the
Jamie in row two. And fourth, the argument entails a truly phan-
tasmic vision of "regular" classrooms, where schoolchildren spend
the entire day eating information from the school trough until
they qualify to become rocket scientists. Perhaps if that were in
fact the case, there would be some justification for giving priority
to the students with the biggest appetites. But on *this* planet,
schools actually do much more than impart information; they also
teach children how to interact with other people in a regular institutional setting. So let's not ask whether Jamie will disable his
nondisabled peers; let's ask what his nondisabled peers will
"learn" if they're forcibly segregated from him.

One thing they'll learn is an implicit lesson I learned as a
child: *The "disabled" are always other people. You don't have to worry
about them. Somebody else is doing that.* All my public schools in the
late 1960s and early 1970s had "special" classrooms—or so I
heard. I actually never saw any of those children until the day
each grade took the playground to demonstrate their spring
dances, whereupon the "retarded" class did the hokey-pokey with
varying degrees of proficiency and enthusiasm. Robert Hayman
tells a similar story of growing up ignorant until the fateful day
he "discovered Mrs. Sweeney's 'special' class":

We had always wondered why the window in Mrs. Sweeney's
door was covered with cardboard, wondered why kids weren't

supposed to look in. It never occurred to us that the cardboard also kept the kids inside from looking out, but then, lots of that kind of stuff never occurred to us. What did occur to us was that Mrs. Sweeney's kids had to be "special" in some pretty strange way, or else there would be no reason to keep us from seeing them.

Regardless of whether you believe education should lead to gainful employment or to general emancipation, you may have grounds for agreeing that it's not a good idea to socialize our children into the belief that "special" children—and the "special" adults they will become—are so abnormal that they can only be administered by being cast elsewhere, out of sight and out of mind.

Sometimes I think it's regrettable that disability law places so heavy a stress on the benefits to the disabled child; for when "inclusion" is handled with the care and sensitivity it deserves, its benefits truly are universal. Indeed, some schools, like the Patrick O'Hearn School in Boston, whose principal, Bill Henderson, is both brilliant and blind, are proud to report that because of inclusion, their nondisabled students have not only become socially and psychologically mature but have registered better test scores in their "traditional" areas (verbal and mathematical) as well. For that matter, there's no reason for us to buy the notion that "normal" children are perfectly sound vessels for the accumulation of knowledge and wisdom. It's easy enough to show that Jamie isn't preventing his nondisabled peers from acquiring age-appropriate skills; but what's more important is to show how thoroughly people like Jamie challenge the very idea of the "normal" or "regular" child. When you start doing your homework on this assignment, the results can be staggering. Recent data gathered from various

North American school districts demonstrate that segregated education, like its earlier institutional incarnations, may lead to a pattern of lifelong dependence, whereby "disabled" people never acquire the skills necessary for life on their own, that after a year of full integration in a Saline, Michigan, school district, the percentage of teachers who agreed with the proposition that inclusion is unfair to "regular" kids dropped from eighty to twelve, and that, as researcher Richard Schattman reports, several "regular" teachers in inclusive schools find "they already had children in their classes with more challenging academic, social, and behavioral needs" than the disabled kids assigned to their classrooms by inclusive policies.

The statistic about teacher expectations is a telling one, since everyone knows that primary school education rests heavily on an economy of self-fulfilling prophecies: Children tend to do better when their teachers expect them to do better. Sometimes teachers are the fiercest opponents of inclusion, for fairly reasonable reasons. They're already underpaid and overworked, and they fear being saddled with the additional roles of speech therapist, behavioral psychologist, and nurse practitioner. They especially fear opportunistic, Dickensian administrators and politicians looking to cut costs by eliminating special education and "dumping" disabled children into regular classrooms without providing the aides and therapists who can make inclusion meaningful. But as seven-eighths of the teachers of Saline, Michigan, can tell you, when you do inclusion right, you're doing the right thing by *every* child in the room.

Richard Schattman's item about the irregularity of regular kids, though, is the real mind bender. Don't we know this one in our bones? Yet why are we so susceptible to the notion that all the regular kids are regular and all the special kids are irregular, like mismatched socks? If some normal kids can have greater "special needs" than do the special needs kids—who, for their part, can be fairly normal—then what does this tell us?

I admit that Jamie's "abnormality" is a real one, not something to be finessed with a series of deft rhetorical maneuvers. Normally, humans have forty-six chromosomes, and when they have more or fewer, that's abnormal, and often lethal. To pretend anything else would be vacuous. "Everybody is different," says one of Flannery O'Connor's cliché-driven characters. "Yes, most people is," replies her neighbor. But there's really a very important political and philosophical principle at stake here. If we're talking about human behavior, achievement, and value, then "normal" is a category constructed only by humans. Our chromosomes, skin tones, language games, and eating habits may vary wildly; most of us can speak, some of us were born with fewer limbs than others, some of us can't remember who we are, and some of us have to put up with a lot of electrical interference in our brains. Many of these variations fall within physical norms: Asian and African babies are legibly different from each other in some ways, yet are (normally) born with the same number of limbs. So there are, broadly speaking, such things as "biological norms." But when we start talking about the human "norm" in a nonphysical sense—the sense we use when we're creating institutions like mental hospitals, prisons, and schools—then we're talking about an *ideological* category. Within the "norm" there can be all kinds of variety, which is why "regular" classrooms normally contain such a smorgasbord of abilities, proclivities, and learning styles; and outside the "norm" there's all kinds of variety, too, some of it quite normal. In an ideological sense, however, the distinction between normal and abnormal human development is a distinction between kinds of variety we will agree to overlook—differences that don't make a

difference—and kinds of variety for which we will create social institutions that "administer" to those with "special needs." How
you carve up these differences depends largely on who and where
you are. For example, if I were king, we would consider it "abnormal" and "pathological" to engage in the kind of real estate development that sees beachfront as an excuse to build luxury
condominiums. I would not incarcerate such developers, but I
would offer them counseling. Maybe even special education.

This questioning of constructed norms is one of the lessons
taught to us by deconstruction, and it's a lesson worth writing
down, particularly since deconstruction has gotten such abysmally
bad press in the last few years. (It's usually represented as a school
of thought that says everything is equal to everything else. But I
can't begin to retrace the long game of "telephone" that led to this
kind of bizarre misunderstanding.) The lesson is this. The "normal" is not a category that exists on its own: it requires the creation of various "abnormals," such that the construction of the
not-normal becomes, in a weird way, the philosophical precondi-
tion for the predication of the "normal." You just can't understand
one without the other: *We* are rational, *they* are mad, and one of the
ways we know we're rational is that we know we're not like *them*.
To put this a tad more skeptically, *we* secure our normality by institutionally constructing *their* deviance from the norm. Beyond
this point, we say, drawing and redrawing the line, your deviance
is abnormal. Yet any large-scale grouping of humans will do two
things: emphasize difference *between* groupings, and suppress the
myriad differences *within* any one group.

The valuable feature of deconstruction is that it's been so successful at showing how this works; its worst feature is that you
usually have to have an intimate knowledge of Western philosophy (and a high tolerance for vexing prose) to get the point. But

the point itself is plain as day: Every time you focus on the differences between men and women, you tend to overlook the differences among men, or the differences among women; conversely, fixating on the differences among women tends to blind you to differences between women and men. Every category operates by juggling these two determinants of "difference": the differences *within* the category are held to be trivial (eye color, number of limbs); and the differences *between* categories are held to be fundamental, or even insurmountable, whether those differences are ascribed to culture or to biology (race, gender). When libertarians presume that the individual is the ground of all ethical action, they ignore the myriad commonalities, family resemblances, and tribal affinities among individuals; and when educators classify our children as delayed, normal, and gifted, they may be saying something important about them, maybe even something true, but they're also underestimating the individual variances within each group and the similarities that run across all three groups. To everyone who might tell me I'm just in denial, that I can't wish away the fact that Jamie's measurable intelligence is below normal, I would respond not by discarding IQ numbers but by citing them: "normal," after all, is everything from 80 to 120, and even these numbers aren't as clear as numbers might be. As James Trent points out, "In 1973, with the stroke of a pen, the American Association on Mental Deficiency changed the criterion for 'mental retardation' from one to two standard deviations below the I.Q. norm." There may be a line between normal and abnormal, but it's an awfully fuzzy one, and it leaves us with the same problem of definitional circularity: The normal is composed of everything that's not abnormal, and the abnormal consists of everything not normal.

In practice, of course, the philosophy behind inclusive education has less to do with deconstruction than with hands-on studies of how education works. For instance, expressive language development is often the area in which children with Down syndrome experience their most dramatic delays. (Jamie is quite typical in this regard.) How should this affect their educational placement? Should a child like James be placed in a regular classroom with children whose language comprehension skills are similar to his but who can speak far more fluently than he, on the grounds that he might model the behavior of more competent speakers? Should he be classed with other children of similar speaking abilities even though he may be more mature, cognitively and emotionally, than his peers? Or should he be "partially included" in a regular age-appropriate class and periodically "pulled out" for individual speech therapy? Psychologists Marjorie Beeghly and Dante Cicchetti report:

> Because children with Down syndrome are typically less retarded cognitively than linguistically, it has been hypothesized that children with Down syndrome would be more communicatively competent during social interactions than would non-handicapped children at a similar level of syntactic development. . . . Several investigators have documented that adults with Down syndrome appear to be more advanced communicatively, relative to their linguistic abilities, when nonlinguistic aspects of communication (gestures, body movements) are also considered.

If that's the case, then our assessments of each others' abilities have to be as finely calibrated as possible, which is why it makes little sense to group children solely on the basis of their verbal and mathematical competence. Thomas Armstrong, following

Howard Gardner's theory of multiple intelligences, thus comes to the conclusion that traditional methods of sorting schoolchildren ignore many students' communicative strengths rather than shoring up their weaknesses precisely by exploiting their strengths:

> All too often a student having problems in a specific area will be given an IEP that neglects his most developed intelligences while concentrating on his weaknesses. For instance, let's say a student with well-developed bodily-kinesthetic and spatial intelligences is having difficulty learning to read. In many schools today, he will be given an IEP that fails to include physical and picture-oriented activities as a means of achieving his educational objectives.

Or take a child with a highly developed tactile sense who's having trouble learning her alphabet. Why not give her letters of rubber, plastic, wood, and sponge, so that she can learn ABCs by holding them? When Jamie started occupational therapy with Mincy—I mean, Nancy—he could hold a pen but could only scribble. He didn't have enough manual discipline to draw an H or an F or a T, even though he could recognize the letters without difficulty. So Nancy brought out her Styrofoam strips and showed Jamie how to *construct* letters with horizontal and vertical lines before teaching him how to draw them. After only a few sessions Jamie was bringing home papers full of enormous Fs and Hs—and learning nifty tricks with Styrofoam, too, like how to tip the lines of an H to make an A, or how to play with curved strips to make an O, a D, and (to his keen delight) a J.

This may seem straightforward and commonsensical enough, but too often it falls on the ears of people who seem to have "reg-

ular" hearing but turn out to be strangely tone-deaf. I once got
into an Internet discussion with a man who was convinced that
"special" students were slowing down his children's classes. I
cited the arguments I've just sketched out above; I offered a few
examples of what some developmentally delayed children can and
can't do; and I concluded by suggesting that schools are as important for what they teach socially as for what they teach academi-
cally. To wit, if we're going to learn how to incorporate the
disabled—those *other* people—into our "regular" lives, schools are
a very good place to start. Conversely, if we can't imagine inclusion in school, it's not likely that we're going to manage it anywhere else; thus, if you want to argue against inclusion in school,
then you're also necessarily arguing against inclusion in any number of other social settings, many of which *depend* on the socialization provided in school. The anti-inclusion advocates see
themselves as proponents of realism; I see them as proponents of
the politics of denial. For the fact is that many millions of us humans *are* disabled, and it's just wishful thinking to expect that
they can all go live someplace where we normal people don't have
to deal with them. But if we *can* manage to integrate special and
regular kids wherever possible in the early grades of elementary
school, we'll not only be teaching them spelling and math, we'll
be teaching them how the disabled and nondisabled might integrate themselves after they're through with school.

From my Internet interlocutor I got back what I considered a
bizarre and depressing answer: Schools do not exist for "social activities," I was told. He wasn't interested in after-school programs
and clubs and sports teams; he was interested in his children's
learning. I actually hadn't said anything about after-school programs; I was talking about the social lessons schools teach even
while they're teaching the three Rs. Yet I've run into this misun-

derstanding time and again since that Internet exchange. All too many parents, legislators, and even teachers seem to think that schools offer models of social interaction only when they're holding "social functions," as if the social interactions in which human children participate were not also fundamental to their learning of social studies—or reading, writing, and arithmetic.

Personally, I regret having been skipped a grade. I was ostracized for most of my grammar school years not only for being an egghead but also for being a twerp, eighteen months younger and many pounds lighter than the rest of the boys in class. In my case, the people who sorted me by academic ability actually wound up inadvertently creating more obstacles to my social maturation. I'm generally opposed to "skipping" as a result, but only on the grounds that if a child's group interactions are interfering with his or her learning, then we should give as much consideration to the social effects of schooling as to the child's academic curriculum. I think we should offer some "gifted" classes just as we offer some "special" classes, but I also think it's narrow-minded and foolish to think we can group children by academic ability alone. I also think it may not be a good idea to base so much of our academic reward system on traditional test-taking abilities. I'll continue to think this way until someone comes up with a stunningly compelling argument that the planet needs more technical wizards and fewer people skilled at sympathetic social interaction.

Our own family practice basically runs the gamut of educational options. For the past three years, Nick has been in one of Champaign's three "gifted" programs, so he attends Dr. Howard, a school slightly out of our district, about a mile away. A large part of his school placement depends on teacher evaluation; they don't simply slot kids by their test scores. To some extent they even tailor the classes to children's needs: Nick can be in one class group for math, another for music, another for social studies. The school is roughly 40 percent nonwhite. We hope Jamie will be going to Dr. Howard in a few years, even if it means we have to move a few blocks north or east.

In the meantime, we think Jamie's schooling options are complicated enough as they are. When he turned three and got that first IEP, we had four or five different school settings to choose from: full inclusion with children his age; full inclusion with younger children; mainstreaming in a regular school with partial inclusion; mainstreaming in a regular school in a special ed class; and a special school for "at risk" children of all kinds. For months we investigated different schools and classrooms, talked to teachers, aides, and principals, pored over pamphlets, and periodically blurted out inarticulate expressions of indecision and bewilderment. The Early Learning Center, a Montessori-like school, would place James with nondisabled three year olds. This sounded great, but when we checked out the school we worried that he might not be able to keep up with the other kids physically. Kenwood offered a brand new special ed class, and Kenwood's principal happened to be the husband of Rita Huddle, Jamie's former therapist. It looked quite good to us until we started thinking, *Well, Early Learning's been doing this for years, and the Kenwood program is new, and that might be all the better, but maybe we should wait and see, or maybe we should visit both schools again*, and so on. Then there was Marquette, the "at risk" school, about which we were initially skeptical—until we met with the teachers and therapists, who were wonderful. Finally, there was Jamie's day care, First United Methodist, where he was fully included with "age-appropriate" children about a year younger than himself.

But our decision was still more difficult than this would suggest. There was also the question of transportation. If Jamie went to Kenwood or Marquette, he would be in a half-day program in the mornings. The rest of the day he would spend at FUM, to which he would be ferried at lunchtime by schoolbus. However, if he went to Early Learning Center he could stay all day, no FUM, no bus. If he went to Kenwood or Marquette, he could be picked up at home by bus as well. But since we couldn't yet imagine our toddler taking a bus at all, we figured we'd probably prefer to drop him off ourselves. The teachers at FUM, meanwhile, didn't want Jamie to leave, and we didn't want to disrupt a routine with which he was very familiar—and very happy. So we hemmed and hawed, and then hemmed and hawed some more.

In the end, we decided on FUM and Marquette: some full inclusion, some special services, and a little bit of riding the bus. For 1994–95, Jamie had a morning class at Marquette, Tuesdays through Fridays, after which he was driven to FUM in time for lunch at 11:30. We had to negotiate his arrival time with the bus company, pointing out that if Jamie didn't get to FUM by then he would miss lunch altogether. Just to make sure everything was all right, Janet showed up at Marquette on Jamie's first day of school to watch him be dismissed from class and boarded onto a waiting bus. Then, she says, she saw him gently hoisted into a seat and strapped in, and she drove behind the bus all the way to FUM with tears streaming down her cheeks.

When Jamie turned four, his schedule reversed itself. On Mondays and all mornings Tuesday through Friday, he goes to FUM, fully "included" in a class of nondisabled three year olds. Tuesday through Friday afternoons, he rides a 12:25 bus to Marquette, where he goes to a class of four and five year olds and is "pulled out" once weekly for one-on-one speech therapy and once a week for occupational therapy. Each school has slightly different organizational routines. At FUM, Jamie learns to read his symbol and to take turns being class leader; at Marquette he hangs up his coat and backpack on his hook, describes the weather, and takes turns using the computer mouse.

We think it's just the right mix, and we're especially happy that we have such a rich and dizzying array of educational options for Jamie in the first place. Besides, I don't mean to suggest that mainstreaming and inclusion policies are so self-evidently right and just as to be immune to criticism. There are any number of problems with the way IDEA is currently administered, and many of them have to do with money. Critics will point to the fact that special ed costs more per student than regular ed, and they'll construe this as a misallocation of resources that hurts gifted children most. But that's not the problem. First of all, special ed *should* cost more than regular ed, particularly when severe physical disabilities are at issue: More vulnerable children need a greater degree of care. So there's no reason to pretend that "justice" demands giving kids *x* number of dollars for every IQ point they register. Second, the argument is incredibly disingenuous. *Every* area of American public education is scandalously underfunded, and blaming disabled children for shortfalls is a particularly nasty form of scapegoating—as if one were to blame the homeless for our nation's lack of low-income urban housing. Conservatives are fond of claiming that school funding is not the prime determinant of school success, and in support of this claim they religiously cite the 1966 Coleman Report, which held that stable and supportive family structures were more crucial to a child's academic success than the number of dollars the state spends per child. I'm more than willing to agree on the importance of stable and supportive families, but when people tell me that it's immaterial that urban district A, 97 percent nonwhite, spends $3,000 per student, whereas suburban district B, 97 percent white, spends $8,000, I say, Fine, if money doesn't matter, let's just exchange these districts' budgets and have the property taxes of district B support the schools of district A. *Then* we'll see how many conservatives cite chapter and verse of the Coleman Report.

For that matter, there's no plausible reason why public schools should be funded from property taxes in the first place. It's the ideal scheme for setting the elderly against children, singles and childless couples against parents, homeowners against tenants, and homeowning parents of children in private school against everyone else. It's a system designed for the production of scapegoats, and it could only have been devised by people who wanted to see public education destroy itself. Better yet, it's recently given rise to a wholly new form of opportunistic politician, like John Engler, the Republican governor of Michigan, who's "reformed" the system by funding education out of even *more* regressive taxes than the property tax—such as the sales tax. Unless we change this funding system at its roots, I fear we will see the dismantling of public education in our lifetimes, and it won't be the fault of the "handicapped" and "retarded" children in Mrs. Sweeney's class or of Jamie's "at risk" classmates at Marquette.

In the coming years, however, it will be all too easy for libertarians, conservatives, and opportunists-at-large to make it look that way. Consider this: The IDEA envisioned a system wherein the federal government picked up 40 percent of the tab for special education; at the moment, federal funds account for only 7 percent. Yet special education isn't all about money, and not all of its shortcomings can be referred to the fiscal policies that inform American public education. Two problems seem to me especially pressing. One is chiefly practical, the other chiefly theoretical, but the distinction between theory and practice probably isn't very useful here. The theoretical impasse chiefly has to do with disability law's uneasy disjunctions between individual idiosyncrasies and broad social mandates, but the way these disjunctions make themselves felt is primarily a practical problem. To wit, the system is beset by misdiagnoses, and both the misdiagnoses and the means of correcting them rely heavily on a bureaucracy that's both vast and disorganized. In one sense that's to be expected, since the project of classifying individual human potential is a nearly impossible one. But few people know just how overdetermined our various misdiagnoses can be—fueled by variables such as race, funding formulas, "excellence" initiatives in local schools, and even the federalized structure of the United States itself.

The last of these variables is more important than many people think, especially when there are fundamental political disputes over who should set educational standards, the federal government or the individual states and localities. The 104th U.S. Congress has proposed shifting the administration of many low-income social programs, from welfare to Medicaid, away from the federal government and over to the states. According to its sponsors, this plan would give average citizens greater access to and control over these programs. But the plan also runs the risk of destroying many of our basic social services by Balkanizing them. There's already too much variability and inconsistency in the way individual states treat their neediest citizens, and defederalizing programs like Supplemental Security Income (or Head Start, or the Women, Infants, and Children food program, or even welfare) will only exacerbate those inconsistencies. Some critics fear that defederalization will produce a "race to the bottom," in which each state vies with its neighbors to cut services still further. Even if this doesn't happen, though, we'll have taken a giant step in the wrong direction. What the United States needs, with regard to fundamental social policy, is precisely more unity, more consistency—not a crazy quilt of services and agencies that vary wildly on opposite sides of rivers and mountain ranges. This nation once tore itself apart over the question of whether federal law could override the states' idiosyncratic and inequitable treatment of their inhabitants; that question led us to civil war, and part of the legacy of the Civil War is the Fourteenth Amendment, which guarantees every American citizen—regardless of whether they live in Massachusetts or Mississippi—equal protection under the laws. It's odd that a plan so corrosive as defederalization would be proposed by the very same people who complain that the United States needs to return to a "common culture," as if we could only forge a common culture by abrading our common social foundations. For if you want to see how chaotic the nation's social policies would become when fully defederalized, just look at how our all-too-defederalized educational system works now.

As *U.S. News and World Report* pointed out in a five-month study of special ed, state-by-state administration takes our already fragile classification systems and subjects them to the vagaries of chance and politics:

> In Ohio, a child with an IQ level below 80 is considered mentally retarded. Move across the border to Kentucky, and the same child is placed in a regular classroom and taught along with all the other students. The anomalies are endless. Should special education students be taught in separate classrooms or regular classrooms? There are few meaningful guide-

lines. The result: in North Dakota, 72 percent of the state's special education students are taught in regular classrooms. In South Dakota, a state with almost identical demographics, only 8 percent of special ed students go to class with nondisabled children.

What's especially striking about the misadministration of special education is that although many people fear that "retarded" and "at risk" children are being dumped indiscriminately into "regular" classrooms, the reverse is much more often the case. The current system actually favors greater *segregation* of disabled students, not greater *inclusion*. The 1993 *U.S. News* study—hardly the work of dyed-in-the-wool democratic socialists—found a host of disturbing patterns nationwide, particularly wherever administrative incentives favored segregating students by physical or mental ability. One such incentive is attributable to the Reagan-era "excellence" movement, which measures local school administrators on the basis of students' performance on standardized achievement exams. Since special ed students are not counted in the total, you've got a system where administrators' "merit pay" raises can depend on their willingness to dump all kinds of "below average" kids into segregated "special" classes. Another incentive has to do with individual states' funding formulas:

No state has more students classified as emotionally disturbed than Connecticut, for example. But it's not that there is more stress, paranoia or pathology there. It's simply that the state's complex funding formula encourages school districts to send emotionally disturbed children to separate schools. . . . [S]ome cities, like New Haven, actually save money when they send children to out-of-district schools, even though these schools can cost more than $100,000 per student, because the state picks up the bulk of the cost.

Conversely, under mainstreaming and inclusion policies, students can often go to schools in their home district—and that means, among other things, the likelihood of lower "special" transportation costs statewide.

When it comes to intelligence and race, ask not for whom the bell curves. Not only are African-American children disproportionately placed in special classes, they're also categorized differently than white children even when they have profiles similar to those of whites. That is, black children are much more likely to be classified as "mentally retarded" when white children are labeled "learning disabled" (the latter designation itself, needless to say, is problematic, encompassing relatively identifiable deficits like dyslexia as well as more nebulous conditions like attention-deficit disorder). Of course, most Americans have come to expect disproportionate numbers of blacks to turn up in various unenviable social locations, whether they attribute the disproportion to systemic racism or to "personal responsibility." But even the *U.S. News* study contended that "the large number of blacks in special ed. programs cannot be explained by socioeconomic factors alone," and told a "tale of two counties" to explain why:

The Perry County and Mountain Brook school districts in Alabama have the same number of special education students. In Perry County, in the state's impoverished, cotton-farming "Black Belt," 236 students are labelled mentally retarded and 14 learning-disabled. The Mountain Brook district is farther north, a wealthy suburb of Birmingham. There, the numbers are reversed: 271 youngsters are classified as learning disabled, only 15 as mentally retarded. Demographically, the two districts could not be more different. Perry County's residents are 96 percent black. Mountain Brook is 99 percent white. . . .

In Mountain Brook . . . school officials bend over backward to classify kids as learning-disabled. The label is less stigmatizing, and it typically results in the placement of students in more rigorous academic programs than if they were classified as mentally retarded. That is clear at Mountain Brook High School, where nearly every student with a learning disability takes all regular classes and 97 percent go on to college.

When you look at how educational policy works in practice, therefore, you find that the ideal of giving every child a "free and appropriate public education" in the "least restrictive environment" runs up against a host of practical difficulties. Local funding formulas can favor greater segregation of "special" students, even if those formulas don't make good fiscal sense; "excellence" and "merit pay" initiatives in school districts can lead administrators to shortchange learning-disabled children; and the categorization of "at risk" children is inflected by the standard American inequalities of race and class. Serious as they are, however, none of these arguments suggests that inclusion and mainstreaming are contrary to the ideal of social justice in that they siphon resources from "gifted" students; they suggest merely that we're not implementing policies of mainstreaming and inclusion as well as we might. It's in this sense that I call these problems "practical" rather than theoretical. Some of them, like the racial composition problem and the incentive-to-segregate problem, actually imply that inclusive education is a positive social good whose realization is being thwarted by local injustices.

There's only one argument against inclusion *in theory* to which I am inclined to give any moral weight, and that's the argument against coercion. Inclusion is not a "one size fits all" policy. I cannot support inclusion as an a priori principle any more than I can support a priori moral absolutes in regard to prenatal testing and abortion. It would be absurd for me to say that the range of human circumstances is so vast, and our moral decisions so various, that we cannot presume to bar people from seeking prenatal testing or from choosing abortion—and then to declare that once they're born, all children must be educated in regular classrooms *regardless* of the range of human circumstances. It would also be hypocritical of me to say this, since Jamie himself is now being schooled in two very different environments and Nick in another environment altogether.

In *Train Go Sorry: Life in a Deaf World*, Leah Cohen makes an eloquent case for the proposition that not all forms of inclusion are equal:

> Mainstreaming's proponents (many of whom are unfamiliar with the special circumstances of deafness but see special programs as a way of isolating and stigmatizing learning-disabled and emotionally disturbed children) believe that the least restrictive environment for all children is the same: regular public school. The goal of social integration must now be achieved at any cost. As desirable as this outcome may be for many children, for some it amounts to bad pedagogy. For the deaf, it means the dissolution of their culture.

What Cohen calls "mainstreaming" here, many people would call "full inclusion": regular public school for all students irrespective of abilities or disabilities. But the reason Cohen's caveat about inclusion is persuasive, whereas Charles Sykes's is not, lies in

Cohen's scrupulous and detailed portraits of deaf communities in *Train Go Sorry*. By means of these portraits, Cohen convincingly tells us—by showing us—that deaf children do indeed have a distinctive culture and language that would be violated by universal, blanket policies of inclusion. I'm not sure I can say the same of children with Down syndrome, or autistic children, or learning-disabled children, but then, that's precisely the point: one size, one policy initiative, does not fit all. To decree that all children, irrespective of individual needs and group idiosyncrasies, shall be educated in regular classrooms is ethically as dubious as to decree that all children will be classified by "intelligence" or "aptitude" regardless of circumstances. Our challenge with regard to inclusive education, then, is actually quite similar to our challenge with regard to reproductive rights: What we need is a system bounded by the broadest possible definitions of freedom and justice, but internally variegated so as to admit multiple competing moral imperatives—imperatives which can only be deliberated with the nuance they deserve if we publicly maintain that some decisions are so difficult that they can only be "private." For education, this means keeping open the widest possible variety of options—not just full inclusion for some disabled students in regular classrooms, but also special ed and special services for children who need them and/or parents who prefer them; some separate classes, and even some separate schools, as options when inclusion does not work; "reverse" mainstreaming, when regular children are taught for part of the day in "special" classrooms; and, not least, sufficient funding for teachers and aides in every area of public schooling. It also means maintaining a complex system in which parents, therapists, administrators, and teachers hash out IEPs and deliberate about what "justice" might mean in case after difficult case.

And *that* means deliberating about values and mores that no one law, not even the best IDEA in the world, can mandate. For Jamie came into the world asking us a question more basic than any I've yet dealt with, in this book or in my life: Assuming that we can even imagine a form of social organization in which citizens like James are nourished, supported, and encouraged to reach their full human potential, why might we seek to create it at all? There's no self-evident reason why we should, and there's no reason to believe that my question's assumption is worth granting in the first place. We have not yet created a form of social organization that vouchsafes equal opportunity to all its "normal" citizens, let alone a society in which the disabled enjoy all the rights of the nondisabled. Ours is a world in which able-bodied men kill each other by the millions for no good reason, in which many societies murder or torture their female children, in which much of the species dies by starvation, violence, chance, or excruciating and preventable disease. Why in the world should we be so arrogant or so ambitious as to imagine that we can devise a society in which all persons—even all persons with disabilities—are given a fair shake?

And what the hell *is* a fair shake, anyway?

In the course of my travels through the literature on disability law and social justice, I came across a curious news item from *Time* magazine, April 29, 1985:

> "There is no injustice in the universe," wrote Educator Eileen
> Marie Gardner in a 1983 paper for the right-wing Heritage
> Foundation criticizing federal aid for ill-advantaged students.
> "Those of the handicapped constituency who seek to have oth-
> ers bear their burdens and eliminate their challenges are seek-

ing to avoid the central issue of their lives." Gardner's views might have gone unnoticed but for the fact that she began work last week as a special assistant to Secretary of Education William Bennett.

Lowell Weicker, then a Republican senator from Connecticut and the father of a boy with Down syndrome, publicly criticized Gardner's views, as well as those of "another newly appointed Bennett aide, Lawrence Uzzell, who wants to abolish the department's National Institute of Education, which conducts and funds research." Bennett, for his part, tried to brush off Weicker's complaints, replying, as *Time* reported, "that Gardner's views were her personal religious beliefs" and denying that "either her or Uzzell's opinions on these matters would affect their official roles." Two days later, however, Bennett apparently decided that Gardner and Uzzell would be an unwarranted embarrassment to the Reagan administration and accepted their resignations. We have not heard from either Gardner or Uzzell since. Bennett, however, has gone on to an illustrious career as America's official Morals Maven, making millions by chastising our national character and peddling *The Book of Virtues* and its byproducts as the cure for what ails us.

But in a way, Gardner and Uzzell have had their day at last. Washington, D.C., is now populated by politicians who claim that taxation is theft, that government has no business fostering the egalitarianism on which the country was founded, and that the best thing wealthy Americans can do with their money is spend it as they see fit. Dick Armey, one of the leaders of the new dispensation, has even denounced the Americans with Disabilities Act of 1990 as "an abomination." Whether the issue is taxation or representation, we Americans spend a great deal of time talking about values and responsibilities, but it seems that few of us talk about things like "justice" anymore unless we're discussing crime—at which point we stop telling each other that life is unfair and begin talking to each other about fundamental rights to life and property. Indeed, so influential is this new-fundamentalist version of laissez-faire libertarian thought that it can be discovered even among liberals, or at least among people who are "liberals" by virtue of their own self-description. Take, for example, the late William Henry, a former culture critic for *Time* magazine, a card-carrying member of the ACLU, and the author of a book entitled *In Defense of Elitism*:

> The world is a rational place in which winners on the whole deserve to win and losers deserve to lose.
>
> Intelligence varies genetically and . . . intelligence by and large determines economic success.
>
> At some point the elitist impulse must be recognized as the only tenable one: to say, at least by the inaction of withholding treatment, that some lives are indeed worth less to society than others. Ideologues will denounce this as fascism. It is really just candor.

Now, as it happens, no one has yet denounced Henry's book as fascist; it won rave reviews from *New Criterion* managing editor Roger Kimball in the *New York Times Book Review* (that bastion of politically correct leftist thought) and from Harvard political scientist Harvey Mansfield in the *Wall Street Journal*. Although Mansfield's curious beliefs have caused him trouble before—most recently when he publicly delivered himself of the opinion that grade inflation at Harvard was the fault of indulgent liberals who were covering for the inferiority of black students—the larger lesson at stake here is all too clear. Some of us simply are worth more than others, and only an ideologue or a deconstructionist would think otherwise. Though one would hope that practicing Christians, whatever their sublunary political commitments, would find this idea repulsive as well.

However much I'd like to enlist practicing Christians in the cause of social egalitarianism, though, I don't want to argue that our current justifications of inequality are un-Christian. I want merely to look at how Henry's principle of "candor" actually works in practice. Let's take a recent example, one that has made headlines from sea to shining sea. Sandra Jensen, a thirty-five-year-old woman with Down syndrome, has an IQ of 70 and a congenital heart defect that puts an increasingly unbearable strain on her respiratory system. She's been more independent than many adults with Down's—living in her own apartment in Sacramento, California, for fourteen years—but in the early spring of 1995 she found she needed a heart-lung transplant to stay alive. Unfortunately, no local hospital would perform the procedure, and in March 1995, Stanford University Hospital administrators rejected her request for treatment on the grounds that people with Down syndrome are not "appropriate candidates" for the surgery. UC San Diego turned her down as well, noting that she is "limited in her ability to have recall and memory." Denial of medical treatment on the grounds of disability happens all the time throughout North America; for that matter, denial of medical treatment on grounds of indigence is getting more common with each passing year. But Ms. Jensen's case was poignant enough to make the pages of *People* magazine in October 1995, whereupon the court of public opinion constructed by *People* became, for Sandra Jensen and for many people like her, the court of last resort.

Like a lot of the stories that appear in *People*, Sandra's has a happy ending. In January 1996, Stanford reversed its earlier decision and performed the double transplant. *People* magazine didn't impel this result by itself: Stanford agreed to the procedure only after California's Medicaid program agreed to provide Sandra with a full-time caretaker to help her with post-operative necessities like exercise and anti-rejection drugs. According to the AP newswire, Sandra became the "first seriously retarded person in the United States to receive a major transplant." The phrasing is interesting. Most of us would agree that a heart-lung transplant constitutes major surgery, but not everyone would consider an independent, thirty-five-year-old woman with an IQ of 70 "seriously retarded." But was justice done in the Sandra Jensen case? Was she an appropriate candidate for the surgery after all, or was she using up valuable medical resources that should have gone to a more "capable" citizen with a higher IQ and a better memory? The best answer to this question, I think, was provided by Dr. William Bronson, a California state rehabilitation administrator and one of Ms. Jensen's leading advocates. According to Bronson, Sandra Jensen's groundbreaking victory was not a victory for Sandra Jensen alone: "This is a miracle," Bronson told the press. "The struggle to get Sandra on the transplant list was really a struggle to get everyone in the country on the list." Of course, not everyone wants to be on that list, but that's not the point. The point is that if Sandra Jensen has convinced us of the justice of her appeal, then perhaps we just might be able to imagine a society in which every living person has an equal right to the medical resources they require. Some people may, for whatever reason, find it desirable to waive that right; but in Ms. Jensen's case or in anyone else's, justice would seem to demand that the right to medical treatment be established *as* a basic human right, regardless of whether an individual person wants to exercise it.

In 1865, the great Russian novelist Fyodor Dostoyevsky outlined his plan to write a novel about crime and punishment. A young man murders an apparently worthless and malicious old woman, but "the laws of justice and truth, of human justice, gain the upper hand. The murderer himself decides to accept his punishment in order to expiate his crime. However," Dostoyevsky added, "I find it difficult to explain my idea." Nor, I would add, is it clear where the idea came from. Literary critic William Dowling tells of a different scenario that centers on the same problem:

> I'm reminded of a story told by a friend of mine about a philosophy seminar he once took with John Searle. The discussion was about the concept of promising, and my friend was having difficulty with how, at a certain point in the act of promising, a new thing called an "obligation" materializes out of nowhere. Where does it come from? Searle's instant rejoinder was: "Look, Schueler: you're in a football game. Your quarterback hands you the ball. You zig; you zag; you run into the end zone. Where do the six points come from?"
>
> A witty rejoinder, as one expects from Searle, but on examination it seems only to translate the original difficulty into other terms: Where, indeed, *do* the six points come from?

Searle's point, obviously, is that six points are as necessary a part of touchdowns—part of the definition of what a touchdown *is*—as obligations are part of promising. As Ludwig Wittgenstein might say, that's simply how the game is played.

But Wittgenstein also notes, in a sinuous discussion concerning definitions, that even lines have thickness—and any football fan can tell you that the boundary of the "end zone" is often anything but self-evident, its definition resting as it does on an official's interpretation of whether the ball has broken the *plane* of the *front edge* of the goal line. Borders are no less powerful for being intangible, to be sure, but the paradox of football is that we do not obviate disputes by defining boundaries with ever greater precision: on the contrary, the very attempt to draw the line "precisely" creates the conditions of possibility for further contestation of the boundary (as in the dispute over whether on-field officials should be overruled by instant replay). So where do the six points come from? And why *six*? What is this idea of "human justice," and why is it so hard to explain? From the book of Genesis to *2001: A Space Odyssey*, humans have not failed to puzzle over the fact that they are intelligent creatures who can conceive of things like "justice" but who murder and betray each other nonetheless. And although Genesis suggests we've fallen from a more divine state and *2001* suggests we're smart tool-making hominids who don't know how to put tools to good use, they leave us in pretty much the same dilemma in the end. We have this odd sense that there is such a thing as "right action," and although we regularly pontificate about what this might be, we don't normally engage in it.

So, dear reader, be you a chimney sweep or a chairman of the board, do you have any obligations to the Jamies in your midst? Why is it possible for us to believe that we may, and so easy for us to act as if we do not? Is it simply that we find it so easy to believe we will never face the prospect of caring for someone—child, parent, friend, countryman—with a disability that requires our help?

Most Earthlings answer these questions by referring them to divinity: The six points come from God, from Allah, from Ba'al, from Shiva, from the spirit or the will of the infinite Is. Unfortunately, however, over the past ten thousand years or so, that answer has precipitated a good deal more disagreement than concord. So let's assume for the moment that we can't explain our ideas of human justice by invoking "divine justice"; let's assume that the idea of justice is simply some weird by-product of consciousness, just as consciousness appears to be an evanescent epiphenomenon of intelligence. And then let's ask where that leaves us.

In recent decades, sociobiologists have posed the question anew, but they've posed it in a most troubling way—and sociobiologists, I think, might be of some relevance to a moral predicament that, in Jamie's case, directly follows from the question of how we administer and interpret significant variations on the human biological norm. They are, so they claim, inclined to take the long view: Since self-sacrificing organisms would seem to be less likely to survive and reproduce than would selfish organisms, how can we explain the existence of altruism? Or is altruism merely a ideological overlay, a deceptive sugar coating, masking the fact that humans, like the rest of the natural world, should by rights be red in tooth and claw?

Such questions become even more seductive when you look at evolution from the gene's point of view, which, for living things, seems to be the longest view available. That's precisely what Richard Dawkins set out to do in his 1976 book, *The Selfish Gene*. Despite his provocative title, which has led to any number of misunderstandings, Dawkins doesn't suggest anything so silly as a specific gene for selfishness; rather, he starts from the premise that when we look at life on Earth, we're really looking at how DNA makes a home for itself. There are some special molecules that can produce copies of themselves; so how is it that over the course of Earth's history (to date) they have managed to be so successful? How have they managed to produce bacteria, vertebrates, reptiles, mammals? Why should they have developed organisms that require sex to reproduce instead of relying on simple cell division? Why should they have devised organisms that lay eggs, that build chrysalises, that undergo the perils of live birth? Why, in other words, are we here, and what might we do about it?

In one sense, Dawkins's perspective is bracing: Genes are the carriers of self-replicating DNA molecules, and in Dawkins's felicitous phrase, we humans are merely the "survival machines" that enable genes to go about their business. But in another sense, Dawkins's perspective is deeply disturbing, particularly when he tries to account for how natural selection preserves some genetic mutations and not others:

> It is its potential immortality that makes a gene a good candidate as the basic unit of natural selection. . . . The few new ones who succeed do so partly because they are lucky, but mainly because they have what it takes, and that means they are good at making survival machines. . . .
>
> [C]an we think of any universal qualities which we would expect to find in all good (i.e. long-lived) genes? Conversely, what are the properties which instantly mark a gene out as a "bad," short-lived one? There might be several such properties, but there is one which is particularly relevant to this book: at the gene level, altruism must be bad and selfishness good. . . . Any gene which behaves in such a way as to increase its own survival chances in the gene pool at the expense of its alleles will, by definition, tautologically, tend to survive. The gene is the basic unit of selfishness.

It's a long leap from a gene to a government, but landmark books like *The Selfish Gene* and Edward O. Wilson's *On Human Nature* (1978) do tend to suggest that over the long run—say, a few hundred million years or so—there's no reason why a species would make provisions for the care of individuals like Jamie. Usually, though, they hasten to add that we should not derive any public policy implications from this. In a 1975 *New York Times Magazine* essay, "Human Decency Is Animal," Wilson wrote that "When any genetic bias is demonstrated, it cannot be used to justify a continuing practice in present and future societies." That's a noble sentiment, and quite right in its refusal to derive a political *ought* from the hypothesis of a biochemical *is*. But as it happens, some sociobiologists aren't as scrupulous as Wilson suggests; on the contrary, over the past twenty years, it has become quite common to see biological determinists using their research to argue for or against public policy initiatives. Interestingly, however, Dawkins himself, echoing Wilson's sentiments, ends his book with the suggestion that heredity is not destiny:

> Even if we look at the dark side and assume that individual man is fundamentally selfish, our conscious foresight—our capacity to simulate the future in imagination—could save us from the worst selfish excesses of the blind replicators. We have at least the mental equipment to foster our long-term selfish interests rather than merely our short-term selfish interests. We have the power to defy the selfish genes of our birth. . . . We can even discuss ways of cultivating and nurturing pure, disinterested altruism—something that has no place in nature, something that has never existed before in the history of the world.

In many ways, Dawkins's conclusion is eloquent and moving. What, then, shall we make of our ability to discuss and nurture an unprecedented and anomalous trait like altruism, whether we conceive it in Christian, utilitarian, or sociobiological terms?

But wait a minute. *That's* not right. Altruism may be unprecedented, and human selflessness may have no place in nature, but almost *everything* human has no place in nature, from World Cup soccer games to the threat of thermonuclear war. Why then should we be so concerned about the anomalous status of altruism? Why shouldn't we focus our attention on the anomalous status of war?

In the humanities and the social sciences, we're generally familiar with the principle that observation is always already informed by interpretation. We know how to deconstruct a premise, an axiom, a first principle, and show how its assumptions inform or dictate its conclusions. Take, for instance, Lawrence Wright's August 1995 *New Yorker* essay on twin studies, which complains that our political squeamishness has squelched legitimate genetic research: "In this country," he writes, "the National Institutes of Health, facing charges of racism, pulled the rug out from under a planned 1992 conference on 'Genetic Factors in Crime' and scaled back research into the causes of violence." Well, do tell. Why, I wonder, should we hold a conference on crime that investigates genetic predispositions to *violence*? Why shouldn't we hold a conference on crime that investigates genetic predispositions to embezzlement? Perhaps my suggestion wouldn't be likely to garner NIH support, but imagine that it did. The point at issue here is this: *Which* forms of human behavior are we expecting to "account for" genetically? Why might we think that violent crime calls out for an evolutionary explanation, rather than embezzlement—or, more seriously still, the bizarre human impulse to devastate the fragile environment that makes life possible in the first place?

This kind of selective vision, I fear, is not accidental in sociobiology; it is fundamental. It was there from the start. As Edward

Wilson himself inadvertently demonstrated in "Human Decency Is Animal," the field *assumed* a specific vision of "human nature" from the outset:

> We commonly find one species of bird or mammal to be highly territorial, employing elaborate, aggressive displays and attacks, while a second, otherwise similar species shows little or no territorial behavior. In short, the case for a pervasive aggressive instinct does not exist. . . .
>
> Mankind, let me add at once, happens to be one of the more aggressive species. But we are far from being the most aggressive. Recent studies of hyenas, lions and languar monkeys, to take three familiar species, have disclosed that under natural conditions those animals engage in lethal fighting, infanticide and even cannibalism at a rate far above that found in human beings. When a count is made of the number of murders committed per thousand individuals per year, human beings are well down the list of aggressive creatures, and *I am fairly confident that this would still be the case even if our episodic wars were to be averaged in.* (Emphasis added.)

All right, we're not that violent a species, and probably we're somewhere well down the charts even if we counted murders committed in war. I think that's a little like saying we don't think there's very much ice on the planet, and that we're fairly confident that this would be true even if we were to look at the planet's polar regions. But why should we start from this position at all? Why should we consider *altruism* so hard to explain in evolutionary terms? Why should we not start from the premise that no other mammalian species has developed practices like "war," "torture," and "genocide," each of which is far more destructive than "lethal fighting," infanticide, and cannibalism—particularly since war, torture, and genocide have rather little survival value for struggling species?

It's possible to argue that torture and genocide differ only in degree from the practices of other species. Cats sometimes toy with mice before killing them, and war may be just another name for "lethal fighting," but what distinguishes us from other cruel and nasty species, in this respect, is our wonderful capacity for social organization. We have gotten together and perfected torture on a mass scale, torture administered by governmental policy, just as we have developed the ability to take lethal fighting to a point unimagined by angry bone-wielding ape-men. Why then should we not try to account, in evolutionary terms, for the development of skills that may endanger every form of life as we know it?

Let me pose these questions another way. Leaving aside the possibility that all the really smart, selfish specimens of Homo erectus were mysteriously killed off by viruses or earthquakes a million years ago, giving us comparatively altruistic saps domain over the earth by default, what if there *were* a genetic component to altruism? What if, say, the altruism gene is discovered to lie somewhere on the twenty-first chromosome, thus giving rise to speculation that people with Down syndrome are just as human as anyone else, only more humane? I wouldn't buy it for an instant. People with Down syndrome are *not* uniformly sweet and angelic. It's a "good" stereotype, as stereotypes go, but it just doesn't fit the facts. It's something like the belief that people with Down syndrome were "put" here to humanize the rest of us. It's nice enough if this actually happens, since there are few among us who would not benefit by being more compassionate, but as a general principle it becomes less attractive the longer you look at it. I mean, personally, I hope none of us was put here for the benefit of others.

But such are the seductions of the argument from design: we like to think that every human trait, whether it's been engineered by God or by natural selection, is here for a reason. Indeed, I'm convinced that most people who think they accept the tenets of evolution actually believe in something more like "meliorism," just as most Christians, when pressed, turn out to be Docetists, believers in the ancient heresy that Christ was not fully human after all (ask a Christian whether Christ had sexual fantasies or moments of irrational hatred and you'll see what I mean). Meliorism is the picture of evolution we get from that famous representation of chimps, ape-men, and humans walking left to right—a string of primates depicting the march of "progress," gradually getting more upright and increasing their hat sizes as they go. To ask at what juncture the concept of "justice" might arrive in this picture is to play into the hands of the social Darwinists: *Exactly*, they say, *justice is contrary to nature, and life is unfair*. 'Twas ever thus. Now get back down there and shovel that coal.

In the end, asking where the idea of justice "came from" may turn out to be a lot like asking about the point value of touchdowns. Maybe the origins of the concept of justice, and the possibility of altruism that it entails, should be sought in provisional forms of conscious, linguistically mediated human agreement rather than in the blind workings of primordial ooze. Those forms of agreement have been around long before the mid-twentieth century, before even the invention of football, and they've generally taken three shapes. One is commonly associated with Christ, and it's worth heeding regardless of whether you believe Christ was divine: Do unto others as you would have them do unto you. One is an ancient variation on this, asking you not to imagine the possibility of reciprocity but the power of emulation: Wouldn't you like to be the kind of person who does *that*? (Or, conversely, wouldn't you like to avoid being the kind of person who does *that*?) And one is the Kantian reworking of the idea of reciprocity: Conduct yourself as if your actions could become universal law.

There are doubtless billions and billions of other possible moral edicts, but these three will serve us well for now. Kant's is notoriously difficult to put into practice, partly because it is an "anti-consequentialist" theory: You're supposed to behave morally without regard to possible consequences. Taking consequences into account leads you to the realm of cost-benefit analyses, the greatest good for the greatest number, the moral calculus—and Kant's theory wanted none of those distractions. In the famous example, it requires you to tell the truth to Attila the Hun even if doing so will bring about the death of an entire civilization. The principle of emulation is similarly vexed, since it relies on the systems of social value and prestige that are already in place. I would indeed like to be the kind of person whom everybody thinks is real cool, but that doesn't say much about whether I should be entrusted with the power to shape social policy. The standard of reciprocity is hampered because it's so difficult to think of except when you're dealing with people one at a time (putting blankets on their sleeping bodies) or in small groups (ordering pizza, tacos, and burgers in an imaginary restaurant). When it comes to larger entities like nations, it may be possible to persuade people to give their lives for their country, but appeals like that don't rely on the principle of reciprocity, mainly because it makes little sense to enjoin people (whether the issue is war or welfare) to do unto 250 million other people as they would have 250 million other people do unto them. Yet there's a crucial commonality to all three moral imperatives. They require the attribute of imagination—not imagination as daydreaming, but imagination as a kind of disciplined aesthetic-ethical exercise that enhances your ability to imagine yourself as someone other than yourself.

Two of the most formidable moral philosophers of our time, both of whose work relies explicitly on the ideal of reciprocity, are Jürgen Habermas and John Rawls. Habermas, whose theory usually goes by the name of "communicative action," focuses on the possibility of locating norms of reciprocity in social practices that enable reflection—chiefly, language. The ideal society, for Habermas, resembles an "ideal speech situation" in which all conversants speak freely in an atmosphere free of domination, coercion, or power asymmetry of any kind, and the possibility of imagining such a society resides, interestingly, in the communicative ideal inherent in language itself. Habermas is routinely criticized, of course—from the right, for being a wishful thinker; from the left, for imagining that some kind of "consensus" will emerge from the ideal speech situation. But interestingly enough, neither the critics from the right nor the critics from the left have been able to argue convincingly that the hypothetical "ideal speech situation," in which all humans discourse as equals, is not in fact ideal.

Rawls takes a wholly different approach, but his 1971 book, *A Theory of Justice*, is nonetheless our century's single most compelling challenge to utilitarian philosophy, and the reason for its cogency is that Rawls, like Habermas, imagines the creation of a social contract in which the ideal of reciprocity precedes any other notion of the right or of the good. In the Rawlsian state, people are governed by two overarching principles, each of which has to be interpreted to fit every new situation and context: "First: each person is to have an equal right to the most extensive basic liberty compatible with a similar liberty for others. Second: social and economic inequalities are to be arranged so that they are both (a) reasonably expected to be to everyone's advantage, and (b) attached to positions and offices open to all." By contrast, utilitarianism holds that the just society is that which creates the greatest good for the greatest number. For most of my life I've considered that principle sufficient to my own needs, and Jamie's as well—since, as I fondly imagined, any decent conception of "the greatest number" would certainly include Jamie. And yes, utilitarianism, as social philosophy, is vastly preferable to any social Darwinist regime in which the battle goes always to the strong, the bread always to those whose test scores declare them to be wise. It's also many light-years beyond the adolescent, libertarian conception of a regime in which individual freedom supersedes all other claims to "justice" in a local or collective sense.

But Rawls's "formalist" critique of utilitarianism is a forceful one, and it rests on three insuperable problems in utilitarian thought. First, utilitarianism permits some individuals to be disadvantaged so that the collective good, averaged over the entire population, can be enhanced. Most egalitarians would think that's all right: We can deprive the luckiest few of some of the fruits of their advantages so that the rest of us can benefit slightly. As Rawls shows, however, there's nothing in utilitarianism to prevent this logic from working the opposite way. Thus, we might achieve the "greatest good" by allowing 10 percent of the population to reap such extraordinary social benefits that the "collective" good of the society is enhanced, per capita, even if the other 90 percent of the population never sees any of these benefits and can only read about them in the papers. Second, utilitarianism, like libertarianism, doesn't challenge irrational selfishness or eugenics; it merely factors these into the mix. As Rawls puts it, in utilitarianism, "social welfare depends directly and solely upon the levels of satisfaction or dissatisfaction of individuals. Thus if men take a certain pleasure in discriminating against one another, in subjecting others to a lesser liberty as a means of enhancing their self-respect, then the satisfaction of those desires must be weighed in our deliberations according to their intensity, or whatever, along with other desires." Rawls's challenge to this is the idea of "justice as fairness," where fairness entails the principles of reciprocity I mentioned above, and where, from the outset, "an individual who finds that he enjoys seeing others in positions of lesser liberty understands that he has no claim whatever to this enjoyment."

Third and last, utilitarianism does not respect individual idiosyncrasy. This seems to be a strange charge to level against utilitarians, especially if you've just charged them with accepting individuals' idiosyncratic desire to discriminate against each other, but as it happens, it follows from the utilitarian conception of the "greatest good." Put it this way: *Who* determines the greatest good, and on what basis? It turns out that the utilitarian answer to these questions assumes that societies might be able to deliberate about such matters as if they were composed of one single individual. "The striking feature of the utilitarian view of justice," writes Rawls,

is that it does not matter, except indirectly, how this sum of satisfactions is distributed among individuals any more than it matters, except indirectly, how one man distributes his satisfactions over time. The correct distribution in either case is that which yields the maximum fulfillment. . . . Here we may note a curious anomaly. It is customary to think of utilitarianism as individualistic, and certainly there are good reasons for this. The utilitarians were strong defenders of liberty and freedom of thought, and they held that the good of society is constituted by the advantages enjoyed by individuals. Yet utilitarianism is not individualistic . . . in that, by conflating all systems of desires, it applies to society the principle of choice for one man.

To think this way, says Rawls, "is not to take seriously the plurality and distinctness of individuals."

Here, then, is where Rawls and Habermas might meet. Deliberations about social justice are not a matter of generalizing from one individual, even if that one individual were so infinitely imaginative that she could experience everyone's attachments and desires as her own. Rather, the ideal of social justice is founded on a collective dialogue—or, more precisely, polylogue—in which all social actors contribute their notions of individual and collective good. There's no reason to believe that such a polylogue will end in consensus, but there's every reason to believe that procedurally it's the best idea we humans have yet devised for hashing out the essential decisions that determine *what* we will value and why—as well as what we will mean by the word "value." If that's the case, then we would do well to seek the ground for human justice in our capacity to communicate with one another, regardless of whether we have sustained serious hearing loss in one ear, regardless of whether we are incapable of uttering proper names, regardless of whether we mumble, regardless of whether we communicate by ASL.

Be our alphabets or our vocabularies what they may, it is through the social practice known as language that we might establish the value of a touchdown or of a human life. The "ground" of justice, in this case, is simply our ability to imagine reciprocity as a ground. Is this ability inherent in us, etched somewhere in the genome? It's hard to imagine why this question might matter. Who can say why the Earth gave birth to creatures who could write books about reciprocity? Geochemists can't even explain why the oxygen composition of Earth's atmosphere has remained so stable for the past couple of billion years. As Lewis Thomas has written, "It is another illustration of our fantastic luck that oxygen filters out the very bands of ultraviolet light that are most devastating for nucleic acids and proteins, while allowing full penetration of the visible light needed for photosynthesis." So let's start from the proposition that we can't fully explain why we're here, and let's create for ourselves a new Chain of Being that expresses our sense of how utterly unlikely we are: First, life is epiphenomenal to matter. From our perspective, it's the most fascinating development we can imagine for things like carbon and potassium, but nothing about the structure of carbon or potassium compels the conclusion that the universe's basic elements just won't be satisfied until they've hooked themselves up into chains that can reproduce themselves. Next, as life is epiphenomenal to matter, so is self-reflective intelligence epiphenomenal to life. Once life is under way on a planet, it's reasonable to expect that conditions will favor self-replicating molecules that can adapt to their environment. But that's no reason to expect that self-replicating molecules should eventually become self-*aware*.

Even in our many representations of human affairs, from Oedipus to Hamlet to Ronald Reagan, we can find no correlation between reflective self-awareness and effective action. Still less is there any reason to link the rise of self-awareness to the rise of language; although the latter might enhance the former, the former doesn't compel the latter. Finally, though we may have evolved, by whatever chance, that sequence of biochemical reactions which Steven Pinker calls a "language instinct," there's nothing to suggest that a language instinct should also carry with it a *reciprocity* instinct. Our languages may all have an internal grammar for which we are hard-wired, but we were using our many languages for quite a long time before we conceived of societies founded on the idea of "egalitarian reciprocity" or "justice as fairness." All we know about this idea is that it's here, it's queer, and we ought to get used to it.

There's no mystery, then, why social Darwinists like Charles Murray spend so much time railing against the political unnaturalness of what they call the "Rawlsian state." They're outraged that evolution has produced a species conscious of evolutionary processes, and they're determined to make sure that we *don't* get used to the idea that we can actually think about evolution, evaluate our innate proclivities, and thereby try to form a society that obeys some rule other than the "survival of the fittest." Such is the fondest dream of the social Darwinist: that they might argue us into abdicating the self-reflexive intelligence bequeathed to us by the mechanics of natural selection.

But once we've gotten used to the idea that we have the capacity to imagine an ideal form of reciprocity, one final question remains: How do we put this idea of "justice" into practice? Here neither Rawls nor Habermas can help my son. Both men, for all their emphasis on reciprocity as the basis of social justice, start from the proposition that before we can discuss the idea of the collective good, we have to shed our individual idiosyncrasies, anything that might prevent us from identifying (and identifying *with*) the collective good in the largest possible sense. Habermas imagines a "public sphere" in which all citizens participate as peers, divested of the attributes that divide us, such as race, gender, age, ethnicity, and sexual orientation. Rawls, even more stringently, imagines that the founders of the ideally just society know nothing about their own idiosyncrasies, nothing about their own most cherished desires:

Among the essential features of this situation is that no one
knows his place in society, his class position or social status,
nor does any one know his fortune in the distribution of natural assets and abilities, his intelligence, strength, and the
like. I shall even assume that the parties do not know their
conceptions of the good or their special psychological propensities. The principles of justice are chosen behind a veil of ig-
norance.

Neither Rawls nor Habermas is suggesting that justice can only
be deliberated by humans without qualities; neither is saying
that we cannot come to terms with citizens like James unless we
shed all the particularities that make us *us*. They're simply
proposing an abstract starting point: If perfect justice is to be envisioned by imperfect human beings, then let us begin by envisioning some hypothetical "neutral" human being who will do
the envisioning—a human being who will not even know her
own conception of justice.

But from where *we* stand, in my household, knowing what we
do about who we are, we think that both Rawls and Habermas
are succumbing to a curious Enlightenment fantasy, the idea that
once we boil away all the idiosyncrasies and impurities of the irrational human race, we can come up with some perfectly neutral,
rational, disinterested character who can play the language-game
of justice as if it were a contest in which he or she had no stake.
As long as justice depends, even theoretically, on the deliberations of humans who have no interests, no disabilities, no "special
psychological propensities," no passionate desires to see the world
and to see it in a specific way, then Rawlsian and Habermasian
ideas of justice will remain "academic" exercises in the worst
sense of the word—the sense we use when we speak of an "acade-

mic" question, a question that does not matter. Feminist philosophers like Nancy Fraser and Seyla Benhabib have already made the case for us: If Rawls is right in criticizing utilitarianism for its inability "to take seriously the plurality and distinctness of individuals," then we shouldn't begin to imagine, even provisionally, a system of justice that gets deliberated by "unmarked" individuals who have been theoretically purged of all individual proclivities and predilections. There isn't a chance in the world that James Lyon Bérubé could come to the table independently of "interests," independent of cognitive and social idiosyncrasies legible to all, independent of either a genetic makeup or a social apparatus that constructs him as "abnormal." The society that fosters Jamie's independence *must* start from an understanding of his dependencies, and any viable conception of justice has to take the concrete bodies and "private," idiosyncratic interests of individuals like Jamie into account, or it will be of no account at all.

There was a time when I would have considered any system of "universal justice" hopelessly naive. Indeed, before James was born I frankly didn't think very highly of appeals to our "common humanity." I thought such appeals were well intentioned but basically inconsequential. Clearly, Muslim and Christian do not bond over their common ancestor in Australopithecus. Rwandan Hutu and Rwandan Tutsi do not toast to their distinctive status as speakers of language and creators of art. The rape of Bosnia, and Bosnian women, does not stop once Serbian soldiers realize that they too will pass from the earth.

Yet we benighted humans possess one crucial characteristic: the desire to communicate, to understand, to put ourselves in some mutual, reciprocal form of contact with one another. This desire hasn't proven any better at disarming warheads than any of the weaker commonalities enumerated above, but it stands a better chance nonetheless. For among the most amazing and hopeful things about this species is that its offspring show up, from their day of birth, programmed to receive and transmit even in the most difficult circumstances; the ability to conduct mutual communicative relations is embedded in our material bodies, woven through our double-stranded fibers. Granted, the sociohistorical variables of human communication, like the variables in everything else about us, are more significant and numerous than any genetic determinism can admit. All the same, the ability to communicate lies in our software somewhere, and better still, it's a program that teaches itself how to operate each time we use it.

Whether you want to consider reciprocal communication a constant or a variable, though, the point remains that it's a human attribute that requires other people if it's going to work. Among the talents we have, it's one we could stand to develop more fully. It's only natural: among our deepest, strongest impulses is the impulse to mutual cueing. Nothing, nothing will delight James so much as the realization that you have understood him—except the realization that he has understood *you*, and recursively understood his own understanding and yours. Perhaps I could have realized our human stake in mutual realization without James's aid; any number of other humans would have been willing to help me out. But now that I get it, I get it for good. Communication is itself self-replicating. Sign unto others as you'd have them sign unto you. Pass it on.

■

Epilogue

▲

Many of them have almond-shaped eyes, obliquely set; and this feature, with the squat nose and wiry hair, gives the Mongol aspect from which they derive their name. The hands are usually broad and the fingers short, and often the little finger is incurved. The feet are also characteristically clumsy. There is reason to believe that they are essentially *unfinished* children, and that their peculiar appearance is really that of a phase of foetal life.

—G. E. Shuttleworth, *Mentally Deficient Children: Their Treatment and Training*, 1900

Fond parents will frequently insist that their Mongol child can speak when his vocabulary is limited to a repetition of such sounds as "dada," and "mamma" to which he associates no meaning. . . . Parents often state that their Mongol child began to talk at 3 or 4 years of age, or rather to repeat a few words but after a few months the child ceased to speak and vocalization became limited to grunts and harsh cries.

—Kate Brousseau, *Mongolism: A Study of the Physical and Mental Characteristics of Mongolian Imbeciles*, 1928

I couldn't believe my eyes. It was worse than any institution I have seen in visits to a dozen foreign countries. . . . In our country, we would not be allowed to treat cattle like that.

—Niels Erik Bank-Mikkelsen, director of Danish national services for mental retardation, on visiting Sonoma State Hospital in California, just *before* Governor Ronald Reagan had cut $17 million from the state budget for state hospitals and mental institutions, 1967

It is really about how much love and compassion that you have. That's what really counts about values.

—Mitchell Levitz, a twenty-one-year-old man with Down syndrome, November 1992

In March 1995, *Harper's* magazine ran a letter from Steven Pinker in which he responded to an essay that marked my first attempt to write about Jamie. In his reading of my discussion of the textual representation of people with Down syndrome, Pinker apparently took me to be saying that "words and phrases" were to blame for unsavory political attitudes. Accordingly, he set out to set me straight, lest I fall into the English-professor trap of thinking that language is coextensive with thought: "Bérubé notes," he wrote, "that although 'retarded' and 'delayed' are synonyms, neither with any literal pejorative sense, the former (and older) word has become an epithet. Exactly so: any unpleasant or emotionally charged concept will soon taint the word that denotes it, calling for a 'polite' replacement. Unfortunately, the replacement does not cleanse the concept, but rather becomes tainted itself." The letter overall was eloquent and friendly, and closed with a few words of advice to those of us who might want to change what we consider to be unsavory political attitudes: "I take the point of Bérubé's essay to be that there is a greater range of functioning among Down syndrome children than most people think and that, for both ethical and practical reasons, every Down's child ought to be treated as if he or she were in the upper part of this range. Focusing on words and phrases is misspent energy. Once the message gets out, the language will change accordingly."

The reason Pinker wrote to *Harper's* was that I had asked the magazine to send him a copy of my manuscript, thinking that we might have the grounds for an engaging discussion of the competing claims of biological determinism and social constructionism—nature, nurture, and everything in between. But I was surprised that he'd associated my argument with the now discredited Sapir-Whorf hypothesis that our language absolutely determines our thoughts. All I'd said was that there are "intimate links between words and social policies," and I never suggested that one always dictates the other.

But when it comes to the political potential of mere linguistic change, I'm afraid I have to disagree with Pinker on other grounds. When a word becomes an epithet and is eventually supplanted by a "polite replacement," the replacement word *may* become "tainted" in turn—or, as people argue over whether the replacement is an improvement, it may briefly make us self-conscious about what the epithet might mean. Then there are words like "nigger" that mysteriously persist no matter how often people of African descent demonstrate their humanity, thus casting doubt on the proposition that our language changes once the message gets out. Speaking of which, what does it mean when people take up the terms in which they have been dehumanized,

when black folk call each other "nigger" and gay and lesbian people nominate themselves "queer"? Has the language changed, in
these cases, simply because a message has gotten out, or are people trying to change the very meaning of the message that dehu-
manizes them?

My thoughts about thought, language, and change might be
neatly summarized by Ludwig Wittgenstein:

> In a law-court, for instance, the question might be raised
> how someone meant a word. And this can be inferred from
> certain facts.—It is a question of *intention*. But could how he
> experienced a word—the word "bank" for instance—have
> been significant in the same way?
>
> Suppose I had agreed on a code with someone; "tower"
> means bank. I tell him "Now go to the tower"—he under-
> stands me and acts accordingly, but he feels the word "tower"
> to be strange in this use, it has not yet "taken on" the mean-
> ing.

So we may someday call banks "towers" and retarded people "delayed," but there will undoubtedly be a period during which the
new terms have not yet "taken on" their meanings even though
people seem to be using them correctly; and in that interim period, there will surely be debate, reflection, and general self-
consciousness about what "stigma" is and how it operates. Thus,
even when people like me and Steven Pinker disagree over theoretical accounts of linguistic change, it's like the song says in
Oklahoma!—the cognitive psycholinguist and the postmodernist
literary critic can be friends.

This particular disagreement may seem like a classic case of
nitpicking academics missing the boat (or, as they say in ASL,
train go sorry), but as a matter of fact, the question at hand here is

central to everything we say (and everything I've written so far). How do we represent ourselves to ourselves, and what is the material and political force of our representations?

Think of it this way. Much of the literature on "political correctness" in the past few years has focused precisely on the production of elaborate euphemisms, "nonjudgmental" phrases that are easy to parody: *differently abled, vertically challenged, folically compromised*. It's weird that there should have been a national scandal and media feeding frenzy about this kind of thing, not only because it's relatively innocuous as social changes go but especially because it's been going on for decades, ever since "Negroes" became "black" and congresswomen asked to be called congresspersons. Of course, some of these semantic niceties are trivial, and of course some of them amount to rearranging the deck chairs on the *Titanic*—haggling over "physically challenged" or "differently abled" while Congress considers repealing both the Americans with Disabilities Act and the Individuals with Disabilities Education Act. For its part, the Down syndrome community has its own versions of these disputes. As far as I understand the current status of our language, it's more proper to say "child with Down syndrome" than to say "Down syndrome child," on the grounds that the child should come first. We've even been known to have heated arguments that center entirely on an apostrophe, bickering over whether to say *Down* or *Down's* (the issue here having to do with whether our children should be semantically possessed by J. Langdon Down, as if they were DS versions of Jerry's Kids). And we never, never say that someone "suffers from" or "is afflicted by" Down syndrome, because it's preposterous to speak as if you know someone is "suffering" from his or her disability.

As this book demonstrates, I care more about social policy than about "Down syndrome child," more about whether Jamie can *say* possessive "s" than whether he is marked by one. But you can talk about potatoes and tomatoes all you want; I see no reason to call the whole thing off. In our society, *representation matters*. Some linguistic differences, like some cognitive or genetic differences, are indeed too tiny to make a difference, but some can help to make all the difference in the world. Put that another way: If Steven Pinker is right in suggesting that "once the message gets out, the language will change accordingly," then how can the message get out in the first place, except by way of the medium we call "language"?

I don't mean "language" here in the restricted sense that Hamlet uses when he's asked what he's reading—"words, words." Visual representations are a language, too, which is why we can "read" them. In the 1950s, one of the textual instruments that fundamentally changed the "normal" person's perception of people with Down syndrome was *Angel Unaware*, Dale Evans Rogers's memorial book about her daughter Robin, who was born with Down syndrome and died of mumps at the age of two; in the 1990s, one of those textual instruments was the character of Corky, a teenager with Down syndrome played by Chris Burke on ABC's prime time TV series, *Life Goes On*. Whatever the differences between them, these representations were effective because they made it possible for nondisabled folks to imagine, understand, and sympathize with people who have Down syndrome. For some reason we don't yet understand, we seem incapable of empathizing with other humans in the abstract, and we need to have them *represented* to us before we can imagine what it might be like to share their feelings and their dreams. Part of the burden of representation, for human populations that have long been "dehumanized," is precisely to demonstrate that "dehumanized" people do in fact *have* feelings and dreams—just as you do.

Jamie dreams, too. He knows he does—or at least he says so. He likes to pretend to be asleep, and he likes to pop up and say, "Wake up!" Lately, he especially likes doing this in Nick's bed. Last year, he made the epochal transition from a crib to the lower half of a bunk bed with Nick, and *this* year, he learned, much to my distress, how to climb up into Nick's half of the bunk. Somewhere along the way, he also learned what a dream is, and he learned it in part by seeing textual representations of dreams—one in the exquisite Japanese children's film *The Adventures of Milo and Otis*, from a scene where Milo the cat falls asleep in an owl's dreaming nest, and one in the book *Sleepy Dog*, in which the sleepy dog in question dreams that he is running and eating hot dogs. Jamie's gradual recognition of these scenes was almost tangible: *So that's what's going on when I think I'm awake but I'm really asleep. What a revelation to know that other creatures do it, too.* It wasn't long after *Milo and Otis* became Jamie's favorite film that I could ask him, upon greeting him in the morning, if he'd had a *dream*, at which he would perk up, say, "Hm!" and claim (in answer to my next question) that he'd dreamed about a whale and a dolphin. Although I have no doubt that whales and dolphins are important components of his private mental life, I place little faith in these reports of his. Still, I know he knows he can dream. And now you do, too.

The question of how we represent each other to each other, in other words, is both an aesthetic question and a deeply ethical one. The only thing odd about this is that we live in an age when aesthetics and ethics are considered—at least by the self-proclaimed "traditionalists" in my field, like Harold Bloom—to be two utterly different realms of value. But if we take a step back from our own century and look at the emergence of something called "aesthetics" in the seventeenth and eighteenth century, we'll find something curious. As literary historian and theorist John Guillory points out, the discourse of "aesthetics" was once deeply entwined with other discourses of cultural value, like moral philosophy and political economy. Only recently—say, about two hundred years ago, when artists began working under market conditions vastly different from those which prevailed in the era of court patronage—did people start making the argument that aesthetic value was a form of value unto itself, referable to no other scale of evaluation.

In many ways this development was a welcome one, since it freed art (and criticism) from being judged solely for how it served the church or the state; but in one way it's given us a sadly impoverished way of talking about textual and visual representations—as if we could judge their "intrinsic" aesthetic value without any reference at all to their representational content. Such was the sorry outcome of the deliberations over the presentation of the United States' first Bollingen Prize for Poetry, awarded in 1948 to Ezra Pound for his Pisan Cantos. The poems in question contain some of the most revolting, virulent anti-Semitism ever put in verse form, and at one point Pound even says, in so many words, that the Jews are leading the hapless Gentiles to slaughter in great numbers. This is a strange thing to say under any circumstances, but in the wake of the Holocaust it might well be called obscene. Nonetheless, the Bollingen Committee, headed by T. S. Eliot, held that it was artistically illegitimate to judge a work of poetry for its "content." These were simply great poems, and could not be gauged by the same measure we use to evaluate mere "ordinary" language. Some fifty years later, this decision may look as obscene as the poetry it once glorified. Still, it would be a mistake to think that this kind of understanding of "the aesthetic" has passed from the scene. On the contrary, recent years have seen a minor publishing industry form around the project of protecting the purity of "aesthetic value" from the depredations of depraved, politically correct critics like me who would dare to apply "extrinsic" criteria to mere textual representations.

Let's pause a moment over the proposition that "representation" is always both a political and an aesthetic matter. After all, many humans do tend to live under governments that claim to be "representational," and most of us tend to read texts (of whatever kind) with at least one eye on their representational content. Aesthetics was always a matter of discerning the beautiful, but until the nineteenth century, the project of discerning the beautiful was indistinguishable from the project of discerning the *good*. Aesthetic excellence involved the creation of artistic forms that were fit and pleasing (whatever that might mean); likewise, justice involved the creation of social forms that distributed goods in a way that was fit and pleasing (whatever that might mean). This link between aesthetics and justice did not necessarily produce either artistic or social forms we might consider pleasing today. For instance, the notion of the Great Chain of Being, which holds that everything has its proper place from lower to higher orders, could authorize brutal social hierarchies every bit as easily as it ranked the genre of epic higher than the genre of lyric on the grounds that the former dealt with more elevated subject matter. If you believed in the Great Chain of Being, as did most European intellectuals in the eighteenth century, you could very well believe as a result that it is right, just, and pleasing that the common people starve and freeze while we superior, learned folks sit in Baroque drawing rooms and discuss aesthetics with wit and discernment.

To say this is not to say that the ancient idea of aesthetics was by any means blinkered or primitive. It was simply a way of apprehending and evaluating our representations of the world and of each other. The purpose of art, as the Latin poet Horace famously put it two millenia ago, was to delight and instruct. Accordingly, it should not take much imagination to suppose that, under these criteria, art was supposed to instruct us *about* something, and to delight us for some reason. Thus, it would be no more illegitimate to applaud a work of art because it showed you the way the world was (or the way the world might be) than to applaud a work of art because it showed you that despite all their faults, humans can create artifacts of stunning and remarkable beauty.

Here in the twentieth century, whatever we may believe about aesthetics and politics, we Americans argue about representations all the time: the representation of poor people in Congress, the representation of Arabs in Disney movies, the representation of African-Americans in the wake of the O.J. trial, the representation of African-Americans who aren't represented by the best lawyers that money can buy. In the past four years I have found that I have a vested interest in some of our representations, so much so that I now feel compelled to see any movie or read any book that depicts a character with a developmental disability. In practical terms, this means renting *What's Eating Gilbert Grape?* from our local video store and looking again at *One Flew Over the Cuckoo's Nest*. It means being disturbed that *Educating Peter*, a documentary about a boy with Down syndrome, inadvertently suggests that all kids with Down's have behavioral problems; and it means arguing about *Forrest Gump* for a few hours with my parents.

My father, who spoke out against the Vietnam War as early as 1965, largely agreed with conservatives' assessment of the film, but from the opposite side of the aisle. It was reactionary; it pathologized the entire 1960s counterculture; it left the impression that antiwar protesters were foul-mouthed, ill-clad, violent adolescent jerks. "You saw the movie, Michael," he said to me on my last visit home. "Did you see Robert Lowell in the antiwar scenes? Did you see Martin Luther King saying he wasn't gonna study war no more? No. All you saw was an Abbie Hoffman caricature." I told my father he was absolutely right and that furthermore, the movie's last half hour was maudlin and manipulative beyond endurance, marked by not one but *two* heartrending deaths, almost bathetic enough to lead you to expect little Forrest Junior to be struck and killed by the school bus that picks him up in the final scene. But Dad, I said, I just don't have the emotional apparatus I once had. There's a great deal I find aesthetically objectionable about the film, on formal and on ethical grounds, but still, this is a movie that just might change the meaning of "mental disability" in our culture. From Sally Field declaring "there is no normal" when she's told that Forrest is five IQ points below the norm, to Forrest's sage, pragmatist insistence that stupid is as stupid does, this is a movie that refuses any correlation between achievement and "intelligence." So for me, the question is not, What does this movie say about postwar American history? The question is, What bizarre turns in postwar American history have made it possible for *Forrest Gump* and *The Bell Curve* to appear in exactly the same cultural moment?

Representations matter. That's why advocates of the disabled are so concerned about polite words, popular movies, and visual and textual representations of every kind. Our world, as William Wordsworth once put it, is that which our eyes and ears half create and half perceive; and it is because Wordsworth is right that we need to deliberate the question of how we will represent the range of human variation to ourselves. Will we think it outrageous to hear of disabled children in regular classrooms, or odd to come across a child with Down syndrome modeling T-shirts in a flyer for Sears? Or will we think it objectionable to see *no* disabled children in regular classes, no children with Down syndrome in mail order catalogues? In either case, what will then become, to paraphrase Forrest's mother, of what we normally think of as "normal"?

Jamie has come a very long way since the days he spent supine in the ICU. He also has a very, very long way to go. He's just starting to learn to dress himself and to go to the bathroom, and once he manages that, his work is far from done. He will be a teenager before we know it, and we will have to talk to him about adolescence, sexuality, responsibility, and maturity. Not long after that, we will have to worry about whether he will live independently, whether he will find employment, whether he will live in a country that provides health care along with employment, or whether he will live in a country that discourages some of its poor and disabled people from working precisely *because* it is incapable of imagining national health care as something other than an evil, coercive government program. And then, when he's thirty or forty, we can begin to worry about the incidence of Alzheimer's in people with Down syndrome, and we can agonize over which scenario might bring us more emotional pain: the thought of our outliving him, or the thought of his outliving us.

Along the way, Jamie will learn that he has Down syndrome, and that although we do not know the limits to what he can achieve, we know that there *are* limits. Hardly a day goes by that I do not pause over this conundrum. It took the planet almost five billion years to create organisms that were conscious of being organisms. It took hominids another five million to produce children with Down syndrome who could grow up to know that they have Down syndrome. Only in the past few decades has there been a world in which people with Down syndrome know about Down syndrome—its biochemical causes, its developmental effects, and its various textual representations. What will come to pass, I wonder, when my child becomes a man, a man who knows he has a developmental disability that will be with him all his life?

I have read the words of adults with Down syndrome who say that they are tired of having Down syndrome, that they wonder what it would be like if they were born without a disability, that they're proud of what they've accomplished but frustrated by the effort it takes them to fulfill their desires. One of the reasons I've read these words—aside from my vested interests—is that people with Down syndrome have lately begun to represent *themselves* in public, in books, on television. Here, for instance, are the words of Mitchell Levitz, who not only gives me the inspiration for this epilogue but also testifies to an emotional maturity greater than that of any hundred nondisabled adults I know:

I do want to drive, but it's difficult for me to have the skills to drive. My father doesn't see me driving until a certain age. Dad, he sees me driving at twenty-three, which is next year, but I think that's not going to happen. I don't think I'm gonna have the skills by twenty-three or twenty-four. Or at all.

There will be other methods of transportation. I don't think I will ever get those skills. It's difficult for me to face, but I'm learning to accept the fact that I may not be able to do some things that my sisters are doing. Which is a main fact which I will understand.

Not every adult with Down syndrome has Mitchell's sublime equanimity, but if we're concerned with the relation between social justice and textual representation, then that's not important. What's important is that in the face of incalculable odds, we humans have fashioned a social-political-discursive-medical-legal apparatus that not only produces better and better representations of people with Down syndrome but also produces textual representations of people with Down syndrome *authored by* people with Down syndrome. Chris Burke published his autobiography, *Special Kind of Hero*, in 1991; Mitchell Levitz and Jason Kingsley published their collaborative book, *Count Us In: Growing Up with Down Syndrome*, in 1994. Until these books appeared, people with Down syndrome had to rely for their representation on the talents and good will of people without Down syndrome; henceforth, Jason and Mitchell and Chris and their peers can—and will—speak in their own voices.

In these pages, I have tried to represent James to the best of my ability. I have done so in the belief that my textual representations of him might make his claims on the world as broadly and as strongly as possible. I know full well that textual representation is only one form of representation. Nothing I write will redraw a political district; nothing I write will change the chemical composition of Jamie's cells; nothing I write will affect his ability to hear. He has had, to date, two ear operations to combat chronic ear infections; and as I write, he sleeps soundly in the room next to our study, his aural passages kept clear by surgically implanted tubes. As he sleeps, and as I write, we debate the value of physical "treatment" of people like him: tongue surgery, vitamin therapy, nootropic drugs that combat the overproduction of oxidants and free radicals in the cells of persons with Down syndrome. And as he sleeps, and as I write, we debate the meaning of words like "normal," "retarded," "disability," and, underwriting all these, "justice." My task, ethically and aesthetically, is to represent James to you with all the fidelity that mere language can afford, the better to enable you to imagine him—and to imagine what he might think of your ability to imagine him.

When Jamie was younger and just learning to feed himself, we eagerly anticipated the day when he would be able to eat at a "big" table—in a restaurant, in our dining room, in the houses of our friends. We used to say that we were setting a place for him at our table, and we meant it as literally and as metaphorically as our language would allow. In the past two years, as he's grown, he's learned to eat tacos, burgers, and pizza—and, more recently, potatoes, rice, and corn. He's even learned to take vitamins. Most of all, though, he's learned how to set a table. Although he folds the napkins badly and distributes the silverware somewhat randomly, he knows where to put the plates and where to get the forks, and he knows how to set his own place, with his own plate, with his own fork and spoon that say "Jamie." My job, for now, is to represent my son, to set his place at our collective table. But I know I am merely trying my best to prepare for the day he sets his own place. For I have no sweeter dream than to imagine—aesthetically and ethically and parentally—that Jamie will someday be his own advocate, his own author, his own best representative.

Acknowledgments

I have never had so much help and guidance, page by page and paragraph by paragraph, as I have received in the writing of this book. From start to finish, Stacie Colwell was the most impressive and savvy research assistant I have ever heard of: from annotating (and, in many cases, translating) Medline research abstracts and the results of endless Lexis searches, to writing up twenty pages of single-spaced notes (in ten-point type) on the first draft of the manuscript, Stacie strengthened this book in innumerable ways I could not possibly have anticipated. I am deeply indebted also to Amanda Anderson, not only for the many acts of kindness chronicled in these pages but also for her characteristically rigorous and bracing reading of troublesome chapters. From Philip Graham and Richard Powers I received indispensable advice on how to do things I don't normally have to do in literary criticism and theory, like setting scenes and framing dialogue. Linda Healey, my editor at Pantheon, offered me encouragement and intellectual challenge in equal measure, whether the subject was sociobiology, inclusive education, or prenatal testing. For her omnidirectional intelligence and keen eyes I am very grateful. And to my agent, Colleen Mohyde of the Doe Coover Agency, I owe thanks for her crucial help in conceptualizing this book and shaping it into a narrative intelligible, I hope, to specialists and general readers alike.

When I first published an essay about Jamie in *Harper's* magazine in December 1994, I was deluged with mail from parents, advocates, and researchers, many of whom shared their stories and/or their published work. I have tried to incorporate some of that material into Jamie's story, partly in the belief that Jamie's story is not exclusively about Jamie, but also in the knowledge that if other parents and researchers hadn't paved the way for us, we'd probably never have had the opportunity to find out what raising Jamie could teach us. I'm sorry that I can't recall and thank by name everyone who's offered their help, their expertise, and their kind words, but I must at least acknowledge Allen Hance, Roby Harrington, Marta and Patti Peluso, Amy and Jeff Margolis, Emily and Charles Kingsley, David Hunt, Paul Baker, John and Ethel Magnus, Rayna Rapp, Kathleen McClusky-Fawcett, Katherine Dettwyler, Julie Cronk, Jean Rhodes, Max Kläger, Donna Connell, Rosemarie S. Hughes, Abby Lippman, Patrick McDonagh, Elaine T. Kisisel, Maurice Elliott, Philip Ferguson, Fr. Martin Feeney, Joseph A. Panza, James O. Henry, Jack Fowler, Jennifer Hershey, Cassie Sauer, Rubin Pfeffer, Leigh Hafrey, Jesse Scofield, John R. MacArthur, and Sr. Rosie Maas. For similar reasons, I am unable to thank every therapist and medical professional who's helped Jamie stand on his own two feet, but I cannot leave unmentioned the remarkable work of Rita Huddle, Sara Jane Annin, Ofra Tandoor, Kate Garth, Terri McKenzie, Jamie Smith, Anne Osterling, Nancy Yeagle, and Doctors Donald Davison and Kenneth Weiss. And, of course, we will forever be grateful to all Jamie's teachers and aides at First United Methodist and Marquette.

My parents, Anne and Maurice Bérubé, have doubtless been this book's biggest boosters over the past year. While my father compiled newspaper articles, *Phi Delta Kappan* special issues, and research essays by colleagues and students, my mother annotated the manuscript and argued arcana with me chapter by chapter. My sisters, Jean and Kathy, tracked the book's progress as well, giving me updates on the political climate in Washington, D.C. (where Jean is a lawyer) and Norfolk, Virginia (where Kathy supervises a work team of disabled adults). Nicholas and James were not only wonderful children throughout but also good research advisors, helping me pore over the videotapes that chronicle their past few years. The Lyon family offered me companionship, support, and ideas aplenty. And Janet Lyon, as ever, was my ideal reader, my most severe editor, my occasional co-author, and my life's partner in this as in all things. Without her love and perseverance none of this—our book, our lives, the lives of our children—would be possible.

Champaign, Illinois
April 1996

Sources

■

▲

CHAPTER ONE

My information on genetics is drawn chiefly from George W. Burns, *The Science of Genetics: An Introduction to Heredity* (New York: Macmillan, 1980), 4th ed.; David T. Suzuki et al., eds., *Introduction to Genetic Analysis* (New York: W.H. Freeman & Co., 1981), 2d ed.; and Michael R. Cummings, *Human Heredity: Principles and Issues* (St. Paul, MN: West Publishing Co., 1994), 3rd ed.

For statistics pertaining specifically to children with Down syndrome I consulted primarily Lynn Nadel and Donna Rosenthal, eds., *Down Syndrome: Living and Learning in the Community* (New York: John Wiley & Sons, 1995), and Karen Stray-Gunderson, ed., *Babies with Down Syndrome: A New Parents Guide* (Kensington, MD: Woodbine House, 1986).

For individual families' stories of their children with Down's, my three major sources were Willard Abraham, *Barbara: A Prologue* (New York: Rinehart & Co., 1958), The Magnus Family, *A Family Love Story* (Salt Spring Island, British Columbia, Canada: The Magnus Family, 1994), and Jason Kingsley and Mitchell Levitz, *Count Us In: Growing Up with Down Syndrome* (New York:

Harcourt Brace, 1994). Emily Kingsley's story of Jason's birth can be found in Nadel and Rosenthal, eds., *Down Syndrome: Living and Learning in the Community.*

CHAPTER TWO

The texts cited on abortion rights are as follows: Naomi Wolf, "Our Bodies, Our Souls," *The New Republic*, October 16, 1995, pp. 26–35; Christine Allison, "A Child to Lead Us," *The Human Life Review* XV.3 (1989), pp. 97–102; John Noonan, *The Morality of Abortion* (Cambridge, MA: Harvard University Press, 1970); Judith Jarvis Thomson, "A Defense of Abortion," *Philosophy and Public Affairs* 1.1 (1971), pp. 47–66; Lewis M. Schwartz, *Arguing About Abortion* (Belmont, CA: Wentworth Publishing Company, 1993); Peter Singer, "Killing Babies Isn't Always Wrong," *The Spectator*, September 16, 1995, pp. 20–22. For Rayna Rapp's essay, see Rapp, "Accounting for Amniocentesis," in Shirley Lindenbaum and Margaret Lock, *Knowledge, Power, and Practice: The Anthropology of Medicine and Everyday Life* (Berkeley, CA: University of California Press, 1993), pp. 55–76.

My information on the Jones Institute for Reproductive Medicine in Norfolk came from Marie Joyce, "A Break on Down Syndrome Efforts? Jones Institute Will Screen Embryos Prior to Implanting Them in the Uterus," *Norfolk Virginian-Pilot*, February 22, 1995, pp. A1, A9. More recently the *Virginian-Pilot* ran a follow-up essay by Marie Joyce: "New Test for Down Syndrome: Jones Institute Offers Screening to Couples Before Embryo Implants," January 14, 1996, pp. B1, B4.

On the FISH-PCR test, my source is a medical abstract published on Medline: I.V. Soloviev, Y.B. Yurov, S.G. Vorsanova, F. Fayet, G. Roizes, and P. Malet, "Prenatal diagnosis of trisomy 21 using interphase fluorescence in situ hybridization of post-replicated cells with site-specific cosmid and cosmid contig probes." Laboratoire d'Histologie Embryologie-Cytogenetique, Université d'Auvergne, Faculté de Médecine, Clermont-Ferrand, France. *Prenatal Diagnosis* 15.3 (March 1995), pp. 237–48.

CHAPTER THREE

All direct citations in this chapter come from James W. Trent, Jr., *Inventing the Feeble Mind: A History of Mental Retardation in the United States* (Berkeley, CA: University of California Press, 1994); Robert L. Hayman, Jr., *Smart Culture* (New York: New York University Press, 1996); and Dave Barry, *Babies and Other Hazards of Sex* (Emmaus, PA: Rodale Press, 1984).

The chapter's synopsis of Foucauldian thought is drawn from the following works of Michel Foucault: *The Archaeology of Knowledge*, trans. A.M. Sheridan Smith (New York: Pantheon, 1972); *Discipline and Punish: The Birth of the Prison*, trans. Alan Sheridan (New York: Vintage, 1979); *The History of Sexuality. Volume 1: An Introduction* (New York: Vintage, 1978); and Paul Rabinow, ed., *The Foucault Reader* (New York: Pantheon, 1984).

CHAPTER FOUR

The Kingsley citation comes from Nadel and Rosenthal, eds., *Down Syndrome: Living and Learning in the Community*. All other direct quotes are from Ludwig Wittgenstein, *Philosophical Investigations*, 3rd ed., trans. G.E.M. Anscombe (New York: Macmillan, 1958), and Steven Pinker, *The Language Instinct: How the Mind Creates Language* (New York: William Morrow and Co., 1994).

CHAPTER FIVE

The story about Luke Zimmerman, "Down Syndrome Player Is Inspiration to Football Team," was released by the Associated Press on November 8, 1995.

The following are my primary sources on inclusion, main-streaming, and disability law: *Educational Rights of Children with Disabilities: A Primer for Advocates*, by Eileen L. Ordover & Kathleen B. Boundy (Washington, D.C: Center for Law and Education, 1991); Barbara Ebenstein, "The Law and Inclusion," *Exceptional Parent* 25.9 (1995), pp. 40–44; Charles Sykes, *Dumbing Down Our Kids: Why American Children Feel Good About Themselves But Can't Read, Write, or Add* (New York: St. Martin's Press, 1995); *Restructuring for Caring and Effective Education: An Administrative Guide to Creating Heterogeneous Schools*, ed. Richard A. Villa, Jacqueline S. Thousand, William Stainback, and Susan Stainback (Baltimore, MD: Paul H. Brookes, 1992); Marjorie Beeghly and Dante Cicchetti, "An Organizational Approach to Symbolic Development in Children with Down Syndrome," Cicchetti and Beeghly, eds., *Symbolic Development in Atypical Children* (San Francisco: Jossey-Bass, 1987); Thomas Armstrong, *Multiple Intelligences in the Classroom* (Alexandria, VA: Association for Supervision and Curriculum Development, 1994); Howard Gardner, *Frames of Mind: The Theory of Multiple Intelligences* (New York: Basic Books, 1983); Joseph P. Shapiro et al., "Separate and Unequal: How Special Education Programs Are Cheating Our Children and Costing Taxpayers Billions Each Year," *U.S. News and World Report*, December 13, 1993, pp. 46–60; Leah Cohen, *Train Go Sorry: Life in a Deaf World* (Boston: Houghton Mifflin, 1994).

The rest of the chapter's sources concern the question of justice. "Discord over the Disabled," *Time*, April 29, 1985, p. 50; William A. Henry III, *In Defense of Elitism* (New York: Doubleday, 1994); Roger Kimball, review of *In Defense of Elitism, New York Times Book Review*, October 16, 1994, p. 30; Harvey Mansfield, "Why Equality Is Ridiculous," review of *In Defense of Elitism, Wall Street Journal*, September 6, 1994, p. A18 (Mansfield's comments on black students and grade inflation were reported in the *Chronicle of Higher Education*, March 31, 1993, p. A27); Diane M. Gianelli, "Transplant Denied: Careful Use of Scarce Organs, or Discrimination?" *American Medical News*, September 18, 1995, pp. 3, 27; Marjorie Rosen and Jamie Reno, "By the Numbers: Refused a Transplant Because of Her Low IQ, Sandra Jensen Defends Her Own Right to Life," *People*, October 16, 1995, pp. 67–68; "Woman with Down Gets Heart-Lung Transplant," Associated Press, January 24, 1996; William C. Dowling, "Intentionless Meaning," in W.J.T. Mitchell, ed., *Against Theory: Literary Studies and the New Pragmatism* (Chicago: University of Chicago Press, 1985), pp. 89–94; Richard Dawkins, *The Selfish Gene* (Oxford University Press, 1976); Edward Wilson, "Human Decency Is Animal," *New York Times Magazine*, October 12, 1975, pp. 38–50; Lawrence Wright, "Double Mystery," *The New Yorker*, August 7, 1995, pp. 45–62; Lewis Thomas, *The Lives of a Cell* (New York: Viking, 1974); for introductions to many of the major works of sociobiology I am indebted to Connie Barlow, ed., *From Gaia to Selfish Genes: Selected Writings in the Life Sciences* (Cambridge, MA: The MIT Press, 1991).

Finally, my brief discussion of Rawls and Habermas relies on John Rawls, *A Theory of Justice* (Cambridge, MA: The Belknap Press of Harvard University Press, 1971), Jürgen Habermas, *Moral Consciousness and Communicative Action*, trans. Christian Lenhardt and Shierry Weber Nicholson (Cambridge, MA: The MIT Press, 1990) and *The Theory of Communicative Action*, trans. Thomas McCarthy. 2 vols. (Boston: Beacon Press, 1984–1987).

EPILOGUE

The sources of the chapter's epigraphs are as follows: G. E. Shuttleworth, *Mentally-Deficient Children: Their Treatment and Training,*

2d ed. (London: H. K. Lewis, 1900); Kate Brousseau, *Mongolism: A Study of the Physical and Mental Characteristics of Mongolian Imbeciles*, revised by H. G. Brainerd (Baltimore: The Williams and Wilkins Company, 1928); James W. Trent, Jr., *Inventing the Feeble Mind*; and Kingsley and Mitchell, *Count Us In: Growing Up with Down Syndrome*.

The passage on eighteenth-century aesthetics is drawn mostly from John Guillory, *Cultural Capital: The Problem of Literary Canon Formation* (Chicago: University of Chicago Press, 1993), but this discussion is also heavily influenced by Oscar Kenshur, " 'The Tumour of Their Own Hearts': Relativism, Aesthetics, and the Rhetoric of Demystification," in George Levine, ed., *Aesthetics and Ideology* (New Brunswick, NJ: Rutgers University Press), pp. 57–78, and Terry Eagleton, *The Ideology of the Aesthetic* (Oxford: Basil Blackwell, 1990). The final passage from Mitchell Levitz appears in *Count Us In*.

My literary sources in the book are William Faulkner, *The Sound and the Fury*, corrected edition (New York: Vintage, 1990); Richard Powers, *The Gold Bug Variations* (New York: William Morrow and Company, 1991); Marcel Proust, *Remembrance of Things Past*, trans. C. K. Scott Moncrieff and Terence Kilmartin (New York: Vintage, 1981); W.E.B. Du Bois, *The Souls of Black Folk* (New York: Bantam, 1989); Flannery O'Connor, "Good Country People," in *A Good Man Is Hard to Find* (New York: Harcourt Brace, 1955). The passage from Dostoyevsky concerning his plans for *Crime and Punishment* can be found in the translator's introduction to the Penguin edition. Fyodor Dostoyevsky, *Crime and Punishment*, trans. David Magarschack (Harmondsworth, Middlesex, England: Penguin Books, 1951).

Index

abortion:
  debate about, 48–49
  "gray areas," moral
    decisionmaking in, 60–63
  hypothetical question
    regarding Jamie, 49–50
  killing of providers by
    abortion opponents, 65–66
  life's beginning and, 56,
    66–67
  "natural" rights and, 63–65
  prenatal testing and, 46–48,
    54–56, 67–69, 70, 73,
    76
  "probabilities" argument
    against, 56–60
  viability and, 61
Abraham, Willard, 29
"Accounting for Amniocentesis"
  (Rapp), 67–69
Adventures of Milo and Otis (film),
  256
aesthetics, 256–59

African-American children,
  222–23
aggressive instinct, 237
Allison, Christine, 54–55, 73
alphafetoprotein (AFP) test, 74
altruism, 233–39
American Association on Mental
  Deficiency, 110
American College of
  Obstreticians and
  Gynecologists, 74
Americans with Disabilities
  Act, 227, 254
amniocentesis: *see* prenatal
  testing
Anderson, Amanda, 98, 99,
  106, 116, 144, 145
Angel Unaware (Rogers), 255
Annin, Daniel, 114
Annin, Sara Jane, 113–14, 177
antifoundationalist philosophy,
  150, 152
Armey, Dick, 227

Armstrong, Thomas, 211–12
Augustine, St., 148–49, 151

Bank-Mikkelsen, Niels Erik, 251
Barbara (Abraham), 29
Barry, Dave, 126–27
Beeghly, Marjorie, 211
Benhabib, Seyla, 248
Bennett, William, 227
Bérubé, James Lyon "Jamie":
    appearance issue, 118–19
    birth of, 4–6, 7
    books, love of, 167–68
    cognitive development, 119, 182–88, 191–97
    cost of medical care, 41–44
    dancing by, 147
    in day care, 172–78, 215–17
    developmental milestones, 127–28
    dreaming by, 256
    education of, 200–201, 215–17
    expectations regarding, 118–19
    facial asymmetry, 118–19
    feeding of, 35, 37, 89–90, 92–93
    fetal development, 6–7, 8–9
    future prospects, 261–62
    hearing problem, 130–33, 136–37, 192

ICU stay, 7–8, 10–14, 35–38, 40
illnesses and infections, 95, 144–45, 146
imagination of, xviii
individual autonomy, 176
"Jamie as Jamie" issue, xi–xiii, xvi–xviii
language learning, 160, 191–94
lists, love of, ix
maps, interest in, 185–86
marvel, capacity for, 128–29
as medicalized child, 40–41, 88–90
memory of, 168, 186, 188
mimicry by, xvi–xviii
modeling by, 174, 176
music, love of, 146–47
occupational therapy, 200–201
physical characteristics, 20
physical health at three, 83
physical problems at birth, 7–8, 11–12
physical therapy, 114–17, 121–25, 171
praise, response to, 125–26
representation of, 263–64
sign language, use of, 160–67
sitting up, 116, 124–25, 129–30
speech therapy, 168–70, 191–92

spinal damage, 117–18

television appearance, 177–78

vacation in New England, ix–xviii

vocalization, first, 93–94

vomiting problem, 96–97

walking by, 123–24, 147–48, 171–73, 174, 177

words, first production of, 170–71

Bérubé, Michael:

adaptation to caring for Jamie, 89–94

Brazil visit, 169, 170

ear injury, 132

grammar school years, 214

guilt feelings, 118

intelligence tests, 180–81

"Jamie as Jamie" issue, xi–xiii, xvi–xviii

Jamie's birth, 4–6, 7

Jamie's ICU stay, 10–14, 35–38, 40

Jamie's intelligence testing, 183–85

maps, interest in, 185

memory of Jamie's first year, 119–21

prenatal testing decision, 6–7, 45, 46

reading in childhood, 190

representation of Jamie, 263–64

sadness of, xi, 134–36, 141–44

Special Sitters training, 99–100, 106

stress, response to, 95–96

teaching career, 3, 6, 96, 145

vacation in New England, ix–xviii

vows regarding Jamie, 38–39

Bérubé, Nicholas "Nick," ix, 3, 8–10, 12, 13, 84, 90, 97, 127, 158, 167–68, 190

asthma problem, 9, 134–35

education of, 214–15

intelligence of, 182, 185, 186, 187

Jamie's relationship with, 125–26, 147–48

language acquisition, 151–52

maps, interest in, 185

signing with Jamie, 166–67

tape recording of early speech, 140–41

Bloom, Harold, 256

Board of Education of Hendrick Hudson School District v. *Rowley,* 201

Boundy, Kathleen, 199

Bradbury, Ray, 21

brains of humans, 15–16

Bronson, William, 230

Brousseau, Kate, 250

Buck, Doris, 109, 111

Buck, Pearl, 111

Buck v. *Bell,* 108–10
Burke, Chris, 20, 255, 263

Catholic Church, 57, 66–67
cell division, 16–18, 21
Chevras Dor Yershurim, 69
children with disabilities: *see*
disabled children
Chomsky, Noam, 161
Christmas Carol, A (Dickens),
51
chromosomes, 18–20, 21, 22
Cicchetti, Dante, 211
Clarke, Arthur C., 16
Cohen, Leah, 224–25
Coleman Report, 217–18
communicative action, 241
contraception, 67
Count Us In (Levitz and
Kingsley), 31–32, 263
CPR, 99–100

Daniel R. R. v. *State Board of
Education,* 201, 202
Davison, Donald, 41, 177
Dawkins, Richard, 233–34,
235
day care, 172–78, 215–17
deaf communities, 224–25
Decartes, René, 155–56
deconstruction, 209–10, 236
defederalization, 219–20
definitions, 231–32
deinstitutionalization, 112

Dickens, Charles, 51
differences among humans,
22–24
disabled children: as "luxuries"
society can't afford,
52–53
pro-lifers and, 50–51
see also Down syndrome
children; social services for
the disabled; special
education
DNA, 3–4, 16–17, 233–34
Dostoyevsky, Fyodor, 231
Do the Right Thing (film), 164
Dowling, William, 231
Down, J. Langdon, 25, 107
Down syndrome:
carriers of, 21
chromosomal origin, 18,
19–20, 22
"cure" for, 77–78
Foucauldian view of, 103
historical perspective on,
24–25
incidence of, 19, 25
maternal age and, 21–22
mosaicism, 21
prenatal testing's focus on,
71–78
prevention issue, 77
"purpose" of, 34–35, 68–69,
238
self-representation by persons
with, 262–63

subtle effects, 20–21
terminology issue, 25–27,
    32–33, 254
Down syndrome children:
at-home care, early instances
    of, 27–28, 30–32
institutionalization of,
    28–30, 73
learning capacity, 138–39
nondisabled population's
    perceptions of, 179–80,
    182–83
see also Bérubé, James Lyon
    "Jamie"; parents of Down's
    children
Drake, Nick, 147
Du Bois, W. E. B., 143
Dumbing Down Our Kids (Sykes),
    203–4

Easter Bunny story, 114
Ebenstein, Barbara, 202, 203
Educating Peter (film), 259
education:
    funding of, 218
    see also special education
Edwards' syndrome, 19, 20
Eliot, T. S., 257
emulation, principle of, 239–40
Engler, John, 218
eugenics, 52–53, 108–11
evolution, 14–15, 239, 246
Exceptional Parent (magazine),
    135

family resemblances, 153–54
Faulkner, William, xiv-xv,
    194–95
First United Methodist (FUM)
    day care, 172–78, 215–17
Forrest Gump (film), 259–60
Foucauldian thought, 102–5,
    106, 107
Fraser, Nancy, 248

Gallagher, Larry, 147
Gardner, Eileen Marie, 226–27
Gardner, Howard, 182, 212
Garth, Kate, 194
genetics, 33–34
    altruism and, 233–39
    cell division, 16–18, 21
    chromosomes, 18–20, 21, 22
    differences among humans
        and, 22–24
Gold Bug Variations (Powers),
    16–17
Goodnight Moon (book), 168
grammar, 192–94
Great Chain of Being, 258
Guillory, John, 257

Habermas, Jürgen, 241, 244,
    246, 247
Hance, Allen, 98
Hayman, Robert, 111, 205–6
health insurance, 42–45, 261
Henderson, Bill, 206
Henry, William, 228

heroic "lifesaving" measures, 62
history of mental retardation,
    107–12
Hodgen, Gary D., 76
Holmes, Oliver Wendell,
    108–10
Holte, Bjorg, 114–15, 121
Horace, 259
Huddle, Rita, 113, 177
"Human Decency Is Animal"
    (Wilson), 235, 236–37
Human Life Review, 54
Huntington's disease, 70–71

Ideas, Platonic, 152, 153,
    154–55
imagination, xviii, 240–41
inclusive education, 201–7,
    210–14, 223–26
In Defense of Elitism (Henry), 228
Individualized Education Plans
    (IEPs), 200–201
Individuals with Disabilities
    Education Act (IDEA),
    198–200, 203–4, 218, 254
infant mortality, 17
institutionalization, 28–30, 73,
    108, 112, 251
intelligence, 14–15
    Jamie's cognitive
        development, 119,
        182–88, 191–97
    memory and, 186–87,
        188–90

testing for, 180–85
understanding and, 189–90
Inventing the Feeble Mind (Trent),
    107–8

Jensen, Sandra, 229–30
Jesus Christ, 114, 239
John Paul II, Pope, 67
Jones Institute, 75–76
justice, 86
    aesthetics and, 258
    altruism and, 233–39
    definitions and, 231–32
    divine justice, 232–33
    as fairness, 243
    laissez-faire libertarian
        thought and, 226–29
    language and, 244, 245–46,
        248–49
    medical treatment, right to,
        229–30
    origins of, 239–46
    practice of, 246–49

Kant, Immanuel, 240
Kennedy family, 111
Kimball, Roger, 228
Kingsley family, 30–32,
    138–39, 263
Klinefelter's syndrome, 18

language:
    abuse of, 165
    grammar, 192–94

justice and, 244, 245–46, 248–49

representation and, 254–55

sign language, 160–67

theories of, 148–60

thought-language relationship, 251–54

Language Instinct (Pinker), 157–59

Lee, Spike, 164

Levitz, Mitchell, 31, 251, 262, 263

life, epiphenomenon of, 245

Life Goes On (TV show), 20, 255

Life of Brian (film), 105

Lyon, Bud and Sarah, 53, 91

Lyon, Janet, ix, xii

  adaptation to caring for Jamie, 91–94

  guilt feelings, 118

  hearing problem, 132

  Jamie's birth, 4–6, 7

  Jamie's ICU stay, 10, 14, 35–38

  pregnancy with Jamie, 6–7, 8–9

  prenatal testing decision, 6–7, 45, 46

  sadness of, 134, 136, 141–44

  spatial orientation, 195

  teaching career, 3, 6, 96, 145

  vows regarding Jamie, 38–39

mainstreaming, 202–3

Mansfield, Harvey, 228

Marquette school, 215–17

McKenzie, Terri, 191

medical treatment, right to, 229–30

meiosis, 17–18

meliorism, 239

memory, 119–21, 186–87, 188–90

Mentally Deficient Children (Shuttleworth), 250

miscarriages, 17, 19

mitosis, 16, 17–18

mongolism: *see* Down syndrome

Mongolism (Brousseau), 250

Morality of Abortion (Noonan), 57

mosaicism, 21

Murray, Charles, 246

mutual realization, 249

national health care, 44–45, 261

"natural" rights, 63–65, 86

Noonan, John T., 57, 58, 59, 63–65

normal and abnormal development, distinction between, 207–10

Oberti v. *Board of Education,* 203

obligations, 231

obstetricians, 37–38

occupational therapy, 200–201

O'Connor, Flannery, 208
On Human Nature (Wilson), 234
Ordover, Eileen, 199

Paglia, Camille, 104–5
parallel instruction, 203
parallel talk, 191–92
parental leave, 10
parents of Down's children,
   135–36
  caretaking issue, 27–32
  decisionmaking by
    prospective parents on
    proceeding with a
    pregnancy, 78–88
  IEPs and, 200–201
  respite care, 100–101
  see also Bérubé, Michael; Lyon,
    Janet
Patau's syndrome, 19, 20
Patrick O'Hearn School, 206
People magazine, 229–30
Philosophical Investigations
   (Wittgenstein), xii,
   149–50
physical therapy, 114–17,
   121–25, 171
Pinker, Steven, 157–59, 161,
   245, 251–52, 255
Plato, 150, 152, 153, 154–55
polylogue, 244
polymerase chain reaction (PCR)
   technology, 71–72
Pound, Ezra, 257

Powers, Richard, 16–17, 23
prenatal testing (amniocentesis),
   53–54, 63
  abortion and, 46–48, 54–56,
   67–69, 70, 73, 76
  Bérubé-Lyons' decision
    against, 6–7, 45, 46
  coercive uses of, 70–71
  Down syndrome, focus on,
   71–78
  morality issue, 69–70
  policymaking on, 73–76
  preventive function, 76–
   78
privacy rights, 87–88
promising, 231
Proust, Marcel, 120–21

Quine, W. V. O., 152, 157

Rapp, Rayna, 67–69
Rawls, John, 241–44, 246–
   48
Reagan, Ronald, 111, 251
reciprocity, principle of, 239,
   240–46
Remembrance of Things Past
   (Proust), 120–21
representation, xix, 198
  aesthetics and, 256–59
  Bérubé's representation of
    Jamie, 263–64
  disability and, 259–61
  language and, 254–55

self-representation by persons with Down syndrome, 262–63

respite care, 100–101

Rogers, Dale Evans, 111, 255

Rowley, Ann, 201

St.-Croix, Étienne, 67–68

Sale, Kirkpatrick, 11, 105

scandal of induction, 152, 159

Schattman, Richard, 207

Schwarz, Lewis, 60

Science of Genetics, The (textbook), 25

Searle, John, 231

Seguin, Edward, 108

self-consciousness as measure of humanity, 62–63

Selfish Gene (Dawkins), 233–34, 235

Sendak, Maurice, 167

Shuttleworth, G. E., 250

sign language, 160–67

Singer, Peter, 61–63, 66

Sleepy Dog (book), 256

Smith, Jamie, 192

social contract, 101–2, 241

social Darwinism, 246

social services for the disabled, 13–14

America's paradoxical approach to, 105–6

beneficial effects, 113–14

control issue, 102–7

defunding of, 121–22, 135

history of, 107–12

respite care for parents, 100–101

social contract and, 101–2

sociobiology, 233–37

Souls of Black Folk (Du Bois), 143

Sound and the Fury (Faulkner), xiv–xv, 194–95

"Sound of Thunder" (Bradbury), 21

special education:

African-American children and, 222–23

coercion problem, 224–25

conservative criticism of, 203–5, 217–18

cost concerns, 217–18

defederalization and, 219–20

IEPs, 200–201

inclusion issue, 201–7, 210–14, 223–26

Jamie's education, 200–201, 215–17

laws on, 198–200

mainstreaming, 202–3

misadministration of, 220–23

misdiagnoses problem, 219

multiple intelligences and, 211–12

nondisabled students, benefits for, 206–7

special education (*cont.*)
normal and abnormal
development, distinction
between, 207–10
parallel instruction, 203
segregated classrooms,
205–6, 221–22
socialization function,
213–14
teacher expectations and,
207
variety of options, importance
of, 225–26
Special Kind of Hero (Burke),
263
Special Sitters training, 99–100,
106
speech therapy, 168–70, 191–92
Stanford University, 229, 230
sterilization, involuntary,
108–11
Supreme Court, U.S., 108–10,
201
Sykes, Charles, 203–4

Tandoor, Ofra, 122–25, 129–30,
171, 177
Tay-Sachs disease, 76
Theory of Justice (Rawls),
241–44, 246–48
Thomas, Lewis, 245
Thomson, Judith Jarvis, 57–58
Tolson, Melvin, 180
Train Go Sorry (Cohen), 224–25

translocation, 21
Trent, James, 107–8, 111, 112,
210
triple screen test, 55, 71, 74
trisomies, 18–20
trisomy 21: *see* Down syndrome
Turner's syndrome, 18

understanding, 189–90
U.S. News and World Report,
220–23
utilitarianism, 241, 242–44,
248
Uzzell, Lawrence, 227

"Vision of the Future"
(Kingsley), 138–39

Weicker, Lowell, 227
Where the Wild Things Are
(Sendak), 167
Wilson, Edward O., 234, 235,
236–37
Wittgenstein, Ludwig, xii,
149–50, 152, 153–54,
188–89, 231, 253
Wolf, Naomi, 49
Wordsworth, William, 260
Wright, Lawrence, 236

Yeagle, Nancy, 113, 177, 196,
212

Zimmerman, Luke, 179–80